Harvard Historical Studies, 109

Published under the auspices
of the Department of History
from the income of the
Paul Revere Frothingham Bequest
Robert Louis Stroock Fund
Henry Warren Torrey Fund

RELUCTANT ICON

Gladstone, Bulgaria, and the
Working Classes, 1856–1878

ANN POTTINGER SAAB

Harvard University Press
Cambridge, Massachusetts
London, England
1991

Library of Congress Cataloging-in-Publication Data

Saab, Ann Pottinger, 1934–
    Reluctant icon: Gladstone, Bulgaria, and the working classes,
    1856–1878/Ann Pottinger Saab.
        p.   cm.—(Harvard historical studies; 109)
    Includes bibliographical references and index.
    ISBN 0-674-75965-6 (cloth: alk. paper)
    1. Gladstone, W. E. (William Ewart), 1809–1898—Views on Bulgaria.
    2. Bulgaria—History—Uprising, 1876—Foreign public opinion,
    British.   3. Working class—Great Britain—Political activity—
    History—19th century.   4. Public opinion—Great Britain—
    History—19th century.   I. Title.   II. Series: Harvard historical
    studies; v. 109.
DA563.5.S23   1991
949.77'015—dc20

90-25526
CIP

Contents

Acknowledgments

Twenty years have gone into the making of this book. I began some months before the birth of our younger child. His high treble mingled with my dry scholarly murmur on tapes of some of the earlier chapters. We argued over the computer when he wanted to play "Lode Runner." This autumn, he went away to college.

There is another sense in which this book is "a chapter of autobiography," if it is not presumptuous to borrow Gladstone's happy phrase. I was trained by William L. Langer in the classical tradition of diplomatic history, which reaches back to Sir Charles Webster and H. W. V. Temperley. Like most of my generation (and I must confess later than many), I became disenchanted with its narrow, artificially rational focus. The search for a new approach was facilitated by a graduate colloquium I have taught most years since 1973, in which we looked at different historical methodologies, using mainly works on British history. The result contrasts with my earlier work; whether it is better will be for my readers to decide.

To acknowledge the debts incurred during a period which includes most of my adult professional life is a task both daunting and pleasurable. First of all, I must thank the staffs of the many British libraries and archives I have been privileged to use. Their warm acceptance of a colleague from overseas has been an essential support. Specifically, I wish to thank the British Library for permission to quote from the Morris Papers and the Gladstone Papers; the Bodleian for permission to quote from the Disraeli Papers; the University of Birmingham for permission to quote from the Chamberlain Papers; and the University of Sheffield for permission to quote from the Mundella Papers. Sir William Gladstone graciously allowed me to quote from those of his ancestor's papers which remain with St. Deiniol's Library in Hawarden. I have reprinted passages from *The Gladstone Diaries*, ed. M. R. D. Foot and H. C. G. Matthew, 11 vols. to date (Oxford: Clarendon Press, 1968–) by permission of Oxford University Press. R. T. Shannon kindly allowed me to use materials published in his magisterial *Gladstone and the Bulgarian Agitation, 1876.* Short pieces are quoted with the concurrence of *Punch* and the Public Record Office. And I am grateful for authorization to use revised versions of articles which originally appeared in the *Journal of Modern History* (University of Chicago Press), *Muslim World,* and the *International History Review.*

Among the many friends who read this book in one or another of its interminable drafts, I want especially to express my gratitude to Dr. Agatha Ramm. She taught me a great deal about Britain and its history and society; saved me from innumerable mistakes; broadened my knowledge of the literature; and never hesitated to tell me when it was time to tear up a chapter and start over. Not even a thesis advisor *could* have given more than she has given me, at a later stage in my career and without the slightest institutional obligation. And very few thesis advisors *would* have offered such friendship and hospitality, not only to me but to my entire family.

Another reader who made major suggestions and unstintingly invested his time in this project is Peter Stansky. Colleagues at the University of North Carolina at Greensboro who went over drafts include Ronald D. Cassell, David Mackenzie, and Karl Schleunes. Frank T. Melton, also of UNCG, was the source of much useful information; so was Robert C. Shipkey.

Many friends in the United States and abroad have supported me with their enthusiasm over the years and have come to my rescue when particular problems loomed. I should like to mention especially Sir Hugh Lloyd-Jones and Mary Lefkowitz, Colin Matthew, Matthew Anderson, and Alan Sked. Helen and Robert Maclennan were most kind when, writing from the United States, I needed help with parliamentary petitions. Without their timely intervention, I should not have been able to carry out an important piece of my investigation.

The University of North Carolina at Greensboro has underwritten this project through grants from the Research Council, and the interlibrary loan staff of the Jackson Library has cheerfully filled uncounted requests for obscure publications needed "yesterday." Tim Barkley and Toni Brown designed the table and figures. Dr. Elisabeth Zinser, during her tenure as Vice Chancellor for Academic Affairs, found ways to finance a crucial summer research trip. Dean Robert L. Miller has been an unfailing resource for everything from conversation to computer paper on Sunday. Finally, the staff of the Harvard University Press, notably Elizabeth Suttell and Lauren Osborne, have continued a tradition of editing which makes publishing an educational experience; it has been a joy to work with them.

My family has lived with this project almost as intensively as I have. I can never say enough about my husband's patience and unselfishness, or about David's adaptability. Finally, I want to thank Georges, our older son, now a computer engineer. I know how good he is at what he does because I was his first pupil.

Reluctant Icon

I ◆ Introduction

In 1876 a series of massacres in the Ottoman province of Bulgaria scandalized Britain. Many, priding themselves rightly or wrongly on their moral sensibility, reacted as though Britain's trusted friend had been revealed as a monster. For some forty years, support of the Ottoman Empire had been official British policy. British ambassadors had played commanding parts in Constantinople and had not hesitated to lecture the Sultan, to contrive ministerial changes, and, so they firmly believed, to direct policy. They assumed this attitude because they thought that in members of the Ottoman government they had found apt and willing pupils. A widespread and astonishing confidence prevailed in England that, whatever past and continuing deficiencies might exist, the Ottoman Porte, as the government of the Empire was known in Europe, was determined to westernize and in fact was becoming more British every day. Ongoing massacres, starting with the bloodshed at Aleppo in 1850, were signs that this westernization was more irritant than accomplished fact, and that social change, particularly when it aimed to raise the status of the subject populations, could provoke a backlash which called the results of reform very much into question.

Significantly, the British failed to assimilate these clues until the 1870s, when a firestorm of protest broke out over the havoc in Bulgaria, almost the last in the succession of massacres. Under the leadership of William Ewart Gladstone, a loose coalition of Nonconformists, Radicals, and High Churchmen, drawn primarily though by no means entirely from the middle classes and the so-called labor aristocracy, created a climate of indignation strong enough to limit substantially the government's options in the ensuing crisis in the East.[1] Although Russia went to war against the Ottoman Empire in 1877 and thus replicated the crisis of 1853–54, Britain did not intervene militarily as during the Crimean War; apart from a carefully circumscribed demonstration by the fleet, British action was strictly diplomatic. Although Russia's most extreme pretensions, as embodied in the Treaty of San Stefano, were modified by agreements which were later extended and formalized at the Congress of Berlin, the settlement nonetheless extended full independence to Serbia, Romania, and Montenegro and set up part of Bulgaria as a Russian "satellite." Austria occupied Bosnia and Herzegovina; Britain, by the Cyprus Convention, occupied Cyprus; and farther to the west, France received hints that an eventual takeover of Tunis would be condoned. Something very like a partition—or at least a mutilation—of the Ottoman Empire had taken place; and Britain, far from taking active steps to prevent it, had actually joined in the scramble. In subsequent years, Britain's influence at the Porte declined drastically. Although Lord Salisbury hoped to regenerate a smaller, more viable Ottoman empire in Asia, the heart had gone out of British efforts, and the Porte's faith in British good intentions had been fatally wounded. Gradually the Ottomans turned elsewhere—ultimately, by the First World War, to Germany.

This shift in British policy obviously invites study, and many authors have examined it at the level of high politics. The relatively early work by R. W. Seton-Watson, W. N. Medlicott, and David Harris has recently been supplemented by Richard Millman's research in private papers. In addition to these books, which concentrate on diplomacy, Richard Shannon's classic treatment, *Gladstone and the Bulgarian Agitation*, focuses specifically on public opinion.[2] Indeed, given the excellence of that examination, some explanation is due as to why the subject might be worth revisiting. Shannon essentially limits himself to the period between May and December 1876; in contrast, I go back to the aftermath of the Crimean War and forward to the Congress of Berlin. I have thus tried to integrate the later history of the agitation, which Shannon characterizes as "the more restricted and . . . somewhat different phenomenon of pressure groups,"[3] with the more spontaneous protest of 1876. Doing this has required a different conceptualization; whereas Shannon, despite bows to the view of the agitation as a social protest movement,[4] primarily describes it as an affair of high politics, I analyze it as an instance of collective behavior, drawing on the sociological framework developed by Neil Smelser.[5] New sources have become available since Shannon wrote; he was not able to utilize Gladstone's diaries or the private papers which remained at

Hawarden. And some sources of great importance were excluded by his time frame. Petitions to Parliament were not numerous in 1876 because Parliament adjourned almost before the agitation started, but they poured in by the hundreds and thousands in 1877 and 1878. These sources elucidate the structure of the agitation and show how it changed.

All this tends to modify Shannon's portrait of Gladstone; without denying the complexities and capacity for self-deception highlighted by Shannon, Gladstone seems both more sincere and, after his initial hesitations, more deliberate. Furthermore, my view enhances the influence assigned to those groups normally excluded from political decision making who, through the agency of the Bulgarian agitation, were able to introduce their views into the process and significantly affect the outcome.

This view of the British Eastern crisis of 1876–1878, in concentrating on low politics and on the connections between low politics and high politics insofar as they can be recovered, assumes that government policy, including foreign policy, must bear a rough relationship to some sort of national consensus. This observation has been illustrated repeatedly in twentieth-century democracies. But even states which are not democratic, not based on explicit, formal participation by the citizens, cannot implement a foreign policy, or indeed any policy, unless there is some support, either expressed or implied, from society at large. For example, some recent studies of Hitler's regime have suggested that his difficulties in mobilizing bureaucrats, many of them inner émigrés, to carry out his plans represented a serious barrier to full implementation of his policies.[6] Victorian England, although not a democratic state on the twentieth-century model, seems to occupy a middle ground. By the last third of the century, the upper and middle classes and a substantial proportion of the urban working classes were legally allowed to participate in the government. New groups were gaining the ability to influence governmental decisions. It is therefore necessary for diplomatic historians to look at the views and the activities of individuals and groups in society who were not part of the political process at the highest level, but who, nevertheless, when aroused, could sometimes bend official planning. Such an examination fits into the broader historical concern with political outgroups, with the relatively powerless and the disadvantaged. Furthermore, it attempts to demonstrate what these individuals thought about foreign policy, why they thought as they did, how these beliefs functioned (both as an understanding of the surrounding world and in terms of efforts to find common ground among groups), as well as what happened when language was translated into action, first in the national and then in the international arena.

The years 1876–1878 marked an important shift in British policy toward the Near East. A foreign policy sanctified by forty years of tradition, embraced by two generations of political leaders, and validated by a series of experts, was called into question. Britain, the foremost power throughout the eastern Mediterranean up to the mid-1870s, drew back. Although Britain did not formallly relinquish the commitment to maintaining the Ottoman Empire until 1914, when the Turks entered the war on the German side,[7] British interests had long before been refocused. Little enough of Turkey-in-Europe survived after 1878: the British in effect wrote off what there was. The British attitude toward Constantinople, the Straits, and Asia Minor with its scattered Armenian population remained problematic. Although some, following Salisbury and Layard, urged the strategic centrality, political viability under Ottoman rule, and economic significance of these areas, many, especially among the Liberals, wanted to treat them as European rather than uniquely British concerns, and to redefine strictly British interests along a line running through Cyprus, the Suez Canal, and Egypt, with Mesopotamia and the Persian Gulf as eastward extensions. Furthermore, the Liberals had severely scrutinized the whole program of imperialism through official commitment of resources (as opposed to moral suasion).[8] If it is true that this rethinking of British policy was significantly affected by the Bulgarian agitation, then this is a notable example of "pressure from without."[9]

From one point of view, the British ultimately arrived at a more reasonable understanding of their interests. Cyprus, the Suez Canal, Egypt, and the Persian Gulf were better defined entities geographically and were more defensible militarily; in fact, Britain continued to control these areas until the 1950s. Kuwait was under British control from 1899 to 1961. Mesopotamia and Palestine, mandated to Britain between the wars, were always less manageable, but, geographically, they rounded out a strong British position in western Asia. By contrast, the Balkans, a large land mass open to invasion both by Russia and by Austria-Hungary, had always presented daunting strategic problems. It was clear as early as the Crimean War that the British, invincible though they might believe themselves to be at sea, struggled if confronted with Russian land might, even when the French cooperated and bore a disproportionate share of the burden. It was certainly wise to come to terms with inevitability and let the Balkans go.

Constantinople, the Straits, and Asia Minor were trickier. Although the interior of Asia Minor was indefensible by Britain, much like the Balkans, the Straits area could easily be dominated from the sea. Throughout the crisis of the 1870s, Disraeli had fantasies of seizing some strategic point as a bargaining counter.[10] Without the stimulus of the agitation, joined to pressure from important members of his cabinet, he might have implemented such a plan, with significant consequences for the shape of the peace and for future Anglo-Ottoman relations.

Britain's partial retreat in the 1870s brought problems. It certainly implied a pull-back in the Great Game and hence reduced competition with Russia. (Indeed, in the early 1900s the British and the Russians would articulate their concerns in the remaining contested area, Persia, and would use that understanding as the basis for a diplomatic entente.) But the retreat ended constructively, largely because of internal problems in Russia. Various revolutionary groups posed increasing domestic threats to the Russian government, and Russia's appetite for foreign adventure diminished accordingly.

As it turned out, the most serious consequence of Britain's new policy could hardly have been foreseen in 1878. The unification of Germany in 1871 and the alliance with Austria, which became the keystone of Germany's foreign policy after 1873, created for the first time a strong diplomatic center in Europe. In a sense Bismarck's role as the "broker" at the Congress of Berlin was a recognition of Germany's new status within the European state system; but since the emphasis was placed on his being an "honest broker," the potential of the new arrangement for disturbing the balance of power was not yet clear. In actuality, the British lost the possibility of exerting influence on central Europe from the east, through a second front. They were to pay the price for this in the First World War in the Gallipoli campaign and again in Crete and Greece in the Second World War. Britain had traded long-term deterrence for middle-term manageability.

Could the traditional British policy of active support for the Ottoman government realistically have been continued? Most British historians believe that this would have been impossible after the Bulgarian massacres. As A. J. P. Taylor put it, the Bulgarian massacres were "the political crime of the century"[11] and destroyed Ottoman credibility for ever. However, this widely held evaluation rests upon a view of the Ottoman Empire which has been substantially modified since Taylor wrote. Recent excellent studies both by Turks and by outsiders demonstrate conclusively that the Bulgarian massacres, far from being the "crime of the century," were one in a series of massacres and indeed, with the exception of the Armenian massacres in the 1890s, represent the end of a trend, rather than the beginning.[12] Furthermore, the Bulgarian Christians were not the innocent victims portrayed by contemporary British polemicists. A great many Muslims suffered as well, and because of the many conversions to Islam in Bulgaria, many of those Muslims brutalized were ethnically identical to the Bulgarian Christians. In short, civil war superimposed upon political revolt complicated the simplistic picture of religious persecution by foreigners put forward in British propaganda.

Indeed, by 1876 the Ottoman Empire (through the Tanzimat reforms) had made noteworthy progress toward modernization and a working pluralism. The crowning achievement of this movement was the brief constitutional experiment in 1876–77, during which a legislative assembly representing the different religious and ethnic communities functioned in Constantinople in partnership with the Sultan.[13] The Ottoman Empire in 1876 was actually much closer to the image which the British had embraced with such enthusiasm when they went to war in support of the Empire in 1854, and one is tempted to suppose that if they could support the unreformed empire in 1853–54, they could certainly have underwritten the reformed Ottomans in the 1870s. In fact, it is highly possible that the rapid failure of the Ottoman constitutional experiment was due in some degree to lack of support by the European powers.

How did Britain's disillusionment with the Ottoman Empire come about? At first glance, the program of Gladstone and his fellow agitators might seem to owe little to knowledge about or study of the realities of the Near East. In that sense, the policy of the British government was perhaps "policy made in the streets" in the derogatory sense of the term. Yet the Bulgarian agitation was only one factor in a larger process of decision making and the result was certainly far from irresponsible or uninformed.

British leaders tended to see the Ottoman Empire in rather shallow terms that reflected national interests. Put another way, they functioned within the world view condemned by Edward Said as Orientalism.[14] Consistently, diplomats in Constantinople, even those with many years' experience in the area such as Lord Stratford de Redcliffe, tended to tag Ottoman statesmen as members of the English party, the French party, or the Russian party. Such labeling, while convenient for writers of dispatches, did little to explain the mechanisms of Ottoman politics. Naturally, Western observers were never analytical in a modern social scientific sense. The massacres were reported as unique events and judged in moralistic terms; status changes between religious groups and the backlash felt by those who were losing status went unrecognized. Gladstone, in an article in the *Quarterly Review* in 1858, raised the possibility that earlier disturbances in Montenegro, Crete, Lebanon, Izmir, and Jidda might be part of a pattern or, as he put it, were likely to be "based in causes of profound influence, which make the whole soil of the Turkish Empire heave convulsively with a volcanic movement." Yet he concluded optimistically: "The end of the struggle will, we trust, be for the happiness of man;" he did not at that time probe the consequences for Britain of his further insight that "the passage to it may be a dreadful one."[15]

The Ottoman Empire was both geographically and culturally distant from Britain. It is thus remarkable that Britons at high levels of the government had experienced and understood Ottoman realities as well as they did. Their understanding relied heavily on the unsystematic advice of "experts," largely self-trained individuals who nevertheless developed considerable knowledge of Ottoman affairs and significantly influenced policy. One type, to be distinguished from casual travelers, is represented by the historian George Finlay, who originally went to Greece at the time of the revolt in the 1820s and met Lord Byron before the latter's death. After Greece became independent, Finlay became a local fixture in Athens, writing extensively for British newspapers. His acerbic point of view preserved the disillusionment which many philhellenes of the 1820s experienced upon close contact with the realities of Greece; he continued to express it long after it had ceased to be fashionable at home. Yet his years of exposure to Greece and his articulate, closely reasoned style of writing assured him a wide following. Even Gladstone, much more pro-Greek, cited Finlay as an authority.[16] Apparently, throughout the 1860s Finlay's love-hate relationship with Greece served to curb facile enthusiasm for the Greeks in England among a generation who had not undergone the disappointment of the 1820s.[17]

Other experts on the Ottomans gained their information through official channels. In the 1860s, both Henry Layard and Lord Stratford de Redcliffe were members of Parliament; both spoke frequently on the Eastern Question. Although the two men differed in party (Layard was a Liberal whereas Lord Stratford was a Conservative), both supported the Ottoman Empire and both believed Britain should be heavily involved in its modernization. In this, both were heirs of Lord Palmerston, and both continued to espouse the Crimean War policy long after most of the English had had second and third thoughts.

Their knowledge of the area, though it led to surprisingly similar recommendations, had been gained in contrasting ways. Stratford had initially gone out to the East in 1809 and had been instrumental in negotiating the Peace of the Dardanelles, which transferred the Ottoman Empire from the French orbit to the British. He had served as British ambassador in Constantinople for long periods thereafter, most notably during the 1840s and the first half of the 1850s, and had won legendary status as "the Great Elchi," in his own estimation the most powerful Western diplomat in Constantinople. Yet Stratford's claim to expertise was far from incontrovertible. He never learned Turkish, did not travel in the country, and for the most part remained secluded in the British Embassy in Pera or the summer embassy in Tarabya (Therapia). His acquaintances were mostly official and his attempts to go beyond prescribed encounters were marred by ethnocentrism. He worked closely for many years with Reshid Pasha, the great reforming minister of the early Tanzimat, yet he never came to terms with Reshid's religion or ethnicity.[18]

Layard, who came East as a nineteen-year-old adventurer with few prospects, was always better able to assimilate. Initially he had worked his way overland to Constantinople and then to Persia; returning to Constantinople on his way home, he decided to stay and served Stratford as an unofficial emissary and later attaché. His most remarkable feat was the excavation of the great mounds in Iraq which covered the biblical city of Ninevah; this adventure, although begun and finished by others, made his name as an archaeologist. This experience and others placed him for many months in distant and relatively primitive provinces and forced him to mingle with the natives. Even in Constantinople, Layard developed many informal contacts among Ottoman statesmen. He delighted in sneaking off from Pera to spend the evenings drinking coffee, smoking, and chatting with Ottoman friends; his contacts were valued by Lord Stratford, who used him as a go-between to Reshid Pasha. It was only after years of this relatively spontaneous exposure that Layard achieved ambassadorial rank and magisterial status in the 1870s.[19]

Another "expert" on the Ottoman Empire, whose acceptance, though perhaps surprising, was wide, was the veteran Ottoman minister in London, Constantine Musurus Pasha. Musurus, an ethnic Greek who had opted for Ottoman service, came to London originally in 1851 after a series of revolving-door ministries. He remained until 1885 and became a London fixture. Before he retired, he had become the doyen of the diplomatic corps. When his wife died during the Sultan's visit in 1867, British high society mourned, and many of the socially prominent attended her funeral (which ironically took place in the Russian Orthodox Church). Some years later, Musurus's daughter married an Englishman of excellent connections.[20] Indeed, Musurus himself enjoyed close contacts in society; for example, he helped Gladstone with "Greek pronunciation."[21] In the early 1860s, upon the initiative of Lord Palmerston, Musurus was given an opportunity to influence articles in the *Morning Post*. These pieces, which stand out from other writing about the Middle East because of their wealth of detail and sympathetic portrayal of the Porte's problems, were repeated in other papers, particularly the *Manchester Guardian*, and seem to have reinforced Palmerston's policy of support for Ottoman reform.[22]

Although not objective, these experts and others did bring a significant body of experience and well-developed opinions to bear on the problems Britain faced in the East. They agreed in suggesting that Ottoman rule, whatever its flaws, was susceptible to improvement and offered the best hope for peace and stability in the area; in contrast, as successor governments run by native Christians began to emerge, they proved to be weak and inclined to regrettable excess.

A number of important British statesmen had traveled to the Near East and had gained impressions of Ottoman society at first hand. Many upper-class Englishmen included Greece on the grand tour; the most adventuresome might visit Constantinople, Lebanon, or Egypt as well. Surely the hazards of travel in Greece in the 1860s, a period when embassy personnel despaired of protecting their staff if they so much as took "long walks,"[23] must have contributed to the general skepticism about the Greeks' suitability for leadership in the eastern Mediterranean, replacing the Ottomans. The abduction of a party of well-connected British tourists and the murder of several hostages in April 1870 sparked a diplomatic confrontation; the travelers' mistake was to take an excursion to the site of the battle of Marathon,[24] an obvious attraction for the classically educated.

Both Disraeli and Gladstone visited the eastern Mediterranean. They took surprisingly similar paths, going first to the Ionian Islands, then crossing to the mainland to be entertained by Ottoman officials in the pashalik of Janina. Gladstone felt seriously uncomfortable throughout his visit. Ottoman customs were unsettling and his experiences confirmed his notions of the laziness and corruption of the Ottoman bureaucracy. Far preferable for this classically trained student of Homer was his brief unofficial visit to Athens to see the Acropolis and hobnob with acquaintances in the capital.

Disraeli, on the other hand, treated his experiences in Albania as high adventure; he even contemplated volunteering to help the Porte put down a local rebellion and was only dissuaded by the fact that the revolt petered out before his arrival. From Albania, Disraeli went on to Constantinople, where he spent several months, and then toured the Holy Land and Egypt. For Disraeli the East appealed to a deep strain of Jewish identity; he recognized and in some sense came to terms with aspects of his family life and upbringing which had seemed hopelessly eccentric in England.[25] In a sense, both Gladstone's and Disraeli's views of the Ottoman Empire were flawed by accidents of personality and background. Gladstone's relative rigidity and tendency to take himself extremely seriously led him to feel awkward in such a very foreign situation, whereas Disraeli's love of adventure and search for his origins led him to feel at home. These personal factors also colored their later policy decisions.

Such tourists did not imagine staying in the Near East; even an old Turkish hand like Lord Stratford regarded Constantinople as a place of exile and yearned for a career in London in Parliament with prospects of the cabinet.[26] The Ottoman Empire did appeal, though, to a type of daredevil or misfit, usually aristocratic in origin, who sought foreign service for adventure and personal heroism. Examples were Sir Adolphus Slade and Hobart Pasha, admirals in the Sultan's navy, or Captain Burnaby, who made the famous ride to Khiva and also traveled through Asia Minor. Such individuals stirred the imagination of less bold friends at home and, in addition to providing good gossip for fellow aristocrats, offered superior copy to the newspapers. Their views were pro-Ottoman; as imperial soldiers of fortune, they had few scruples about serving the Porte, but most of them tended to be deeply suspicious of Russia, England's rival in Asia.

In contrast to such highly placed, official or semi-official, observers of the Middle East, a new group came into prominence in the 1860s and 1870s. These were the missionaries. They dealt with a different population in the East and introduced a novel perspective. Since the

Porte forbade proselytization of Muslims, their work was necessarily with Christians and thus they were able, virtually for the first time, to present the viewpoint of the subject peoples.

Even those Britons who were less well born were somewhat sophisticated about the Ottoman Empire. In a society in which religious commitment encouraged close study of the Holy Land, the frequent public lectures on its archaeology were evidently well attended. Books dealing with the area, either in an ancient or a modern context, held a secure niche in the market. Investors in London or Manchester looked, perhaps not suspiciously enough, at the immediate details of loans and business ventures, and financial news was heavily focused on the pros and cons (more typically the pros) of such investments. A few businessmen and professionals made careers in the Ottoman Empire, such as the lawyer Sir Edwin Pears. Like the missionaries, they usually became long-term expatriates; the title of Pears's autobiography, *Forty Years in Constantinople*,[27] tells the story. Pears became a severe critic of the Porte and especially of Sultan Abdul Hamid; he admitted, however, that he stood almost alone in a foreign colony which lived the good life on Ottoman sufferance. A few workmen went out for projects such as the railways; when they returned, they sometimes testified about their exotic experiences.[28] David Urquhart's Foreign Affairs committees promoted fairly ambitious programs of study of the Ottoman Empire, consciously infused with his anti-Russian and pro-Ottoman bias. After he left England for Switzerland in 1864, though, the committees fell on hard times, and most had failed well before his death abroad in 1877.[29] Only a few, notably the one in Newcastle, remained active. There was also a certain romantic interest in the Middle East, at once vague and avid, diffused throughout British culture. It was fed by familiar works like the *Arabian Nights* and newer offerings like the Eastern fantasies of Byron and Disraeli.

Clearly this latent fascination with the East cut across the usual social divisions of class and religion. So it is not surprising that the Bulgarian massacres aroused protest from people in diverse walks of life and served, for the moment at least, to bind together individuals whose backgrounds and goals were otherwise dissimilar, even opposed. During the same period, Britain experienced a series of protests aimed at achieving strictly domestic goals. Descriptions of the strategies and successes of these internal movements highlight features which obviously parallel the Bulgarian agitation (as the British protest movement came to be known), and suggest that it, too, can usefully be analyzed as a social protest movement. Like all such groups, the protesters faced accusations that they fomented "mob" violence. To gain respectability, spokesmen such as the newspaperman W. T. Stead took up the usual line that "they spoke for the People, for the *common* interest as against the exclusive class interest of the ruling aristocracy." Drawing heavily on the ranks of the Nonconformists, who typically provided the core of such protests, the agitators about Bulgaria, like the earlier Anti–Corn Law Leaguers and those involved in the Contagious Diseases agitation, sought to enhance their respectability by adopting "the language of sin, of the identity of public and private morality, of a distaste for expediency and mere party consideration." They used tactics which had already been developed by other groups, such as the involvement of citizens more highly placed, particularly "magistrates and local councillors" and clergy, "to give their moral authority to the whole." Like the Anti–Corn Law League, they tried to work through existing organizations, such as the chambers of commerce, as well as through their own national organizations. They functioned primarily through the classic protest meeting or "pressure from without" but, again like the Anti–Corn Law League, considered more drastic expedients, including the refusal to pay taxes. Their best hope remained, however, an alliance with a Parliamentary "insider". Earlier, the usual choice had been the Earl of Shaftesbury, that champion of humanitarian causes; in the 1870s it was Gladstone. Just as the Anti–Corn Law League had called forth a "counterorganization" in the form of the Central Agricultural Protection Society, so the Bulgarian agitation by early 1878 faced opposing leagues. Finally, the agitation, like other protest movements, achieved only mixed success: like all such groups—indeed more than most—it served to "co-opt working men in an indirect way into political activity," but at the level of its stated objectives, the results were more negative than positive. As frequently happened, the protest was more effective in ending an unpopular policy than in framing constructive alternatives.[30]

If the Bulgarian agitation can thus be understood, on one level at least, as a classic social protest movement, it becomes feasible to examine it through the conceptual tools developed by sociologists who deal with collective behavior. Empirical models frequently prove valuable in fitting together the chaotic materials generated by years of conventional research. Neil Smelser, in his *Theory of Collective Behavior* (1963), provides one such model.

Smelser states that collective behavior has three attributes. First, it involves mobilization. This was a striking feature of the effectively organized agitation beginning in the second half of 1876. Second, it is shaped by a specific belief, which is based on an evaluation of the facts but takes on a "magical" quality. The Bulgarian agitation did stem from reports of the situation in Bulgaria provided by journalists and travelers, but it quickly took on mythic proportions. In the hands of orators such as W. E. Gladstone and newspapermen such as W. T. Stead, the Turks became almost supernatural figures of evil, and Disraeli a legendary villain. Finally, according to Smelser, collective behavior is "not institutionalized." It arises precisely when the usual channels are considered inadequate to deal with a perceived threat. Certainly this typifies the Bulgarian agitation, which consisted of seemingly spontaneous protest meetings organized to bring pressure to bear on the cabinet outside regular Parliamentary procedures, by people whose participation in the governmental process was recent and still marginal.[31]

Smelser's description seems to apply to the events of the 1860s and 1870s very neatly. Use of his model facilitates the daunting task of organizing and presenting a movement which extended over two years in its active phase and eventually involved hundreds of meetings, thousands of petitions, and tens of thousands of participants all over the country. Since Smelser developed his theoretical framework historically and adduces examples from the twentieth century as well as the nineteenth and from America as well as Europe, his work introduces a comparative dimension that goes well beyond the familiar material of nineteenth-century British protests and helps differentiate what was typical about the Bulgarian agitation and what was not. Such a non-Marxist analysis is particularly appropriate to behavior which was apparently motivated more by social, religious, and political imperatives than by economic goals.

Where Smelser's description becomes, at least for present purposes, somewhat sketchy, specifically regarding the details of mobilization, I have fleshed it out with an original analytical scheme grounded in those particular events. Nevertheless, I remain indebted to Smelser for his emphasis on viewing collective behavior as generalizable process. Finally, it is not necessary to understand Smelser's scheme as deterministic, or his patterns as more than suggestively recurring regularities, though he himself sometimes seemed to do so.

Smelser believed that for a movement to emerge, six factors must be present. A protest (as opposed to random criticism or wide-ranging debate) cannot erupt without all six of these factors, and each factor narrows and shapes the precise character of the movement (the value-added phenomenon), although the factors may develop in any sequence. First, there must be structural conduciveness: a state of society which facilitates the genesis of a social movement, such as a period of transition or dislocation in which relationships between important groups and institutions are no longer clearly defined. Second, structural strain must be related to the condition of conduciveness: for example, a case where the proclaimed ideas of society conflict in a significant way with actual practice. Third, a "generalized belief" must appear and circulate, perhaps associated with a leader capable of mobilizing existing unease by proclaiming ideas which focus general distress. Fourth, there must be a precipitating factor, some specific incident which will catch popular attention, intensify disquiet, and trigger the movement. Fifth, there must be a mobilization process by which individuals and groups are organized to bring pressure to bear on the established authorities. Finally, "the operation of social control," the steps taken by the established authorities in the hope of limiting or taming the movement, plays a vital part in determining a movement's direction and force. (Because the term "social control" has been so widely used by Marxists in a pejorative sense, I prefer the more neutral "response."[32])

From such a vantage point, the significance of the Bulgarian agitation shifts and changes. In addition to its stated agenda concerning foreign policy, it had large repercussions for the structure of domestic politics. It served as a crucible in which new alliances might be forged and was a critical element in the recasting of the bond between Gladstone and the Liberals after the party's electoral defeat in 1874. Significant as was its influence in helping to limit and focus British involvement in the East, its greatest importance lay in shaping the concerns and loyalties which culminated in the Midlothian campaign and in Gladstone's return to power in 1880; its influence on the nature of the Liberal party, on its disorganized passion and passionate disorganization, reached forward through the 1880s and beyond.

The larger questions which the movement raises, if properly asked, bring us closer to the relationship between international affairs and domestic concerns. What elements of myth and what elements of fact combine in policy-making? What mechanisms determine whether collective behavior will focus on an internal or an external grievance? Why should a poorly understood situation in an "exotic" land summon forth fervor comparable to that aroused by domestic problems, which touch individuals in their daily lives? Does the language in common use about foreign countries and foreign affairs "say" anything about domestic struggles? And if a more or less academic situation becomes immediate, if it comes down to peace or war, what happens to the protest? Does it become something else, or are there continuities?

It is a commonplace that "public opinion" somehow "affects" policy, though we cannot always say how; and it is obvious that in certain cases (foreign invasion or total war) international developments determine domestic events. But what are the uses, most often unconscious and irrational, of international events, or myths about them, in the daily rough-and-tumble of political society? And how does the condition, one is almost tempted to say the health, of a political society affect its foreign policy?

2 • The Crisis in the Ottoman Empire

What were Britain's stakes in the eastern Mediterranean? What did the British want from the Ottoman Empire? Quite possibly, at the deepest level, they did not really know. Louis Halle, after a career with the U.S. Department of State, remarked "that the foreign policy of a nation addresses itself not to the external world . . . but rather to 'the image of the external world' that is in the minds of those who make foreign policy."[1] It frequently happens that an image of certain countries, the relationships between them, and the consequences if these relationships are altered, takes root in the shared wisdom of a foreign policy establishment and is then passed from lip to lip, pen to pen, generation to generation, without much reexamination or "reality-testing." When a crisis finally arises, the leaders may react unquestioningly with assumptions which are dangerously out of date.

The initial British commitment to maintaining the independence and integrity of the Ottoman Empire was made during the 1830s, at a time when Russia was believed to be establishing a protectorate over the Empire through the dubious friendship crystallized in the treaty of Unkiar-Skelessi of 1833. The revolutionary and Napoleonic wars had already aroused concern over the eastern Mediterranean. Russia's regular defeats of the Ottomans, starting dramatically in 1774 with the treaty of Kutchuk-Kainardji and continuing at roughly twenty-year intervals thereafter, left no doubt as to which was the stronger and more aggressive power. After 1815, the Tsar's role as the so-called policeman of Europe made Russia synonymous for many Britons with despotism. The Turks accordingly took their place, along with the Poles and the Circassians, among the weak yet courageous and appealing defenders of Liberty.

In the 1830s the idea gained ground that support of the Ottoman

Empire was an important British interest. This assumption was reinforced at the time of the Crimean War, along with the concomitant
notions that the Russians definitely planned domination of the eastern
Mediterrranean and would end the Ottomans' promising attempts to
create a modern, pluralistic state. Of course, there were always doubt-
ers in Britain—skeptics who were not convinced that the Russians
were as heinous, the Turks as progressive, or the maintenance of the
Ottoman Empire as essential as they were commonly supposed to be.
But, despite the inevitable disillusionment attending closer association
with the Ottomans during the war, the very fact that the British had
sacrificed so many lives and so much money to the Ottoman cause
gave the phrase "independence and integrity of the Ottoman Empire"
a special ring in the 1860s and 1870s. It meant that the burden of proof
was on those who did not believe Britain should support Constantinople, rather than on those who did.

But in thus taking on a vast and entangling web of commitments, it
seems in retrospect, and seemed to some Britons even at the time,
as though they had created a system which greatly exceeded their
requirements and was disproportionate to any likely threat. In a certain
sense, this occurred because, for the most part, the British were not
challenged. They had been tempted into a vast overextension of their
influence by the relative lack of competition during much of the century and by their own clear technological superiority on the sea. And
behind—far behind—the myth of the necessity of British support for
the Ottomans there did lie some real strategic and economic interests
which did not just fade away when it became fashionable to attack the
policy. Britain's need of the Porte was exaggerated, but it was not
invented.

At a strategic level, the British had been concerned since the end of
the eighteenth century with control of the communication routes from
the Bosporus and the Dardanelles east to the Khyber Pass because
they blocked the Russians from access to the Middle East and India.
Naturally anxiety about Britain's potentially vulnerable position in India was the major reason for their fear of Russian proximity; the corollary was concern for the routes to India, whether they involved the
Tigris-Euphrates area or the Suez–Red Sea passage. In accordance with
the tendency to embrace foreign policy "images" uncritically, during
much of the nineteenth century the British generalized their concern
to include the strategic balance throughout the eastern Mediterranean
region, and so believed that they had a direct interest in the fate of

the Bosporus and the Dardanelles as well as western Asia Minor and the southeastern Balkans. This strategic involvement with a broad front subject to British manipulation and indirect control created the Great Game.[2] Opponents at the time might pooh-pooh the threat; they could reasonably point out that the distances involved were enormous and the menace accordingly overdrawn. Indeed, it is not clear that the British ever seriously expected a Russian army to challenge them on the plains of India. The worry was instead intrigue and subversion throughout the area, and this anxiety had some basis in fact, especially after the Mutiny in 1857 and the Russian conquest of Central Asia in the 1860s.

In addition to such strategic concerns, the British developed a range of economic interests in the eastern Mediterranean. Vernon John Puryear, in his pioneering *International Economics and Diplomacy*, pointed out that Britain was attracted to this area by its "surplus of desirable agricultural exports." Of particular potential significance was the grain which could be imported from Moldavia and Walachia. After the treaty of Adrianople (1829) permitted the Principalities to sell grain on the world market, imports rose steeply; by the time of the Crimean War, they were potentially critical to Britain's ability to feed its population. Although grain from Russia continued to offer competition, the totals from the Ottoman Empire now far outstripped the Russian share.[3] The situation changed only after 1880, when American grain took over the market.[4] The Ottoman Empire was also a possible source of cotton. Significant quantities of cotton were grown in Egypt, and although its quality was not competitive with that of American cotton, it was superior to Indian cotton and increased its share of the market during the Cotton Famine of the early 1860s caused by the American Civil War.

More important than these imports, however, was the vast market for British manufactured goods which was opened up by the Anglo-Ottoman commercial treaty of Balta Liman, signed in 1838. In a clear bid to tie the British to the Ottoman Empire economically and thus to win diplomatic support, the Ottomans made trade concessions so extensive that "Turkey . . . was virtually a free-trade country" and "British trade suffered fewer legal restraints in the Ottoman Empire than in any other part of the world."[5] British exports into the Ottoman Empire in effect paid a virtually nominal rate of 3 percent.[6] Not surprisingly, Britain's trade with the Empire rose dramatically and came to dominate the field; in the middle years of the nineteenth century, when Britain's industrial supremacy was still relatively unchallenged,

61 percent of Ottoman imports originated in Britain.[7] It seemed possible that this market could be expanded indefinitely, as and if Western goods and the Western life style they symbolized became increasingly attractive to Ottoman subjects.

In the wake of the partnership in the Crimean War, British commercial and industrial circles were extremely optimistic about the potential for profit in an even closer economic link to the Ottoman Empire. The area was considered rich in resources and ripe for development. The major obstacle was perceived to be lack of appropriate transportation facilities. Roads were inadequate and in very bad shape. Harbors, even in major cities such as Constantinople and Izmir (Smyrna), were not provided with docking and loading facilities. And although the British had been angling for a railroad concession since 1836, the Ottomans did not make any grants until 1856, when the British received permission to construct a line between Izmir and Aydin. In the next ten years, the British joined with the French in financing railroad companies to build lines which would open up the interior, but progress was slow. By 1866, only 452 kilometers had been completed, consisting of two lines going into the hinterland from Izmir, one line in Romania ending at Constanţa, and one line in Bulgaria between Ruse (Ruschuk) and Varna.[8]

Improvement of the terminal ports was part of this program, but here too there were problems. Disappointments over payments for the work on the harbor at Constanţa gave rise to a lively discussion between Abdul Aziz and a deputation of merchants and investors during the Sultan's visit to England in 1867.[9] And it soon became clear that the railroads constructed with such agonizing slowness were also slow to turn a profit, in part because most of the railroads fed into agricultural regions, where there was a high demand for transport during the harvest season, but very little flow of goods in either direction at other times. The British tended to blame this failure upon the irresponsibility of the agricultural interests whom the railroads supposedly served. Demand grew for British involvement in Ottoman agriculture, and during the 1860s there was continuing pressure for modification of the system of land ownership to allow foreigners to own land in the Empire and develop its resources directly. The Porte, not unreasonably, was unwilling to encourage the growth of a large class of agricultural capitalists whose interests might lie with Europe more than with the Ottoman Empire;[10] but railroads were another matter. Unable to finance development through its rudimentary financial institutions, the Porte was ready to pay generously to entice foreign capital. Investment in Ottoman railroads was sweetened either by guaranteed interest on the capital or by so-called kilometric guarantees, by which the Porte pledged to pay the difference between the actual gross receipts per kilometer and an estimated return agreed upon in advance.[11] On this basis, as long as the Porte could be held to its obligations, the return was assured; and as late as September 1876, despite the fact that the Porte was £200,000 in arrears, a London stockholders' meeting of the Izmir-Aydin railway voted to negotiate an extension of the line.[12]

Thus in the middle years of the nineteenth century the British had developed important strategic and economic stakes in the eastern Mediterranean. In 1875–76, according to the Blue Book issued for Parliament, British ships passing the Bosporus exceeded in number those under any other foreign flag. In terms of percentages, British shipping accounted for 6 percent of the shipping and 30 percent of the tonnage trading with the Ottoman Empire; 20 percent of the shipping and 35 percent of the tonnage entering the Black Sea; and 18 percent of the shipping and 30 percent of the tonnage going to Russian Black Sea ports. Besides the Russian trade, two other significant areas dependent on the route through the Bosporus were the Danube, where the British controlled 29 percent of the total shipping and 62 percent of the total tonnage, and the transit trade to Persia through Trabzon (Trebizond), which despite declines in the Persian silk trade amounted to £1,000,000 in 1875–76.[13]

The underpinning of this lucrative involvement was continued and extended westernization. Westernization was a prerequisite at two levels. At the most direct level, westernization was essential if the Ottoman Empire was to fit into the British political and economic orbit. At another level, a certain degree of westernization was vital if the British were to continue to believe in the validity of their association with a society which in fact was radically different and in many senses antithetical to their own. In the simplest sense, the Ottoman Empire needed to undergo military reforms if it was to be a worthwhile ally to Britain in the struggle to control the region and contain Russia. In the Crimean War, it was fashionable for Britons to make fun of Ottoman military capabilities, and the Ottoman forces were subjected in various ways to British training or control. Yet the Ottoman forts on the Danube withstood the initial Russian advance in 1853–54; it seems obvious that without the time thus gained for the allies to transport their troops to the East, the course of the war would have been very different. Certainly Britain's control of the area through indirect means depended upon the Ottomans' assuming a fair amount of responsibility. This in turn had been made possible by Ottoman attempts before the Crimean War to modernize their army, including heavy use of military advisers (some of them refugees from Hungary and Poland in the aftermath of 1848, some of them "renegades" like Omer Pasha, a Slav from the Austrian Empire who later became commander in chief). The experience of the war encouraged the continuation and amplification of these reforms. Much of the money borrowed abroad, to the extent that it was available for investment in the Ottoman Empire, in fact went into military expenditures, which reached staggering proportions. In the later years of the century, more than 50 percent of the budget was devoted to such purposes.[14]

In the economic sphere, the need for development within the Empire if it was to be easily exploited by Western countries has already been noted. In addition, since Western goods implied Western ways, advances in westernization would be a critical aid to the marketing of Western products. When only a small elite furnished their palaces with Western chairs, beds or wardrobes, the market for Western furniture was obviously limited. When the majority of the population ate their food with their fingers, the demand for British silverware was of necessity restricted. Similar points could be made about clothing, and in a society suffering from deindustrialization, or the decline of handicrafts due to foreign competition without a compensating changeover to industry,[15] these consumer goods necessarily bulked very large in the exchange.

But westernization was important for reasons other than creation of a market. Traditionally, commerce had been in the hands of Levantines, non-Muslims living in the coastal cities of the eastern Mediterranean whose ethnically mixed and often indecipherable backgrounds might include Greek, Russian, Jewish, Italian, and Lebanese Christian elements, to mention only a few of the more obvious. Besides their commercial skill, these individuals usually spoke some European language as their first language and therefore tended to be quicker students of French or English, the commercial languages of choice. Expansion of British commerce with the Ottoman Empire was bound to enhance their economic position; it was only logical that demands for amelioration of their political and social status would follow. To close the circle, such an amelioration, phrased in England as the demand for Christian-Muslim equality and much touted by the missionaries, was a program that could not fail to appeal to Christian European opinion.

As it happened, the pressures for westernization which were implicit in Britain's interest in the eastern Mediterranean coincided with the purposes of a group of reformers identified with the Tanzimat, the important Ottoman reform movement of the 1840s and 1850s. Men such as Reshid Pasha, Ali Pasha, and Fuad Pasha had traveled and lived in the West on diplomatic assignment, had learned Western languages, and had studied Western writings. They were convinced that the Ottoman Empire must modernize if it was to survive. The principles that they embraced were embodied most strikingly in the two major reform decrees, the Hatti Sherif of Gulhane of 1839 and the Hatti Humayun or Islâhat Fermani of 1856. Both decrees owed something to foreign pressure in times of diplomatic crisis, but they also owed much to the perceptions of certain Ottoman statesmen of the necessary hard choices facing Ottoman society. The Hatti Sherif of Gulhane was a charter emphasizing the security of life, honor, and property. It rather ambitiously called for safeguarding these fundamental rights for all subjects of the Porte, irrespective of religion. In addition, it offered promises of a more equitable system of taxation and a fairer method of recruitment for the army. The Islâhat Fermani went even farther in proclaiming that subjects were to be treated alike irrespective of religion; this was in many respects a drastic modification of the old system, by which Ottoman subjects had been organized in religious communities or millets, whose leadership formed a subject's main channel of communication with the Porte on political as well as religious matters.[16]

It was relatively easy to put promises on paper. The problem, as the Tanzimat reformers recognized at once and European observers more slowly, lay in implementation. One might say that the realization of the Tanzimat program was dependent in important ways on heavy governmental borrowing, chiefly carried out in Britain and France, and reaching the sum of two hundred million pounds sterling by 1877.[17] Even before the Crimean War, Ottoman banks had faced severe cash flow crises originating with the Ottomans' unfavorable balance of trade with the West, which tended to drain hard currency from the Empire. In fact, however, the first loans were taken out to finance the war effort in the Crimea in 1854 and 1855.

After the war, new requirements arose. It was a common grievance in the provinces that taxes were too high and that too large a proportion of the money collected went to Constantinople. Yet as the Tanzimat reformers tried to shift more and more administrative functions away from local notables, who tended to operate in terms of age-old prejudices, to a centralized state bureaucracy more susceptible to education in their Western ideas, a transfer of revenues was almost inescapable. Foreign borrowing offered one form of relief.

The promises of tax reform going back to the Hatti Sherif of Gulhane and its program of modernization proved particularly troublesome. Relatively unsucessful efforts to reform the tax system led to a continuing shortfall in collections as compared with estimates.[18] Even more serious, the reforms that the British urged on the Porte, particularly the efforts toward Christian-Muslim equality, inevitably created social unrest and frequently sparked revolts; it was necessary to spend money, usually borrowed abroad, to maintain troops at the ready and to put down disturbances.

Unfortunately, owing partly to inexperience, the Ottomans quickly slid into a disastrous spiral. Poor currency management led to an almost unchecked flow of paper money, or kaimes. One major purpose of foreign borrowing was to retire the kaimes in favor of money with more solid backing. In addition, an extraordinarily large proportion of the money borrowed went into servicing the loans. It has been estimated that between 1854 and 1914 79 percent of the money borrowed served this purpose.[19] There is no reason to suppose that this overall percentage was lower before 1882 and the establishment of the relatively more efficient, Western-dominated Public Debt Administration. In short, foreign borrowing, although necessitated by the program of westernization and hence a concomitant of Britain's interest in the area, in some ways simply made matters worse. It may well have been even less effective than in other non-European regions,[20] and, as elsewhere, it created new problems without entirely solving the old. What it did do was to give the British, who put up a substantial proportion of the money, yet another important stake in the area.

In the years between 1840 and 1870, Britain's commitments in the eastern Mediterranean seemed to grow steadily—and Britain was not operating in a static situation. The activities and concerns of Britons, whether political, economic, or social, accelerated change in the Ottoman Empire and affected its direction; the results in turn influenced the nature of British interests in a dynamic relationship. Nowhere was this more evident than in the area of Christian-Muslim equality. Partly under British inspiration, the Tanzimat reformers had promoted a broad social evolution, which implied a structural remodeling of Ottoman society. It is not surprising that this large-scale transformation was accompanied by hostile outbursts, ultimately taking the form of movements directed against the very existence of the Empire.[21] Between 1850 and 1876, a series of massacres accompanied the dislocation associated with this program for change. Although all these episodes were similar in type, three have been picked out for closer study. All three were reported extensively in Britain, and any one might well have served as the precipitating factor for a social movement of protest against British support for the Ottoman Empire. Indeed, the last of these incidents, the massacres in Bulgaria, did just that.

Although, thanks to their resonance in the West, the Bulgarian atrocities are the best-known to European and American scholars, the events in Lebanon and Damascus in 1860 and in Crete in 1866–1869 were similar in character and just as bloodthirsty. On Mount Lebanon the number of dead was between 7,000 and 12,000, and some 300 villages were razed. The disturbances in Damascus were reputedly still more destructive, with 25,000 of the Christian minority losing their lives. In Bulgaria, in contrast, 4,000 Christians were cut down, plus a substantially larger number of Muslims. The rumored toll, however, was far higher; missionaries from the United States set a figure of some 15,000 Christians and the Bulgarians themselves reported figures ranging from 30,000 to 100,000.[22] Whatever the true figure, the notorious massacres in Bulgaria were probably no more bloody than the massacres on Mount Lebanon or the urban riots in Damascus, and may well have been exceeded by the latter.

All three disasters resemble social protests elsewhere. They exemplify what Smelser called *"mobilization for action under a hostile belief."* All three arose out of similarly conducive conditions—the disruption caused by the shift in group relationships stimulated by the movement for equality between Christians and Muslims. In each case, the groups in conflict were clearly defined, and were set off from each other by profound cleavages in a society in which religion had traditionally determined ethnicity, and both affected social status. There was a religious gulf between Christians and Muslims, with the situation in Lebanon complicated by the presence of the Druse (a sect related to Islam). Other factors included emerging ethnic and nationalistic differences between Semites and Turks in Lebanon and Damascus, between Greeks and Turks in Crete, and between Slavs and Turks in Bulgaria, and a gap in material well-being and potential involving a Christian position in each case lower politically and socially than that of the Muslims. Although the coincidence of these cleavages was not complete (in Crete and Bulgaria, for instance, there existed a substantial minority of ethnic natives who had adopted the Muslim religion), these gulfs did reinforce each other to a significant degree, and this factor increased hostility between groups.[23]

In all three areas there was a lengthy historical background of disturbance. Lebanon was ruled by the Egyptians in the 1830s and the social confusion attendant on the change from the Ottomans to Mehmed Ali and back to the Ottomans again undermined confidence in the permanence of social arrangements and contributed to a festering unrest, which surfaced in 1840–1846 and again in 1858.[24] Crete went to Mehmed Ali in 1830 as enforced payment for the Egyptians' aid to the Sultan during the War of Greek Independence; this seizure snuffed out a healthy independence movement, which had looked toward union with mainland Greece. As in Lebanon, society on the island was further dislocated when, after nearly a decade under Egyptian rule, it went back to the Porte in 1840. Bulgaria, the scene of periodic internal unrest in the 1850s, was further dislocated in 1861–1863 by Midhat Pasha's attempt to create a "model province," and later mounted a cohesive opposition to the Greek Patriarchate, which resulted in the creation of the Bulgarian Exarchate in 1870.

In addition, each area had suffered the social storm loosed by the Islâhat Fermani of 1856, which decreed accelerated progress toward Christian-Muslim equality all over the Empire. Each area was inadequately policed and protected when trouble erupted. In each case, disturbances elsewhere in the Empire had necessitated a serious decrease in military forces, while the police throughout the Empire were minimal and represented the subject peoples rather than the central authority. In each crisis, matters were exacerbated by disagreement among the rulers. In Lebanon, although the authorities in Constantinople were demanding rapid evolution toward greater social equality, local authorities, such as Kurshid Pasha in Beirut and Ahmed Pasha in Damascus, were far less sympathetic, and the notables, the unofficial local leaders, were flatly opposed, particularly in Damascus. As for Crete, a serious division arose in Constantinople about how to handle the rebellion. Many figures in the government, such as Ali Pasha, urged concessions, while the influential Young Ottomans, who represented an important outside threat to the Porte, mocked the policy of accommodation and demanded sterner steps. And during events in Bulgaria, the Grand Vizier allowed himself to hesitate fatally, confused by conflicting advice from within the Ottoman government and from the Russian ambassador. Finally, all three outbursts were facilitated by excellent communication within groups, fostered among the Christians by the churches, and seconded in the cases of Crete and Bulgaria by an active underground revolutionary network, and by the good weather prevailing in the summer season, at least to start the movement.

Although all three regions were affected by the social movement toward equality which involved the entire Empire and all shared a common condition of conduciveness, other factors provoking hostility differed from area to area. In Lebanon, the strains had become endemic, with Maronite Christians, Muslims, and Druse each developing threatening stereotypes of the other groups.[25] Lebanon also suffered economic dislocation going back to the continuing antagonism between peasants and landlords. Damascus, a center of traditional Muslim crafts, had languished as mass-produced European goods began to stream into the Empire, usually brought in by Christian middlemen. In these tense conditions, a precipitating factor was not far to seek; on May 27, 1860, a group of Maronites raided a Druse village. The first blood set off a chain of massacres and countermassacres.[26] In Damascus, some Muslim youths, who had shouted obscenities at Christians, were forced by the Ottoman governor to sweep the streets in the Christian quarter.

Communication within groups on Mount Lebanon was especially good since it was promoted by religious and client-patron networks as well as by kinship. In Damascus, where the mob seems to have been composed of outsiders drawn in from the countryside as well as natives of Damascus, the mobilization of a crowd may have been less predictable, but there were facilitating circumstances: the outbreaks were shorter and the geographical area more restricted.[27] Lebanon produced its share of demagogues, most notably the Maronite Bishop Touma. The role of Druse leaders, such as Said Bey Jumblat, is less clear, but in the aftermath Said Bey was accused of a prominent role, as were many of the notables in Damascus. The coerced street sweepers may well have acted collectively as role models in a limited leadership capacity. Finally, in both Lebanon and Damascus, there seems to have been official involvement at the local level and many reports charge participation in the massacres by the troops,[28] although the central government did intervene to restore law and order, through

Fuad Pasa's mission, and so reaffirmed the original policy of progress toward social equality.

Events in Crete followed a similar pattern. Longterm cleavages and a tendency for scapegoating had been built into the social structure. Tensions had been exacerbated by efforts to implement the Islâhat Fermani. In many places, Christians had rushed to ring church bells and display flags, tactlessly flaunting newly legalized practices.[29] Christians appeared to be buying up property at an accelerated rate.[30] The Ottoman governor seemed dependent on certain Greek Christian favorites, who were criticized as not even representative of the best of the local Christian population.[31] Actually, this situation was almost unavoidable, since the Islâhat Fermani worked against the privileges of the Greek notables quite as much as against the Muslims,[32] and the traditional leadership was not likely to rally to its implementation. Despite these gains, so irritating to the Muslim community, Christians were far from satisfied. On May 14, 1866, some local Christians triggered insurrection when they delivered a petition to the governor begging for lower taxes and a more evenhanded judiciary.

The beliefs that inspired the movements in Crete and Bulgaria differed markedly, however, from those in Lebanon and Damascus. Whereas the rioters in Lebanon and Damascus simply took out general hostility on the group they perceived as antagonistic, the Christians in Crete and Bulgaria operated on a well-articulated nationalist ideology, and their aggression was organized, particularly in Bulgaria, by a full-fledged revolutionary leadership. As result, each of these two later events evolved from a mere outburst to a full-scale independence movement.

In Crete, the governor agreed to the Greeks' petition simply to buy time while he deployed troops all around the island, supposedly to protect the Muslims. The Greeks in turn took the excuse for rebellion with the aim of union with independent Greece. In contrast to Bishop Touma or the street sweepers in Damascus, the Cretans were led by a group of guerrillas who had formulated ambitious aims, been well coached, and who continued to receive support from mainland Greece.[33] They retreated to caves in the hills and organized an effective civil war, marked by dramatic incidents such as the massacre at the monastery at Arkadi. There a group of Cretan families was besieged and then blown up, it is not clear by whom; nearly everyone died. It was an incident which could be and indeed was played up to effect in the western European press, an early instance of exploitation of the media. The process of suppression further played into the revolutionaries' hands. The initial response was moderate, but under pressure from the Young Ottomans in Constantinople, the government eventually sent their best general, Omer Pasha, to the island to carry out a policy which has sometimes been considered systematic genocide.[34] As in Lebanon, the efforts of the authorities to contain the outbreak were complicated by the fact that many Muslims of local origin used the occasion to settle old scores, thus envenoming the fighting.

The massacres in Bulgaria follow a similar pattern. Endemic strains had been intensified in Bulgaria by a massive immigration of Muslims fleeing from the Crimea and from the Caucasus as the Russians consolidated their control there.[35] Between two and three hundred Circassians and Crimeans, most of them Muslims, settled along the Danube in Bulgaria between 1862 and 1878.[36] This influx threatened to change the precarious numerical balance between Christians and Muslims.[37] Tensions were exacerbated when the newcomers reverted to a seminomadic way of life, plundering wherever possible and taking revenge on non-Muslims in a way new to the area. As in Crete, such strains were intensified by nationalistic beliefs. Furthermore, in Bulgaria the movement was reinforced by the closely coinciding and successful earlier agitation for religious autonomy. Bloodshed during a rising in the mountains around Plovdiv (Philippopolis) and Pazardzhik on May 2, 1876, uncovered a long-range, laboriously developed revolutionary movement, which had organized the Bulgarian Revolutionary Central Committee in Serbia in 1870 and had worked persistently if not very successfully since that time to achieve separatist goals.[38] This group provided leadership behind the scenes. The mobilization had been well organized in advance, and the existence of substantial regional dissatisfaction quickly led to civil war. The Ottoman government again bungled the suppression; as in Crete, there was ill-advised delay.[39] The responsibility lay partly with the Russian ambassador, Ignatiev, who two-facedly urged the Grand Vizier Nedim "to suppress the rebels harshly on one hand and to appoint incompetents to handle military and political affairs on the other, thus instigating further revolts that the Ottomans could not suppress." As in Lebanon, the Ottoman forces at Plovdiv (Philippopolis) were insufficient to handle the disturbances and the alternative was to use locally recruited irregular mercenaries or bashi-bozuks, with the usual results in terms of breakdown of discipline and settling of old scores.[40]

Although events in these three provinces differ in detail, all three resemble each other as examples of collective behavior. All were well reported in the British press. Lebanon and Bulgaria had both been scenes of considerable missionary activity. Britain maintained consuls in Beirut and Damascus. France took up the cause of the Maronites and after some months of threats, finally intervened militarily, creating anxiety in Britain and making events in Lebanon and Syria a matter of more than humanitarian interest. Crete being an island, its inhabitants naturally turned to the sea. Many refugees headed for the coast, in hopes of being picked up by vessels of the great powers. Prominent in the impromptu evacuation effort were Captain Murray of the *Wizard* and Captain Pym of the *Assurance*. Their testimony concerning the plight of the victims, invested with all the credibility due to officers of the British Navy, was an important source. Furthermore, refugees who did manage to embark on friendly ships headed for Greek ports. Thousands eventually reached Athens and its environs. There they were highly visible to British consuls and to the British minister. In Bulgaria, after the alarm had been raised by American missionaries, a series of self-appointed observers, such as the American Eugene Schuyler and the Briton Malcolm MacColl, toured Bulgaria in the summer of 1876 and produced graphic reports which made the Bulgarian massacres a cause célèbre. It seems clear that, based on the information available in Britain, any one of these well-publicized episodes could have become the basis for a social protest movement; that this did not happen until the mid-1870s can be explained by the fact that not until that time were the other factors necessary to produce a social movement in place.

3 ✦ British-Ottoman Strain

The social movement toward Christian-Muslim equality in the Ottoman Empire was a continuing force for dislocation which led periodically to massacre. At least two of these episodes, the events in Mount Lebanon/Damascus and the events in Crete, were reported in grisly terms in the British press. Either one could have served, quite as well as the Bulgarian atrocities, as the precipitating factor for a British social protest movement, had the other preconditions for such a movement been present. A second prerequisite, a sense of structural strain related to this dislocation, was also present throughout the period under consideration. Smelser tells us that "strain . . . always expresses a relation between an event or situation and certain cultural or individual standards."[1] It is not hard to translate this into the context of British-Ottoman relations. The British government was supporting a regime under whose auspices Christians were subject to persecution culminating in slaughter. This naturally created a conflict with the "cultural . . . standards" propagated by Christian churches in Britain and the "individual standards" of many believers. Official policy called for support of Constantinople; individual values suggested that Christians should oppose such a commitment. This value strain might be expected to cause and in 1876–1878 did in fact cause repercussions so striking that it is easy to forget that strain had accompanied British-Ottoman friendship for many years.[2]

In point of fact, during the 1860s, episodes which might have served to precipitate social protest were explained away by a series of rationalizations, a special language, which restored a working integration between official policy and Christian imperatives. Study of this process yields a better understanding of the intellectual aspects of British support: how the manifest value strain could be tolerated for a period of some twenty-five years, and how, as certain rationalizations lost plausibility and others emerged in their place, the identity of British supporters and opponents of the Ottoman Empire changed.

Directly preceding the Crimean War, British support of the Ottoman Empire had been widely justified on the grounds that the Ottomans were reforming and one might almost say anglicizing their state and society year by year. This effort, linked to the Tanzimat reformers, was contrasted with the supposedly unenlightened views of the Christians, who, whether Greek Orthodox or Catholic, often received harsh criticism. As one individual put it at a public meeting in Newcastle: "The Turk was not infidel. He was Unitarian. As to the Russian Greeks or Greek Christians, he said nothing against their creed, but they were a besotted, dancing, fiddling race. He spoke from personal observation."[3] Since Unitarians had been prominent in technological innovation and radical thought, there is an obvious implication that the Ottomans were progressive and modern.

Furthermore, in 1853–54 the Turks were readily portrayed as "victims of Russian aggression." This characterization called into play a whole set of hostile attitudes toward Russia. From the 1830s, as John Gleason has ably explained,[4] many sectors of the British public had seen Russia as the prime despotic power in Europe, cruel to its own peoples and barbarous beyond measure to those it conquered, such as the suffering Poles and the gallant Circassians. Although the Ottomans had not been taken over, the pressures to which they had been subjected during the two Eastern crises of the thirties gave them the status of a third oppressed group. These views, quiescent during the 1840s, were revived with tremendous force in 1853 and 1854; indeed it is arguable that the pressure of public opinion was a principal cause of Britain's entry into war with Russia in March 1854.[5] By that time, the tsar's perceived role as Liberty's greatest foe had been reinforced by Russian policy during the 1848 revolutions. Englishmen had followed the suppression of the revolution in Hungary and had noted that Austrian efforts might well have misfired without Nicholas's timely aid. "A wave of sentiment" greeted the Porte's refusal to extradite the Hungarian and Polish refugees who fled to the Empire. When Palmerston sent the fleet to support the Ottomans against Austrian and Russian pressure, the circle was complete: many of the British public, devoted Palmerstonians, had made the refugees' cause their own. When Louis Kossuth, the Hungarian revolutionary leader, made a triumphal speaking tour of Britain, the message was driven home.[6]

Looking at these constructs from a later perspective, it becomes clear that they were essentially myths. Indeed there were hints at the time that all was not as presented in public meetings and the popular press, but such false notes were explained away. When revolts against Ottoman rule broke out in the Greek provinces of Epirus and Thessaly in January, 1853, the British government faced a potentially serious dilemma. If Ottoman rule was tolerant, why were Christians risking their lives to throw off the yoke? One fairly convincing explanation was that this unrest had been fomented from Athens: Ottoman Greeks had been persuaded of their misery by outside agitators from Greece who were acting from selfish political motives. A second argument was religious. As Lord Shaftesbury expounded in the House of Lords, "the Christians were as much the victims of the Greek Orthodox priesthood as they were of the Ottoman administration." Only a concerted missionary effort to extend Protestantism throughout the Balkans offered solid hope of ameliorating conditions; from this perspective, Britain's course was clear. Nicholas of Russia "did not even allow the circulation of the Bible in the vernacular in his dominions." The Porte, on the other hand, had recognized the Protestants as an incorporated religious group, or millet, in 1850.[7]

The massacres in Lebanon and Damascus called these rationalizations into question, but also provided the occasion for new constructs. The Russian threat was never quite as convincing in the 1860s after the resounding defeat inflicted on that power during the Crimean War, while the freeing of the serfs in 1861 cast doubt on the supposed incorrigibility of Russsian autocracy. Although Russian pressure on Central Asia was a subject of concern, there was no confrontation equivalent to the bout in the 1850s until 1877, after the Bulgarian agitation had influenced British attitudes. The suspicion of Catholic and Orthodox Christianity was less noticeable in the sixties, and may have reflected the unusual tensions of the early 1850s, in the wake of the conversions of some former members of the Oxford Movement like Newman and Manning and the increased immigration from Ireland at the time of the Famine. Danger from outside subversion continued to be a prominent theme throughout the decade, but it was less applicable to Lebanon and Damascus than it was to ethnically Greek regions of the Empire. It would reemerge as a major rationalization at the time of the Cretan crisis, but it was muted in the early sixties.

Initial reports of the massacres laid much of the blame on the Ottoman authorities. It was widely believed that the vali of Damascus,

Ahmed Pasha, had encouraged the outbreak; indeed Lenormant, a French observer in the Lebanon with diplomatic connections, charged that the massacres were a deliberate conspiracy hatched by local authorities.[8] However, as soon as news of the disturbances reached Constantinople, Fuad Pasha, the famous reformer and Ottoman foreign minister, was sent out by the Porte to investigate the situation and to punish the guilty. Although some Western observers believed that Fuad's sentences did not go far enough,[9] many officials in Britain credited him with exemplary severity. Fuad was believed to have restored the good name of the Porte and to have provided an instructive example for provincial officials throughout the Empire.

Other possible explanations were largely ignored in British governmental circles. The Damascene community leaders, or notables, themselves theorized that Fuad, acting on behalf of the vested interest of the Turkish central administration, had moved to break the cohesion of the local Arab Muslim ruling elite.[10] Subsequently scholars took the view that the Porte was itself partly to blame because of the failure to reinforce the regular troops in Damascus despite appeals and warnings from Ahmed Pasha. This had necessitated use of irregular, local levies to quell the disturbances with predictably disastrous results.[11] Finally, there were contemporary accusations in Constantinople to the effect that Fuad had mounted a coup de théâtre to preempt the role of the French expeditionary force which now intervened on behalf of European civilization.[12]

For Britons who tended to share Palmerston's public faith in the soundness of Ottoman leadership, reports of Fuad's mission laid to rest most of the doubts that the massacres may have raised. Local people might get out of hand, but the men ultimately reponsible were both enlightened and tough; the lesson for Britain, then, was to support Constantinople as energetically as possible, in the hope that the reformers, thus strengthened, would progressively gain greater control of unruly subordinates and would gradually accomplish the massive reeducation program that was implicit in westernization. As result, in 1860 the English public was remarkably calm, but there was considerable excitement in Ireland, especially among Irish Catholics. Indeed, the massacres in Lebanon and Damascus could have precipitated an outburst of hostility in Ireland.

Ireland's situation in many respects paralleled conditions in Lebanon. Although Ireland had not suffered from a drastic social change in the immediate past such as was caused in the Ottoman Empire by the Islâhat Fermani, there had been a background of trouble since the abortive revolt in 1848. Like Lebanon, Ireland was divided into opposing communities, Catholic and Protestant, with distinctive cultures and mutual hostility.[13] Political leaders, especially on the Catholic side, encouraged this antagonism. One might expect, therefore, that news of the massacres in Lebanon and Damascus might have touched off a social movement in which Irish Catholics would have acted out anger against their English and Protestant oppressors.

In fact, Catholics who had been involved in Syria tried to incite action. Catholic missionaries provided a link between the two areas.[14] Pronouncements by Catholic leaders right up to the Pope sanctioned action on behalf of the Syrian Christians.[15] The thrust of the mobilization effort centered around the visit to Ireland of Father Gifford Palgrave, an English Jesuit missionary in Syria. At the beginning of September, Palgrave held several meetings in Dublin and in Limerick to raise money for the victims; in his speeches, he drew a parallel between the Catholics in Syria and the Catholics in Ireland. In Dublin, he gave a brief history of the Maronites going back to the persecutions of the fifth century and declared that they had suffered torments only equalled by those to which the Catholics of Ireland were subjected. The Druse and the local Muslims, angered by the privileges given Christians in the Treaty of Paris, had mounted a conspiracy to massacre Catholics throughout the northern Arabian peninsula. The killings of Catholics were similar to events at Tipperary, the scene of an abortive attempt at revolution in 1848 (a remark which brought "loud cheers"). Taken as a whole, the massacres could only be compared to the events in Drogheda or Wexford, the notorious butcheries perpetrated by Cromwell—"(loud applause)."[16]

Palgrave's visit brought forth a pastoral letter from the Archbishop of Dublin which was read in all Catholic churches on September 9 and which proposed "that those who are devoted to smoking or to the use of ardent spirits, have now an opportunity of doing good to themselves and to their neighbour, by applying to a work of charity a portion of what they throw away in maintaining useless or pernicious habits."[17] Father Palgrave carried his message on to Limerick, where a large meeting was held attended by local dignitaries such as William Monsell, M.P., high sheriff of the county and later a junior minister in Gladstone's first government. Following Palgrave, Monsell spoke at length and linked the pro-Ottoman policy of Britain and France to their anti-Papal policy in Italy. "The same hand which elevated the Turk, the professed enemy of Christ, is raised to strike down the Holy Father, the visible head of the Christian Church, Christ's Vicar on earth, the common father of the Christian world . . . (sensation)."[18] Like Palgrave, Monsell did not miss the opportunity to remind his hearers of the anti-Catholic thrust of British policy.

In 1876 in England, such meetings led to petitions and delegations to the Foreign Office; they were the start of a well-orchestrated campaign to change Britain's policy. In 1860 in Ireland, the movement never assumed such dimensions. The Irish Catholics, unlike the English in 1876, had an alternative to violence. During the crucial, initial months in 1876, Parliament was not in session. But during 1860 and the spring of 1861, Irish members of the House of Commons expressed themselves freely on the situation in Lebanon and Damascus, and pressed the government hard about its intentions.[19] Normal institutional channels provided an outlet for Irish excitement. Furthermore, neither the British government nor the Irish Protestants adopted a position which targeted them for hostility. When the French insisted on sending troops to protect their coreligionists and restrain the Porte, the British government reluctantly modified its support of the Ottomans sufficiently to cooperate in limited fashion with the intervention. The Irish Protestants, although they exhibited deep suspicion of Catholics in other contexts, did not take an anti-Catholic stand in this particular instance. They strenuously resisted attempts to cast them in the role of the Druse. The *Irish Times* objected very strongly to an article in the *Times* of London which compared the disorders raised by the Orangemen on Battle of the Boyne Day with the battles between Druse and Maronite. Indignantly the *Irish Times* declared that it was hardly fair to equate a ritual one-day disturbance in Ireland with the protracted feuds of the Lebanese.[20] In fact, the images projected in Irish Protestants' minds by the Maronite-Druse quarrel were not taken from Irish history; they were drawn principally from the Indian Mutiny of 1857. The *Irish Times* declared, on journalistic hearsay, that the mutiny in India had almost caused an imitative massacre in Syria.[21] Both the *Irish Times* and the *Freeman's Journal* compared the troubles in Syria with the Indian Mutiny and equated Said Bey Jumblat, the Druse leader, with Nana Sahib.[22]

It is not entirely clear why the comparison between the Druse and the Sepoy mutineers seemed so appropriate to the Irish. The English, as we shall see, usually reacted differently. The Irish were heavily represented in the colonial effort in India, and therefore the plight of the victims of the Mutiny was perhaps particularly close to Irish families. Or perhaps the religious divisions in Ireland gave its inhabitants a sense of living in danger that was foreign to Londoners. At any rate, Irish Protestants, like Irish Catholics, identified with the victimized Maronites, based on the common fear of persecution at the hands of savages.

It was partly on this basis that the Irish Protestants joined in the efforts to raise money for relief; and this too placed them in a collegial, rather than an adversarial, relationship to the Catholics. Protestants, like Catholics, were stirred by accounts of members of their community who had suffered at the hands of the murderers. In Dublin, money was raised from all groups within the Anglican Church and eventually amounted to £1,000, a small sum compared to what had been raised in London, but significant for a relatively poor provincial city.[23] There were significant limits, though, to Irish Protestants' willingness to be ecumenical. News that the Irish Catholics had requested that the money they raised be given exclusively to Catholics called forth demands for explanation.[24] The numbers were small, but it was apparently reassuring to Protestants to learn that although the refugees were seven-eighths Catholic, one-sixteenth Greek Orthodox, and one-sixteenth Greek Catholic, one hundred and twenty Protestants were at risk as well.[25] Yet despite these hints of sectarian suspicion, the fact remained that Irish Protestants sympathized with the victims and were willing to give their money to help. This willingness inevitably defused the situation and substantially diminished any possibility that Catholics and Protestants in Ireland might turn on each other over this issue.

The British took a rather different view of what had happened in Syria, but they too did not present themselves as villains in Catholic eyes. After all, when the French sent an expedition to Syria, the British did cooperate by dispatching naval forces and by naming Lord Dufferin their representative on the international commission of inquiry. Of course, many Britons were deeply suspicious of France. An article in *Punch* equated French occupation of Syria with their earlier occupation of Rome and called the Sultan and the Pope "the two sick men" of Europe.

> The Pope cries, "Heathen friend, I see
> You've got my doctor too;
> He hasn't done much good to me,
> May he do more to you!"[26]

But the central issue, in the opinion of *The Times*, was common Christianity. *The Times* poked fun at the mistake "that has made pious Englishmen believe that east of a certain degree of longitude Christianity is not Christianity, but a creed which only tends to the abasement of those who profess it."[27] On this understanding, according to *The Times*, French intervention had to be accepted.[28] Nonetheless, the English were not enthusiastic about the Maronites. Whereas most people in Ireland apparently believed that the Druse were responsible for the massacres, the English wavered. Many English accounts suggested that the Druse's well-documented initiation of violence was preemptive and hence, by implication, might be condoned. As new evidence came in, suspicions mounted. In mid-September, *The Times's* Beirut correspondent charged that the Maronites had been organized by the Maronite Bishop Tubiyya (Tobia), a "famous agitator."[29] As the French troops wound into the interior, *The Times* reported that a body of Maronite camp followers were wreaking "cruel vengeance" on the Druse.[30] These accusations seemed to be confirmed in the spring of 1861 when *The Times* reported that the Christian bishops of Lebanon, asked by Fuad Pasha to supply a list of their principal persecutors, had produced 4,600 names. When Fuad had objected to this exaggeration, the bishops had cut down the list to a mere 1,200.[31]

This dislike and suspicion of the Maronites is the obverse of the positive English view of the Druse. Early British contacts with the Druse had been reinforced by reports of Richard Wood in the 1830s, at a time when numerous British officials believed that the Druse could be used as the nucleus of resistance to the Egyptians, who had conquered the area in 1832, and the foundation for the restoration of Ottoman supremacy. It was a view which the Druse themselves reinforced. Wood described the visit of two Druse emissaries to Constantinople, where they contacted him at the British embassy. "Convinced now . . . that they have nothing further to hope from the exertions of the Porte . . . they have adopted the resolution of delivering up their Country to the protection of Great Britain . . . they have assured me that their visit to Constantinople has been undertaken with the main object of ascertaining . . . the Sentiments of H.Ms Government on this important proposal previous to their proceeding to England."[32]

The ambassador, Lord Ponsonby, understood that there could be no extraordinary help for the Druse; but he was not above sending Wood back to Lebanon with Ottoman sanction to raise the Druse and other discontented elements against the Egyptians. After the campaign which restored Syria to the Porte, Palmerston played with the idea of a "special relationship" with the Druse, a vision made the more attractive by the missionary dreams of converting the Druse to Protestantism and using them as the basis for religious influence, parallel to French influence over Roman Catholics and Maronites.[33]

Probably these early contacts made it natural in 1860 for the English to identify the Druse as a familiar and friendly minority. Palmerston evidently believed they were Jewish; others compared them to Scottish Highlanders.[34] Visits to the Druse and to Said Bey Jumblat's ancestral home at Muktara were a not uncommon feature on the English aristocratic grand tour. One Englishman who made such a trip described his approach to the Jumblats' home. "The guide was a young Druze, with a proud and frank bearing. Lithe and clean of limb, possessed of wonderful elasticity and muscular force, which enabled him . . . to clear fissures fifteen feet wide as easily as a Londoner steps over a puddle, he was the *beau ideal* of a mountaineer."[35]

A "typical" scene at the Jumblats' was sketched in Dickens's journal, *All the Year Round*. Said Bey's home was described in terms which mingled the fantastic and the familiar: "The house is like a great baronial castle, surrounded by remarkably large olive trees, planted some distance apart. These seen together with the undulations of the land and the extent of green sward, give the whole property the appearance of an English park placed in a Highland glen." The article continued with a highly sympathetic sketch of a morning at the Jumblats':

> On the divan sat the chief, a fine-looking man of about five and thirty . . . wrapped from head to foot in a sort of long pelisse, or dressing-gown, lined with the finest fur . . . Near the divan, but sitting on the floor, were some five or six secretaries, each having before him a number of those wonderfully-shaped pieces of bad Italian writing-paper, upon which all Arab documents seem bound to be written. Next to them were two Maronite monks, in their dark coarse frocks, who had come to see the sheik on some business or other . . . Further off was a prisoner, with his hands confined by a log of wood, and guarded by four armed men . . . The sheik had been judging his case when we arrived.[36]

This is very different from portraits in Irish or French periodicals, which depict Said Bey as a mad killer.

Indeed the British tended more and more to see the troubles in the Ottoman Empire as the inevitable squabbling of subject peoples; they came to feel a certain sympathy for the Porte, which, like London, shouldered the thankless burden of empire. It seems likely that the excitement of Irish Catholics over the plight of the Maronites actually strengthened this tendency. But there was another, more direct influence pushing the same way. Thomas Edward Kebbel, a minor and cheerfully venal London journalist, relates in his memoirs how he was introduced to the Ottoman minister, Constantine Musurus, and agreed, for a consideration, to concoct leading articles for the *Morning Post*, Lord Palmerston's organ, "sometimes two or three times a week—sometimes, perhaps, not for a month," writing "in support of the Turkish policy" of the minister. Kebbel, who obviously enjoyed this arrangement, states:

> As I was paid for each article by the *Post*, in addition to my share of the subsidy, I did pretty well. But without these honoraria I should have been more than half repaid by my interviews with Musurus, and the singularly humorous and vivacious style in which his instructions were communicated. He used to sit cross-legged on his sofa and dictate his views with a volubility which was sometimes perplexing, and mingled with jokes which were always good ones. He was, I think, most amusing when at a loss for the particular English word he wanted, for he neither spoke English fluently nor pronounced it correctly. He often had to fall back upon his French, and then I was mostly able to help him to the word he wanted . . . He told me a great deal, however, which I was very glad to know, and which I have found very useful since.[37]

Musurus picked up several lines of argument which fitted very well with the Palmerstonian liberal conception of the situation in the eastern Mediterranean. Undoubtedly, this was the main objective in using a Palmerstonian paper as his platform. Possibly because his message was attuned to existing British prejudices, the provincial press took advantage of the ease with which articles written in London could now be reproduced verbatim;[38] in this instance, this practice was followed especially by the *Manchester Guardian*, whose readers had long tended to be Palmerstonian sympathizers.

In a general sense, Musurus argued that the Ottomans were a progressive people whose rule was well calculated to assure religious toleration and freedom in the East. In an article on September 1, 1860, the *Morning Post* announced: "There can be no doubt that in European Turkey Christians are more free in respect of worship than Protestants are in Catholic Austria; and that they are also much more free in point of government than they would be under a Russian or Austrian yoke . . . The Turkish Empire, therefore, as it now exists, affords the best guarantee for Christian freedom wherever that empire exists."[39]

A second point was raised repeatedly by Musurus: once Fuad Pasha had been sent out with a body of troops to pacify Syria, he could do the job alone and did not need assistance from the European powers.[40] The *Morning Post* worried that the French occupation would prove hard to terminate, would be too pro-Maronite, and would set a bad precedent for other ambitious powers.[41] Both these points impressed the *Guardian's* editor as worth printing.[42] As the mission continued, the extensiveness and impartiality of the arrests and executions ordered by Fuad were emphasized.[43] Documents backing up these points were made available for publication in the *Post*.[44] In short, the French expeditionary force had never been necessary and had actually proved counterproductive by exacerbating tensions between Maronites and Druse.[45]

The information fed by Musurus did not persuade the British press, public, or government that cooperation with the French expedition could be avoided. However, it seems likely that in the short term it helped Palmerstonian liberals justify support of the Ottoman Empire in the face of the massacres by distancing the reform-minded central government, as exemplified by Fuad Pasha, from provincial officials and local troops who had run out of hand.[46] But Fuad's mission was a tour de force which the Ottomans, under increasing pressure from conservatives, found it difficult or impossible to repeat. A vindication offered by Musurus which had a longer future in British minds was the idea of the "burden of empire." He attempted to disassociate the Ottoman Turks from the Druse by suggesting that they were very different peoples; consequently, the Ottomans should not be blamed for misdeeds which were in fact the work of the Druse. Such a confusion, the leading article declared, "would not be much less absurd than to identify our Government at the Cape with an onslaught of the Kaffirs upon Catholic colonists."[47]

Apparently Musurus, like the Irish, was struck by the parallel with the Mutiny; but the comparison which emerged from his conversations with Kebbel was dramatically different from the view consistently held by the *Irish Times* and the *Freeman's Journal*. These Irish papers had identified with the victims; in contrast, the leading articles in the *Morning Post* empathized with the Ottoman Turks and their dilemmas of leadership. The *Morning Post* declared: "We could not but believe that if, on the occurence of our Indian mutinies in 1857, we had been in a position to submit to dictation from foreign Governments, we might have been told with great truth that the rebellion was the result of our own improvidence in leaving our interests imperfectly defended by English troops; and that this evidence of our recklessness in the administration of our dependencies was to be taken for proof of our incapacity to restore India to our rule."[48] By the same analogy, the *Post* absolved the Porte from guilt: "the Prince Consort was no more responsible for the Indian mutiny than is Abdul Medjid for the Syrian massacres."[49]

This idea of the burden of empire became increasingly prominent during the 1860s, and after Palmerston's death in 1865, it virtually replaced the old liberal faith in Ottoman potential for progress as the leading rationalization for support of the government in Constantinople. It was forcefully urged when the Turks were accused of massacring Cretans in 1866 and 1867. This revolt was well publicized by British diplomatic representatives in independent Greece, typically the refugees' eventual destination. The Cretans thus had friends in court, who could speak directly into the ears of official London, and as result, their plight became, in a small way, a Liberal cause célèbre. The Duke of Argyll, for example, did not hesitate to accuse the Turks of practicing genocide.[50]

The government and its supporters were ready with their defense. As the Earl of Derby had already put it, any aid to the refugees would lead the Greeks to believe that England was ready to intervene on the Cretan side. This would compound the problem by encouraging the insurgents to prolong their resistance, ultimately creating more refugees.[51] There was a danger, as the Earl of Kimberley warned, that England might slide into "the 'artichoke policy'" of picking away Ottoman territories leaf by leaf until at last one gobbled up the "heart."[52] At a popular level, when a London Greek Committee tried to organize relief, there was a lively debate over the pros and cons of aid. A telling point was made by a letter writer to *The Times* who opined: "as well might servant girls in London club together to send their money to Ireland to encourage the Fenians."[53] Most Britons were able to accept the evaluation expressed privately by Stanley: "We thought that *prima facie* the Porte had the same right to put down an insurrection in Crete as England had in India, or France in Algeria, or Russia in Poland. We could not complain of the Government of the Sultan for doing that which every Government in the world, including that of the United States, had done, and would do again when the necessity presented itself."[54]

As the sixties went on, and Irish Catholic discontent continued and even found support in the United States, the parallels with London's problems appeared more striking than ever. Kebbel tells us that he had learned a great deal from Musurus. When the *Pall Mall Gazette* was founded in 1865 under a conservative editor,[55] Kebbel became an "occasional contributor."[56] It is tempting to assign to his inspiration an anonymous article at the end of 1866 on the long and bitter Cretan revolt. This piece juxtaposes in brilliantly satiric fashion the intractability of Ireland with the sorrows of Crete.

> The new Ottoman Lord Lieutenant of Crete has left for his island, with all sorts of benevolent resolves in his head, and with his pockets full of concessions towards the Christians . . . They will, no doubt, have as much tenant-right as they want, think they want, or cry for; and they will be at once relieved from the odious and illogical oppression of an Established State religion which is that of one-third of the inhabitants only, yet to the maintenance of which all are expected to contribute . . . It is evident that all the Constantinople Liberals are under the impression that with a redistribution of the land and with the established Mussulman Church—if we may be allowed the phrase—removed from its position of supremacy, the Cretan Christians will be perfectly satisfied henceforward, and the island will become again the first gem of the Eastern sea . . . But Turkish Liberals seem to forget that the thing which conquered and misgoverned nations . . . want, is not the reformation of their oppressors, but complete severance and final riddance from their conquerors. It matters not whether the nationality really be or be not a nationality . . . So long as the Cretan looks on himself as of the same political faith and race as the free people of the opposite continent; so long as he scrapes together his savings to get him a steerage passage to that continent, away from his hated masters . . . so long as current politics in that country are swayed by the Cretan vote, and may be compelled to take an anti-Turkish tone at any moment; so long, we are convinced, will there be either smouldering discontent or active disaffection in that green island, in spite of all the tenant-right and equitable church arrangement in the world. Not that such reforms become one whit less a duty to the masters; but they *are* the masters, and that is the root of their offending . . . Now all the thought in the world will not efface the memory of the conquest. We hope that English critics will become less offhand and reckless in dealing with the nationalistic difficulties of foreign Governments, if they find any purpose or application in what we say.[57]

This was a new, more world-weary rationale than the old Palmerstonian creed. The Porte, as an imperial government, faced almost insurmountable difficulties and certain ingratitude in a mission which

Britain, also an empire, could surely understand. The viewpoint appealed to conservatives and complemented the assumption of the "white man's burden" in India in the aftermath of the Mutiny,[58] as well as the lowering crisis in Ireland. The easy optimism was gone and ruling was no longer an intoxicating call to teach and to uplift; now it was recognized as a thankless task.[59] Martyrdom and cynicism blended in sophisticated irony, and both were reinforced by the testimony of experts about the peculiar ungovernability of the Ottoman lands.

Layard, benefiting from his long experience as traveler, archaeologist, and diplomat in the Ottoman Empire, outlined the dilemma in a thoughtful commentary on February 15, 1867, before the House of Commons. Starting from the premise that "the Turks in Europe were very much like what the English were in Ireland, and if there was a difference it was in their favour," Layard complained that the Christians wished to drive the Muslims out of the Balkans. This was manifestly unfair, since many Muslims were converts who shared the same ethnic background as the Christians. Furthermore, the Christians themselves were divided; there was no guarantee that once the Muslims had been disposed of, the Christian sects would not turn against each other. Crete appeared especially problematic to Layard because of its "mixed population;" in contrast to Serbia and the Danubian Principalities, an autonomous Crete would place Christians over a substantial group of Muslims, an arrangement just as unfair as the existing situation. Indeed, argued Layard, experience with the Ottoman Empire and with independent Greece suggested that the Muslim Turks were more likely to keep a check on their bureaucrats than were Christian Greeks.[60]

Layard's emphasis on the Turks' comparative tolerance received unexpected confirmation during 1867. In Serbia, and then more dramatically in the Danubian Principalities, Christian governments connived at or even led in persecution of Jewish inhabitants. Sir Francis Goldsmid, a noted lawyer and prominent spokesman for the cause of the international Jewish community, inquired in the Commons on March 29, 1867, about the status of the Jews in Serbia, which had deteriorated markedly since Serbian independence. During the summer, there were severe persecutions in the Danubian Principalities, where the native Jewish cohort had been augmented by refugees from persecution in Russia. The Moldavians forced many Jews to flee across the Danube into the Ottoman Empire; since the Ottomans were not eager to receive them, many simply drowned.[61] Layard noted that the Romanian government itself was involved. Feeling among Jews in Great Britain ran so high that the government was forced to abandon its usual policy of noninterference in favor of a formal protest at Bucharest.[62] These developments were proof, not only to leading Jews, but also to Conservatives like Lord Stratford de Redcliffe and the Earl of Denbigh,[63] that Christian rule unleashed fanaticism. Only the Muslim Turks could be trusted to maintain a working pluralism.

This theme of the burden of empire persisted even as late as the summer of 1876. On July 10, Disraeli declared in a House of Commons debate: "Wars of insurrection are always atrocious," and he compared events in Bulgaria to the tragedy in Jamaica, where the British governor Eyre had put down a threatened rebellion with well-documented brutality, justified in the eyes of many Britons by the need to prevent the total collapse of law and order.[64] Disraeli was well aware of the problems presented by a religiously heterogeneous population; he wrote to Lady Bradford, "Fancy autonomy for Bosnia with a mixed population . . . autonomy for Ireland would be less absurd."[65] And Hanbury, speaking in support of the Ottoman Empire on July 31, 1876, pointed out: "Other nations [England] found it difficult to govern more than one nationality, and Ireland was an example." He went on to say that fanaticism was very much a matter of one's point of view. "In the sense in which we used it, it meant everything that was bad; but in the mouth of a Turk it meant devotion to his creed and country, and those were not virtues which an Englishman would wish to disparage."[66]

The problem with all this was that it depended for its plausibility on an equation between Constantinople and London which some were no longer willing to allow by 1876. "What . . . would have been said," asked the Marquess of Hartington on July 31, "if a few years ago, when we had to deal with the Fenian insurrection, we, instead of employing Regular troops or an organized police, had invoked the assistance of the Orangemen of the North of Ireland, and the religious bitterness, which then existed in that country had led to excesses of one kind or another? Would Europe have considered it a sufficient excuse . . . that we had not at the moment a sufficient force of Regular troops of police?"[67] Ultimately, Britain's experience with empire could be turned against the Ottomans; for it gave Britons the right to judge—and the judgment might be severe.

The comparison became even trickier if Britain and the Ottoman

Empire were seen to resemble each other, for then attacks ostensibly aimed at one government could easily rebound on the other. Irish Catholics had shown some disposition in 1860 to adopt the Porte as a metaphor for their British oppressors. By a similar process, in 1876 some disgruntled Britons came to see the Turkish government as a metaphor for the Disraeli government. The Conservatives' supposed procrastination in making reforms work; their bad faith in arousing expectations which were not then fulfilled; their bureaucratic justifications of policies which defied common sense and ordinary moral sensibilities; their lack of sympathy, generally speaking, for the dictates of the Nonconformist conscience; their affectation of aristocratic luxury at a time when unemployment, underemployment, and pay reductions were rampant—all were qualities mirrored by the apparently effete, ineffectual, and corrupt Ottomans. In the mid-seventies, when the grievances against the government were diverse, and the institutional support for opposition theoretically afforded by the Liberal party was in disarray, a protest movement directed against the Porte could provide a widely acceptable focus and a convenient outlet. It was an attack which the Conservatives had in part brought upon themselves, for it was they above all who had postulated the parallel between London and Constantinople.

4 • Conflicting Visions of the State

Britain's support of the Ottoman government never came easily. The suspiciously strident Palmerstonian faith in the Ottomans' progress in reform, as much wishful thinking as conviction, survived the crisis in Syria and Lebanon in 1860 largely because of Fuad Pasha's energetic efforts. But the belief in the strength and efficacy of Ottoman good intentions lost its most eloquent spokesman when Palmerston died in 1865. Meanwhile, by the time of the next major crisis in the eastern Mediterranean (the civil war in Crete), things had changed for the Porte as well. The Ottomans' options were limited by the pressure placed upon the government by the Young Ottoman movement, which demanded reassertion of Ottoman dignity. The resulting repression, described in Britain in terms evoking systematic genocide, dealt a body blow to the faithful. Yet the collapse of the consensus which had rallied around Palmerston's views did not mean that Britons immediately turned away from the Porte. A more cynical, hard-nosed justification of British policy, based on a recognition of the difficulties of imperial rule, began to gain credence in the early 1860s and soon supplanted the Palmerstonian attitude as the chief rationale for support of the Ottomans.

No imperial power, it was argued, could expect to be loved; with subjects as judges, every such government must stand condemned. Drawing on Britain's unhappy experiences in India and Ireland, this rationalization had a certain sad plausibility; but ultimately this very comparison undermined it. True, the British had not always been loved by their Irish and Indian subjects, but most of the English, if not all of the Irish, were confident that in the nineteenth century the English had not systematically massacred their colonial subjects. The equation of London and Constantinople juxtaposed two quite different ruling groups. It was therefore attacked by defenders of the status quo who wanted to preserve London's credit by separating England from the Turks, and bolstered by critics who wanted to blacken the British ruling class by assuming the dubious connection.

Meanwhile, British society was undergoing a period of transition or dislocation, in which relationships between important groups and institutions were no longer clearly defined. Symptomatic of this structural ambiguity was a far-reaching debate about the purposes of the state as an institution and the degree to which it should be guided by Christian values.[1] Even after the Reform Act of 1832, England had continued to be ruled by a comparatively narrow elite, made up now of the landed classes and industrial and commercial magnates who dominated elections to the House of Commons. Ministers might bring diverse interests and experience to the job, but whatever the personal or family contacts with business, commerce, or the professions, almost all had ties to the landed interest. The question which by hindsight was implicit in the entire period between 1832 and 1885 was whether and in what way to give a voice to the lower-middle and working classes. These groups had their awareness raised by the agitation leading to the first Reform Act in 1832, but they did not gain any institutionalized channel for self-expression. They characteristically made themselves heard by pressure from without, including collective behavior ranging from the Anti–Corn Law League and Chartism, through the temperance movement and the anti-slavery campaign, to the Administrative Reform Association and the Bulgarian agitation. In the early years political leaders generally condemned such pressure, for it reawakened fears of Radical revolution. Consequently, the typical pressure group felt compelled to devote much energy to proving that it was not an unruly "mob." By 1867, such activities had become somewhat more respectable;[2] but Gladstone's caution in putting himself at the head of the Bulgarian agitation reflects this background, and the intense criticism he received is evidence that politicking out-of-doors was still far from generally accepted.

Such protest movements embraced diverse issues, but shared certain structural similarities. All derived ultimately from the structural conduciveness created by the existence of a politically aware underclass which was not explicitly accorded an individual voice. All were aided by changes in the press, especially in provincial centers, but in London as well. The new journalism depended, for its unique blending of local concerns with up-to-date national and international news, on the space-compressing inventions of the railway and telegraph. For its wide circulation, it relied on the steam press,[3] the repeal of the Stamp Tax (1855) and the duties on paper (1861), and the lower cost of paper, which was now made out of wood pulp. These changes, taken together, permitted many papers to reduce their prices to a penny.[4]

Many of these protests were satisfying, at least in the sense that they offered the participants an opportunity to speak out. As far as practical results went, however, it was usually easier to get rid of an unpopular law or to end an abuse than to frame imaginative new approaches. Eventually the protests contributed to the modernization of the political process in several important ways: by bringing the concerns of the provinces to the attention of the parliamentary leadership in London; by creating an ideological bridge which eventually helped to shape the character of the reformed political parties, especially the Liberals;[5] and by elevating the vision of local protesters through contact with charismatic national figures such as Gladstone.[6]

What exactly was the conducive situation which spawned the Bulgarian agitation? And why, when most successful examples of such activity were focused on domestic grievances susceptible at least in theory to precise solutions well within the imagination of the participants, did this particular campaign target a foreign policy problem, about which most of its followers knew little, and whose ramifications were hard to predict?

During the 1860s and 1870s, through a far-reaching and long drawn out process of political change, the precursors to modern political parties gradually developed. In the early decades of the century, there had been no mass organizations. Connections with constituents were largely limited to election time, while the leadership in Parliament was so closely knit that the different groups sometimes resembled factions more than ideological party wings. The Whigs (one element in the future Liberal party) had played a large role in the passage of the 1832 Reform Act, and were especially tightly linked by kinship, marriage, and long association.[7] In the 1830s, they wholeheartedly (and from their point of view quite rightly) preferred cooperation with the conservatives to presiding over a Radical eruption, while the Radicals, by the late 1830s, saw little point in "sustaining 'whig conservatism against the tory conservatism.'"[8] Peel's promising conservative coalition fell apart over the repeal of the Corn Laws, when Peel sacrificed his party to what he perceived to be the national interest; his opponents, the protectionists, including Disraeli, went into a decline lasting twenty years.[9] Although the Peelites were an important force in the coalition governments of the 1850s, they did not command a majority. Under Gladstone's inspiration, they often identified themselves more with efficient administration, particularly good fiscal management, than with larger social goals.

Meanwhile the industrialized sector of the English economy continued to grow. The changing balance between land and trade eventually lent weight to periodic efforts to revise the franchise further, such as those mooted by Lord John Russell under the impact of the 1848 revolutions on the continent.[10] However, Lord Palmerston blocked further electoral reform until his death in 1865. The focus turned instead to a different way of broadening the political base—modernizing political parties. Between the beginning of this process around 1860 and its culmination some twenty-five years later, things were in flux, and the degree of cohesiveness and the effectiveness of the local organizations varied enormously from one community to another. In Manchester, for example, efficient Liberal party machinery controlled by the local industrial magnates took shape early.[11] The same was true of Rochdale.[12] Other communities, such as Leeds, were not able to integrate the activities of competing Liberal clubs representing different segments of the party until comparatively late, sometimes as late as 1880.[13]

Superimposed upon this process was the Second Reform Act of 1867. Upon Palmerston's death in 1865, it was clear that something would have to be done about the franchise; but neither Gladstone's recently united Liberal party nor Disraeli's Conservatives had really thought in detail about precisely what. The result was the rather comic and ill-informed scrambling to pass the Act, a measure which turned out to be considerably more sweeping than anything initially envisioned. It increased the electorate by 82.5 percent, or 1,120,000 voters.[14] The effects on Britain's political system were gradual. Although there was "essential continuity of political life before and after 1867,"[15] the boroughs now operated under something approaching universal manhood suffrage. This opened the way to democracy at two levels: conceptually, since it would only be a matter of time before the counties followed; and organizationally, since the sheer mass of new voters in the boroughs and the large proportion from the working class demanded new techniques of electoral management.

The leadership on the front bench, men who had entered politics in the 1840s or 1850s or even earlier, had to devise new ways to fight elections, to educate and to mobilize new voters who were often more conscious of class interests, and to channel the emotions thus produced through more inclusive political parties toward more broadly attractive goals. To bring this about, they badly needed the skills of a new breed of politician, more like the American party boss—men like Joseph Chamberlain, the Radical industrialist and M.P. from Birmingham.[16] They also needed to come to some agreement about the place of working men in the political parties and the extent to which they should be encouraged to become active participants helping to shape their own future, as opposed to mere spectators who would be allowed to record their opinions at the end of the electoral campaign by casting a vote. Finally, waiting outside the settlement provided in 1867, were the agricultural laborers, who became increasingly self-conscious during the 1870s. A successful union was organized in 1872 by Joseph Arch, a highly charismatic, self-educated, hedge-cutter, Primitive Methodist preacher, and voter under the old forty-shilling freehold provision. Although its first objectives were economic relief, the union soon turned to the question of the franchise.[17]

The situation was complicated by the fact that the working class even in the boroughs was by no means a united bloc. Hanham has identified four main groups of leaders especially concerned with the working class. The first group was the "Junta" of trade union officials, based in London and organized through the London Trades Council. Prominent in this circle was Henry Broadhurst, the stonemason, who had once walked several thousand miles across southern England in search of work. He found it in London, on the bell tower of the Houses of Parliament, where he would later take his seat in 1880 as M.P. for Stoke on Trent.[18] A second group, eventually centered on the Trades Union Congress, consisted of provincial trade union leaders. The most active politically were the miners, whose unusually strong sense of community made them the "pioneers of labour representation." They provided "the first two working-class M.P.s" in 1874. Third was the broad spectrum of Radical clubs. Their membership included, at the extreme, agitators like Charles Bradlaugh, whose widely propagandized atheist convictions had made him notorious. In 1880, his bid to enter Parliament despite his views on religion, led to his imprisonment in the Clock Tower, the last occasion on which anyone was incarcerated there.[19] The final group included middle-class philanthropists like Samuel Morley, the cotton manufacturer and proprietor of the *Daily News*, men "whose radicalism appeared to be only skin-deep,"[20] who were willing to subsidize working-class activities, but only as long as they seemed congruent with the larger purposes of the system.[21]

At least the more prosperous levels of the working classes became very much involved with franchise reform in 1866 and 1867. Parallel to and in fact much larger though less wealthy than its "middle-class rival, the Reform Union . . . centred in Manchester," was the predominantly working-class Reform League, considered by some to be "by far the largest and most perfect political organisation in the country."[22] At crucial moments both in 1866 and 1867, the Reform League staged demonstrations in Hyde Park in favor of extension of the franchise. How much effect this pressure from without had upon the passage of the act is debatable,[23] but it did provide experience and visibility to a number of working-class leaders later active in the Bulgarian agitation and other causes.

Not surprisingly, reactions in Parliament ranged from anxiety through consternation to outrage. Even Gladstone, though he seemed to symbolize the best hope for realizing working men's dreams, was disappointingly slow to affirm their "worthiness" as full-fledged associates and partners.[24] George Howell, a former Chartist and brick-layer[25] and a Reform League leader, insisted that there should be "a thorough organisation of the Liberal Party in which . . . the working men shall be consulted and called into active political life."[26] This was a prospect which many thoughtful establishment leaders found frightening. The 1832 Reform Act had enfranchised many persons of modest resources in the counties, including some tenants, yet the sense of shared interests binding rural communities together had been strong enough to preserve the landlords' position.[27] Would the habit of deference remain similarly strong among the new urban voters, or would they demand to play a part in their own right, rather than simply approving or disapproving what others did for them? And if an accommodation could not be reached within existing parties, might they not go their own way and found their own group, presenting themselves as an independent "force in the next election?"[28]

To prevent this outcome, the Liberal whips entered into secret negotiations with a small group of Reform League leaders, including George Howell, W. R. Cremer, and Thomas Mottershead. What Liberal managers like George Glyn wanted first and foremost was information about the opinions and probable voting behavior of the new working-class voters in the boroughs, and they were willing and able, thanks primarily to Samuel Morley, to pay the expenses of the informants who gathered it. The task quickly expanded to include, in many districts, the formation of Liberal electoral committees, which tried with considerable success to bring the old party managers and the new working-class voters together. It became, as Hanham has described it, "a transitional stage" on the road to full-scale modern party organization: "the old self-perpetuating committees still survived, but they were supplemented by party clubs and working-men's associations."[29]

There was an implicit dilemma, however. Whom should working men support? Could they trust good men of proven ability and experience whatever their origins, or was it essential that some candidates have a specifically working-class background? In many constituencies, representation had already been parcelled out by gentlemen's agreements between different groups in the party or between Liberals and Tories, and there was obvious resistance to making a place for candidates whose most striking recommendation was their humble origin, especially since in most cases it seemed unlikely that they could win. There seemed to be only one sensible answer: avoid factionalism and concentrate on defeating the Tories. Except in situations where one Liberal candidate could be induced to withdraw in favor of another more sensitive to working men's concerns, Howell, Cremer, and their associates did their best to rally the new voters behind existing candidates. The one exception was Sheffield, where Mundella asked for and obtained Howell's help in his campaign against Roebuck, an eccentric old warhorse of a Radical who had fatally alienated working men by his well-publicized opposition to trade unions. A few working men did stand in the general election of 1868, most of them at the last minute, without opportunity for proper prior cultivation of their constituencies; all were defeated.

This result was something of an embarrassment. Although the role played by Howell, Cremer, and their colleagues had been private and strictly secret, awkward questions were asked in the Executive Council of the Reform League about some of the defeats; a particularly nasty altercation developed over Charles Bradlaugh's loss at Northampton and the extent to which Howell and Cremer might actually have contributed to it. Glyn was forced to recognize that he might have been a bit too clever. Pressure for at least token presence of working men in the House of Commons existed and was not going to go away.[30]

The immediate victim of the election was the Reform League itself. As meetings of its Executive Committee became mired in recriminations, its usefulness became questionable, and it was disbanded.[31] To fill the vacuum, middle-class leaders like Mundella and Morley founded the Labour Representation League in September 1869, with the express purpose of getting working-class leaders and those committed to the interests of working men into the House of Commons. It played a role in the 1874 election by putting up thirteen candidates; most of these were defeated, but there were some working-class successes. Thomas Burt, a leader of the Northumberland miners, was elected for Morpeth, and Alexander Macdonald won one of two seats in Stafford. The League was not directly involved with Burt's candidacy but did influence events in Stafford, both by introducing Macdonald to the constituency and by campaigning for him afterward.[32]

Nonetheless, in the mid-1870s efforts to adjust to the new franchise seemed stalled. Electoral reform had raised expectations which could not be met in the short term; the difficult situation had been compounded when the responsiveness of Parliament declined under the impact of the "legislative congestion" resulting from the rush of reform proposals put forward for debate in the climate of change.[33] Between 1870 and 1879, Hanham posits a new phase in the gradual emergence of party organization. While the Conservatives, under the able management of John Gorst, worked to proliferate Conservative associations throughout the country, the Liberals seemed to be in disarray. Indeed, disillusionment with the effectiveness of their unwieldy grouping led to "a resurgence of anti-party, or sectarian, pressure groups on the model of the Anti–Corn Law League."[34] The Bulgarian agitators formed one such group. W. T. Stead, the gifted journalist who whipped up enthusiasm initially in the small northern industrial town of Darlington, stated in the *Northern Echo*:

> Ten years ago such an outburst would not have been so significant. The householders have been enfranchised since then . . . These men who gather in thousands to denounce the Turks and demand that these atrocities shall cease . . . are electors. To a man they have votes, and they will use them . . . It is the first time that the householders have spoken out about foreign policy, and the emphasis of their speech shows that they mean to be heard. It is the appearance of a new force in the arena of Europe.[35]

The problem of how to involve the newly enfranchised working classes in politics extended beyond the business of winning elections to embrace the question of how to govern afterward. The new voters brought their own viewpoints and life-styles to the political process and formed conflicting visions of the state. Many urban Radicals, both middle-class and working-class, were vehemently antireligious. More typical working men were militant, uncompromising Nonconformists; hence, one of the implications of broadening the franchise was extending the vote to Nonconformists on a scale which at last approximated their real numbers.[36] The wealthiest Nonconformists, the great industrial magnates and factory owners, had had the vote at least since 1832; now they were reinforced by legions of less prosperous, and probably even less worldly, fellow believers. The new electors especially entered politics with hope: "buoyed up by the great Nonconformist revival of the 1860s, Dissenters saw . . . the occasion for an assertion of the political priorities of Nonconformity."[37] These new men, many of them steeped in the long tradition of Radicalism, tended to go beyond more experienced Nonconformist voters in seeing the nation's leaders as rich, corrupt, sophisticated, centered on London, and blinded by the landed interest. Many issues which seemed in Chapel circles susceptible to a simple black and white answer were treated officially in morally neutral terms. And despite the Liberal victory in 1868, the doubling of the number of Nonconformist M.P.'s,[38] and the installation as prime minister of Gladstone, the "People's William," the misguided political establishment continued to follow dubious values and even to force them upon others. One example was the Education Act of 1870, which affronted Nonconformist families in one of the ways calculated to hurt most: through their children.

The Education Act grew out of the demand for widespread literacy which had been created first by the Industrial Revolution and now more particularly by extension of the franchise.[39] The goal of reformers such as Chamberlain and his National Education League, proponents of the new ideas in their most extreme form, was a national educational system, "universal, compulsory, unsectarian and free."[40] But what role could they assign to the existing (incomplete) structure of denominational schools, where attendance was voluntary and fees were charged? Most of these were Anglican, although the Methodists also sponsored a substantial number; there were Roman Catholic schools as well, which would eventually seek recognition. From the point of view of most Nonconformists, and certainly from the perspective of the National Education League, the so-called denominational schools were suspect. Indeed, the League proposed to replace them with a totally new system.

Unfortunately, these concerns came to the fore in the difficult months of 1869 and 1870,[41] when there was unease about setting precedents for Irish education,[41] and when Gladstone's own highest priority was the achievement of a settlement in the Irish land question. Partly owing to preoccupation, Gladstone accepted, against his personal judgment, a compromise devised primarily by W. E. Forster.[42] The compromise, even after amendment in Parliament, satisfied no one. Forster understood that a new system along the lines envisioned by the League would affront the vested interest of the denominational schools and their network of supporters; even more to the point, it would be vastly expensive.[43] Accordingly, he called for a dual system, which would leave most existing denominational schools in place. New schools would be founded according to a different plan only where existing schools were deficient or lacking.

As finally passed, the act provided for a one-year transition to determine the adequacy of local schools. After this time boards could be elected in districts that so chose to set up "board" schools where needed. They would be supported out of a new tax or rate. The boards would determine what sort of religious instruction could be given in these schools, a stipulation which seemed to assure that most classes would in practice reflect the Anglican point of view.[44] To be sure, children might be exempted from the study of religion in cases of conscience.[45] Most Nonconformists were especially disturbed by provisions for doubling the Parliamentary maintenance subsidy to denominational schools.[46] Many Nonconformists, exaggerating the disabilities put on them, believed that their very "right to survival" was involved.

Since most Nonconformists were Liberal and a Liberal cabinet had sponsored the bill, the issue was critically divisive for the Liberal party. Chamberlain's National Education League managed to gather signatures from more than two-thirds of the English and Welsh Dissenting ministry on a petition opposing some features of the act, and Gladstone's refusal to listen contributed to the Liberal defeat in 1874.[47]

The experience seemed to dramatize once again for Nonconformists the comfortable relationship between the political establishment and the Church of England. Gladstone suffered personally. He was the party leader who had presided over the debacle; and his betrayal of the Nonconformists was the more wounding because unexpected. Of the possible attitudes toward religious education, Gladstone had adopted the least widely acceptable, that is, denominationalism, or religious instruction offered by teachers following their own personal convictions. Secularism, the complete omission of religion from the curriculum, he rejected after a brief flirtation; undenominationalism, the nonsectarian grounding in broad Christian fundamentals which was the most popular solution, he flatly opposed, finding watered-down religion worse than none at all.[48]

This background of trouble contributed to the Bulgarian agitation.

Nonconformists of modest background, newly enfranchised, were prominent in the agitation. However, not all the new voters were Nonconformists; and neither were all the protesters. In London, which became a major center of agitation, the Nonconformists were notably weak, especially among the working classes.[49] To be sure, there had been some highly successful missionary efforts, financed by middle-class money. Samuel Morley, the textile manufacturer and "New Model" employer "who was reputed to be one of the wealthiest men in England," had provided most of the money for the construction of the Memorial Hall on Farringdon Street, in an area built up as slum clearance in the City;[50] in 1878, it became the center for meetings of Nonconformist ministers opposed to aid to the Ottoman Empire. Morley was also the chief underwriter of the annual series of cultural meetings organized in the mid-1870s by the Reverend G. M. Murphy of Borough Road Congregational Church in Lambeth.[51] Murphy read and discussed the news on Saturday nights at large gatherings; in January 1878 one such meeting allegedly approached two thousand.[52]

But many London working men rejected religion and distrusted the cultural improvement offered by the well-to-do. They found a natural home in the flourishing world of working-class clubs. The clubs were made up of artisans earning about thirty shillings weekly, men able and indeed eager to educate themselves and form an opinion on the issues of the day. The clubs met weekly, typically on Sundays, in a pub or in their own buildings, for drinks, good fellowship, and—most important of all—for lectures and discussion. They were "at once the mutual improvement societies of the metropolitan artisan, and a springboard for political agitation."[53] Although initiated as a middle-class gesture toward working-class improvement and heavily dependent until 1884 on money from patrons like Samuel Morley, the clubs took on a life of their own. No "political test" was imposed on members, and many of them, like the Eleusis Club of Chelsea or the Patriotic Club of Clerkenwell Green, became centers of working-class radicalism.[54] Most were militantly anticlerical, if not atheistic. Indeed, Charles Bradlaugh, the former solicitor's clerk who had become a controversial free thinker, was a favorite speaker on the club circuit; his National Secular Society, thanks to its fine headquarters in the Hall of Science, was "the most discussed club in the metropolis,"[55] an example which transcended the model by shooting out branches all over the country.

Radicals, working men, and Nonconformists had been the foot soldiers of popular protest throughout much of the nineteenth century, and it is no surprise that they were active in the Bulgarian agitation. More remarkably, the agitation also appealed to High Churchmen, and in a somewhat similar way.

For rather different reasons from those of the other groups, High Churchmen had cause to doubt the responsiveness of the state to their own deeply felt ethical values. Trouble was rife inside the established church during the nineteenth century as the British gradually moved toward greater secularization of politics and hence of the state. The removal of the civil disabilities upon Nonconformists in 1828, upon Catholics in 1829, and upon Jews in 1858 was part of this process. But as the state's links with the established church contracted, what guide was left for the state when its actions had ethical ramifications? Both Gladstone and Disraeli considered this problem, Gladstone anxiously in *The State in its Relations with the Church* (1838), Disraeli romantically in his novels, especially *Coningsby* (1844) and *Tancred* (1847). Both men believed that truly effective states rest upon explicit moral foundations. Disraeli, never greatly concerned with the logic of abstract questions, probably lost interest in the issue as he gained experience. But Gladstone, although he retreated from his original belief that the church must steer the state, never gave up the conviction that the two must be closely coupled, and that the Western, Christian state must be infused with Christian teachings.[56]

This problem of church and state pervaded Victorian political life in a more general way. If the church was to be involved in a meaningful sense in day-to-day politics, then the focus within the church would probably shift to practical concerns, that is, to social action. Indeed, this side of religion became increasingly prominent in the nineteenth century; it pulsed through the Evangelical movement, and in part motivated statesmen such as Shaftesbury and Gladstone (whose background, after all, was Evangelical) to the leadership of social protests such as the Bulgarian agitation. However, a certain worldliness was implicit in this realistic approach. Was Christianity nothing more than do-goodism? Was God bound by the measure of man's social vision? As early as the 1840s and 1850s, many sincere Anglicans began to search for a religious position which would offer escape through transcendence rather than reform. This group subscribed to the Oxford movement, and it is no accident that Gladstone, who was closely associated with Oxford during those years, was deeply affected by this view of religion, which emphasized the mystery and omnipotence of

God and His ways as contrasted with the ultimately shallow nature of our earthly striving.

Some followers of the Oxford movement took these ideas to a possible logical conclusion. Manning and Hope, Gladstone's friends, converted to Roman Catholicism. Gladstone himself, deeply attracted though he was by the High Church position, was never in the slightest danger of taking this step. He believed that God placed each individual in a specific religious context, which provided him with a "school of character and belief"; virtue was to be attained by following the path marked out, not, except in the most exceptional circumstances, by choosing another.[57] To do so, he remarked in another context, would be like picking "some other house where the Father is richer, or the Mother fairer."[58] More viscerally, Gladstone could not accept the authority of the Pope. Indeed, in the early 1870s the Vatican Council and the Declaration of Papal Infallibility triggered a crisis of conscience for Gladstone probably unmatched at any period of his life except the difficult years of the late 1840s and early 1850s. He was saved from this depression mainly by the support of liberal Old Catholics such as Döllinger, who was critical of extreme Papal pretensions and much closer to Gladstone's own position. But because of Gladstone's deep concern with these problems, he remained in close touch with both High Church and Catholic leaders, with their speeches and their writings, and eventually, when he was no longer prime minister, took part in the controversy. His perspective isolated him from other Anglicans at a time when his views on the Education Act had cut him off even more sharply from many Nonconformists.

Meanwhile, during the late 1860s a major controversy erupted over Ritualism. This movement was an offshoot of the earlier Oxford movement, but rather than emphasizing doctrinal mysteries, it concentrated on ceremonial practice, borrowing heavily from Rome and attempting through new solemnity to differentiate the celebration of the liturgy from mundane activity. As Peter Marsh puts it, "Ritualism was an aesthetic expression, the tangible poetry, of the Oxford Movement."[59] Ritualism appealed to the affluent young of Oxford and Cambridge, who found in its unabashed romanticism a cure for world-weariness. Meanwhile, migration to the cities provided the occasion for building new churches; and London, in particular, quickly became a center for Ritualist practice in these new parishes.[60] Ritualism gained in the slums because it provided an antidote for worshippers who suffered material or spiritual impoverishment, but it offended many middle-class Victorians by its theatricality. Even High Churchmen, who might have been expected to feel an affinity, were far from uniformly enthusiastic; many thought the movement unwise, while others flatly opposed it.[61] However, when a series of cases involving Ritualist practices were brought before the Judicial Committee of the Privy Council, the Ritualists at first found support.

Their progress was grist to the mill of certain outside critics of the established church such as Edward Miall, whose Liberation Society argued passionately in favor of disestablishment. One of Miall's more persuasive arguments, as he worked continuously to broaden his base, was the prospect that the Ritualists might gain control of the establishment and legally foist their views on the majority of churchgoers. Miall, who had built up the Liberation Society from its founding in 1844 until it became "the best organized and most powerful political lobby in the country," became Liberal M.P. for Bradford in 1869 and resolved to press for disestablishment. Miall, a Congregationalist, counted mainly on the support of other Nonconformists. He capitalized on their desire to achieve real equality within society and joined the Radical attack on the clergy of the establishment as worldly and self-seeking gentlemen and defenders of the status quo.[62] Originally, Miall hoped that under the leadership of the Liberal party in 1868–1874 and in the aftermath of Irish church disestablishment, his plea for disestablishment in England might receive favorable hearing. The question seemed to become more critical with the passage of the Education Act in 1870, when the need to prevent the coercive machinery of the establishment falling into the worst possible hands was greatly enhanced. The remedy for Miall was obvious: end establishment once and for all.

Although the Liberal party included many Nonconformists and some Radicals, most of the leaders in Parliament were Anglican and most subscribed to the mission of the established church as a leaven in politics. Nonetheless, if Gladstone, as prime minister, had been convinced, Miall's program might have had a chance; but Gladstone, despite his stand on Ireland, considered disestablishment in England anathema. He argued against it in Parliament both in 1871 and in 1873. Many of his arguments were practical. He suggested, quite rightly, that the bulk of English opinion was strongly against disestablishment, and he underlined the difficulty of disposing of the church's very sizable endowment, which far surpassed that of the Irish church. But most important to Gladstone was the critical role the church had played in uplifting the political life of the state. He declared: "The Church of England has not only been a part of the history of this country, but a part so vital, entering so profoundly into the entire life and action of the country, that the severing of the two would leave nothing behind but a bleeding and lacerated mass. Take the Church of England out of the history of England, and the history of England becomes a chaos, without order, without life, and without meaning."[63]

Despite their lack of success, the activities of the Liberation Society exacerbated the tensions in the early 1870s in several ways. From the point of view of the Nonconformists, the rejection of disestablishment by Parliament and by Gladstone demonstrated that the proestablishment implications of the Education Act of 1870 had been no accident. Powerful circles in England were indeed consciously determined to keep Nonconformists in second place; a frontal attack simply revealed their strength. But at the same time, the serious and well-organized assault upon the establishment terrified many churchgoers, including many High Churchmen.

It was against this background that the attack on Ritualism culminated. Archibald Tait, the Archbishop of Canterbury, had tried for a number of years to curb the Ritualist movement, because he believed that it was unrepresentative of most Anglicans and threatened to divide the church. When his preliminary efforts proved unsuccessful, he began to consider action through Parliament, but Gladstone, fearful that open controversy would simply win new converts for disestablishment, did not encourage him. Things did not look much better when Disraeli assumed power in 1874; but urged on by Queen Victoria and supported by his bishops, Tait went ahead anyway. He introduced a much attenuated bill, the Public Worship Regulation Bill, into Parliament to limit certain Anglo-Catholic practices and to control Romanizing tendencies.[64]

The bill's divisive implications for the Liberal party were quickly apparent. The Whig wing of the party had long cherished an antipathy to Ritualism; it militated against their desire "to placate nonconformists and to reassert Church nationality." High Churchmen, on the other hand, though not universally friendly to Ritualism, instantly opposed this effort by the state to regulate the church.[65] The issue was particularly delicate for Gladstone. He was known, rightly, as a High Churchman and was suspected, unjustly, of Catholic leanings. Over the years he had attended both High Church and Ritualist services, had corresponded with prominent Tractarians and Liberal Catholics, and had demonstrated continuing interest in dreams of reuniting Anglicans with Catholics and Greek Orthodox. Another man than Gladstone might prudently have evaded the problem. The bill came up during the summer of 1874 when he was vacationing in Wales, and no one really expected that the aging statesman would appear for the debate. Not only did he come and speak against it, but he did so despite considerable stress, as his diary demonstrates. Yet in the end, the bill did pass. As on other occasions in the past, many of Gladstone's fellow Liberals wished he had remained silent. Indeed, Sir William Harcourt asked in exasperation, "Did the House suppose that his right hon. Friend the Member for Greenwich had come back that day for any other object than, if possible, at the last moment, to wreck the Bill?"[66] Gladstone spoke from his deep conviction; "he confessed he thought that even the partial conversion of the House of Commons into an ecclesiastical Synod—constituted as it was, and appointed for other purposes—would be found to strain very severely not only the temper of the House, but its position and its workings in the Constitution."[67] This position pitted him against Harcourt, whose strenuous support of the bill came as a surprise. The result was that "the split in the Liberal leadership was now revealed for the first time since the election" earlier in 1874.[68] It compounded the isolation brought upon Gladstone by the Education Act and the related resounding defeat at the polls, and was apparently one of the major factors convincing him to continue on the course he had begun right after the electoral defeat: to announce his definite, and as he believed final, withdrawal from the Liberal party leadership.[69] He summarized his sense of alienation many years afterward: "I felt myself to be in some measure out of touch with some of the tendencies of the liberal party, especially in religious matters."[70]

But Gladstone was not the only one to be cut off from his normal political base by the controversies of the early 1870s. More traditional High Churchmen felt that they had been betrayed by the Public Worship Regulation Act. An impressive coalition of members of both parties joined in support of the bill, because it seemed to be a blow struck against creeping crypto-Catholicism in the Church of England; the cause was the more popular because of the latent anti-Irish feeling never far below the surface. When both Harcourt and Disraeli spoke up for the bill, neither Liberal High Church sympathizers such as Gladstone and his followers nor Conservatives like Lord Salisbury and his supporters could find much consolation within existing party groupings. But out of the controversy a new, and rather strange, coalition could be discerned, whose main lines would be replicated in the Bulgarian agitation. This coalition linked religious conservatives such as Gladstone, Canon Liddon, and the Marquess of Bath with Radical warhorses such as Henry Richard, P. A. Taylor, A. J. Mundella, and Henry Fawcett, all of whom opposed, more or less categorically, the constraints of religious establishment.[71]

Thus, the main elements of structural conduciveness from which the Bulgarian agitation arose had emerged by 1875 when Gladstone "definitively" retired. The British state seemed to be losing its ethical moorings at just the moment when it had embraced a large group of new voters to whom ethical considerations were peculiarly important. Both Nonconformists and High Churchmen had felt threatened by recent political developments and neither of these groups, which became crucial to the atrocities agitation, could see an immediate means of making their weight and point of view effective in political deliberations. Both groups felt particularly frustrated about the possibility of bringing their values to bear upon political decisions.

The newly enfranchised working classes felt even broader alienation from participation in the political process. Their disaffection went beyond uneasiness at the moral character of their government to outrage at its wealth and self-seeking materialism and to an unwillingness to recognize such leaders as truly representative of England. The radicals of the working men's clubs, also newly enfranchised, distrusted Nonconformity and were deeply hostile to the Church of England, but were equally disillusioned with their rulers. Indeed, for working men as a group, the political experience of the years following the passage of the Second Reform Act had belied its promise and suggested that they were only to be invited to commend the actions of the elite, not to share with them in governing. Furthermore, agricultural laborers in the same material situation as these new urban voters were denied the franchise through an inconsistency that could not be defended for long. Such mixed messages put a strain even on traditionally strong bonds of deference.

The Liberal party, which had been to a greater or lesser extent a vehicle for all these groups, was in disarray. The new leaders, men like Harcourt, were not sensitive to their concerns, while Gladstone seemed to have lost his touch. And all this came at a period of economic downturn. There are too many instances in which dire economic distress in the late 1870s and the 1880s did not lead to social protest for the historian to propose any simple cause and effect relationship; but surely it is relevant that the long boom in the trades which supported England's heavy industry and the so-called artisan elite, trades such as metalworking, engineering, and skilled construction, as well as the less-prestigious mining, was coming to an end, particularly in London. Both employers and laborers felt the pinch.[72]

The Bulgarian agitation would provide a "magic" solution for these disparate groups, who longed to address moral, ethical, and political concerns through effective public action under an inspired leader. It also seems possible that the ill-assorted nature of the disaffected groups decisively influenced the choice of a grievance. Given the fact that the Nonconformists, the High Churchmen, the secular working-class radicals, and the agricultural laborers represented distinct and even opposing communities, it would have been extremely difficult for them to coalesce around an issue internal to England. What was needed was a symbolic grievance; a cause that would allow them to protest religious intolerance, the persecution of Christianity, and the corruption and unresponsiveness of government, without ever having to deal with cases familiar enough to bring out their deep and well-founded disagreements.

5 ✦ Gladstone's Pursuit of Singlemindedness

To an extraordinary degree, William Ewart Gladstone has become identified with the beliefs of the Bulgarian agitation. His leadership so overshadowed the others that Shannon has to remind us that Gladstone joined the movement only belatedly and that his commitment to the cause was a matter of debate as late as August 1876 and even thereafter.[1] True, Gladstone's involvement with Ottoman affairs went back some twenty-five years, at least to his membership in the Aberdeen coalition which had prosecuted the Crimean War; but he had never been an enthusiastic partisan of the Empire and during the 1860s sedulously avoided commentary. The Eastern Question called into play two quite different and contradictory impulses in Gladstone's nature. At one level, the level most often seen by the public and harshly criticized by his enemies, Gladstone was a firm advocate of moral commitment in politics. Although he had given up his early insistence that the church must dominate the state, he never wavered in his conviction that politics, and history as politics acted out over time, must be infused with moral purpose or lose all meaning. Yet, as can be seen from the volumes of his *Diaries* dealing with his first great ministry in 1868–1874,[2] Gladstone's lively political sense made him a more realistic and accommodating leader than might have been predicted based either on public speeches or on analysis working back from the fight over Home Rule. The *Diaries* abound with instances of consultation, sincere solicitation of views, extraordinarily time-consuming efforts to persuade, and, in a significant number of instances, readiness to swallow his own opinion in the face of a majority decision. In other words, Gladstone was a realist who had had a long and at times painful schooling in the art of playing the political game.

From a practical point of view, the demands of the "Great Game" or the Eastern Question had been clear for many years—support of the Ottoman Empire. Gladstone was too canny a politician to throw this over lightly. As late as the difficult days of 1869–1871, when the Cretan crisis, Egyptian debts, brigands in Greece, the quarrel over the leadership of the Bulgarian church, and the revision of the treaty of Paris occupied the Foreign Office, Gladstone operated competently and responsibly within the normal strategic guidelines of British foreign policy. He justified British policy characteristically, on the grounds that it had been developed in conjunction with other great powers through the diplomacy of the Concert of Europe. Yet it is clear that he was never entirely comfortable as a supporter of the Ottoman Empire. His disquiet went back at least as far as the Crimean War, which was also the first occasion on which he took a major public stand on the Ottomans' behalf.

In July 1876, Gladstone, looking back from half a political lifetime upon the question, felt compelled to defend Britain's Crimean War policy as he understood it. He was, after all, the "only person" now a member of the House of Commons who had borne official "responsibility" for that policy. He explained the decision to ally with Constantinople in terms of two broad objectives: first, to protect the Ottoman Empire against foreign attack; second, "to defend her from corruption and dissolution within."[3] Clearly, the first of these imperatives had been the more influential. In a conversation with Aberdeen early in the crisis (February 22, 1853), Gladstone had said: "We were not fighting for the Turks, but we were warning Russia off forbidden ground . . . If, indeed, we undertook to put down the Christians under Turkish rule by force, then we should be fighting for the Turks; but to this I for one could be no party."[4] Throughout the conflict, Gladstone remained troubled by what he called "the responsibilities of needless war," and it is quite possible, as Richard Millman suggests, that a festering sense of guilt inflamed his later virulence against the Turks.[5]

In the years after the Crimean War, Gladstone apparently felt freer to voice his doubts about the Ottoman Empire. During 1856, he entered into correspondence with the Romanian statesman, Bratianu, and was indoctrinated by him with enthusiasm for the Romanian national cause. In an article in *Gentleman's Magazine* in July 1856, he announced that Russia "had been sucked into Turkish affairs by the criminal debility of the Ottoman Empire," and painted a rather far-fetched picture of the Ottoman state being replaced by a Greek empire in Constantinople, which would serve as a barrier against Russia on the one hand and the Pope on the other. Most of Gladstone's supporters, including the Duke of Argyll, found these fantasies embarrassing.[6] Although he later retreated from this extreme position, the support for Romanian national aspirations was no caprice. In the House of Commons on May 4, 1858, Gladstone urged the government to support union of the Principalities in coming negotiations. He foreshadowed his later views by declaring that, if his countrymen were worried about Russian expansion into the area, they "ought to place a living barrier between her and Turkey. There is no barrier . . . like the breasts of free men."[7]

Certainly Gladstone's support for the Romanians and their national aspirations was unequivocal here. The implications, however, were less anti-Ottoman than might at first be supposed. On the evidence of the speech, Gladstone apparently believed that Moldavia and Walachia had always enjoyed a position of virtual independence, and he dismissed the Porte's claim of a right to control the area as a recent and unauthorized innovation. Still, Gladstone had laid down the fundamental argument to which he returned in 1876: independent Balkan states might oppose Russia more often than they helped her, and might do so more effectively than a moribund Ottoman Empire. Furthermore, he assumed in the speech that Ottoman rule would be maintained in the area around Constantinople and in the southern Balkans; the question was how to guard the approaches which had proved so vulnerable to Russian attack in 1829 and 1853. He concluded with a commitment to Britain's traditional policy, which, in its somewhat half-hearted reaffirmation of international law as laid down by the Concert of Europe, set the tone for his thinking about the Eastern Question for many years. "What I assume is," he said, "that it is a great object of European policy to prevent the extension of the Russian power in the direction of Constantinople, and that the Power which now occupies that city is to be maintained as a matter of European policy. I give no opinion, I only recognize the obligations of treaties."[8]

Later that same year, in an article in the *Quarterly Review* that was primarily a long and closely reasoned critique of Palmerstonianism, Gladstone laid down the main lines of his position toward the Ottoman Empire. No admirer of the Turks, he referred to their initial conquest of the Balkans in the fourteenth and fifteenth centuries as "that great savage incursion of brute force, which came, like a deluge of blood rained from the windows of heaven, upon some of the fairest countries of the world." Turning to more recent times, he charged that Palmerston's great mistake was to believe that the Ottoman Empire could be regenerated from the head, from Constantinople. Rather, it was the provinces that were budding with new energies. The wise policy was to encourage as much local self-government as feasible. "Nor is there anything in this practical freedom inconsistent with the interests of the Ottoman Power," he asserted. The Sultan would be relieved of a great deal of difficulty, while his "tribute and title" would be assured; the provinces, permitted to govern themselves to a degree "varying according to their rights, traditions, and comparative maturity," would be hostile to Russia and well-disposed toward the Sultan as their "contentment, prosperity, and strength" burgeoned. Quite possibly over the long term the Ottoman Empire might fall; but not right away and not before a responsible policy on the part of European powers such as Britain and France had prepared a smooth transition to autonomous national states. It was, potentially, a rosy vision. There was one threat to this beneficent evolution, and Gladstone presciently described it: an outbreak of "the whole mass of smouldering Mahometan fanaticism."[9]

Up to this point, Gladstone's understanding of the Eastern Question had been gained indirectly. In 1858, the Conservative government chose him for a mission to the Ionian Islands, an experience which would give him firsthand experience of both Greeks and Turks. The situation in the Islands was a tricky one, and Gladstone was selected partly because he had a reputation for philhellene sympathies, but also partly because Derby hoped to inveigle him into membership in the Conservative party.[10]

The Islands, which had passed back and forth with dizzying rapidity between Venice, France, Russia, and Britain during the Napoleonic Wars, had been confirmed to Britain as a protectorate at the Congress of Vienna. The first Lord High Commissioner, Sir Thomas Maitland, familiarly known as King Tom, had instituted a government which blatantly assigned all real control to the British, despite a complex constitution which managed to put most upper-class Ionians on the government payroll. By 1848, discontent with British rule could no longer be contained. Seaton, the Lord High Commissioner, suggested a far-reaching "liberalization" of the government.[11] Despite this sop to local opinion, revolts broke out. The Crimean War complicated matters further, because the British, allied with the Ottomans, wanted the neutral Ionians to support the war effort.[12] In 1858 a nasty quarrel pitted the then Lord Commissioner, Sir John Young, against the local authorities on the most important island, Corfu. Young responded with wholesale dismissals, but London worried that this tactic might be illegal.[13] Gladstone was supposed to resolve the impasse while offering suggestions for the future of the protectorate.

Gladstone was not yet well acquainted with modern Greeks, but he was predisposed to sympathy.[14] Even more than most Victorians, Gladstone was imbued with the heritage of Greek civilization. He read Greek texts, frequently tutoring his children in Greek, and wrote extensively on Homeric subjects.[15] No less an authority than Sir Hugh Lloyd-Jones has testified that his ideas, although simplistic by standards of modern scholarship, remain worth study.[16]

But Gladstone's view of Greek antiquity was in some respects eccentric. It was shaped both by his need to relate it to Christianity and by his efforts to come to terms with contemporary society. Gladstone thought that the Greeks, like the Hebrews of the Old Testament, understood something of God's promise of a fuller revelation, and he worked out an elaborate equation of the Greek gods and goddesses with Christian concepts such as the godhead, the principle of evil, and the logos. He evidently believed that Greek history demonstrated the possibility of arriving at "traditional Christian values" through "natural" means, apart from the aid of Biblical revelation. Such ideas permitted Gladstone to accept modern, secular society in "the hope or expectation" that it could have "purpose or prescriptive patterns" such as had been discovered earlier by religion.[17] Study of Greek thought was integral to Gladstone's gradual transcendence of his original, more or less theocratic view of politics.

At the same time, Gladstone stood very much in the tradition of Matthew Arnold's view of the classics. The moral prescriptions offered by the Greeks could command the loyalty of new men as well as aristocrats. They might differ in home training, but both were typically educated in the classical tradition. Greek thought could insure continuity of the norms of conduct in a time of rapid social change.[18] Significantly, these intellectual concerns with the meaning of Greek culture seem to have been very much on Gladstone's mind at periods when he was dealing with modern-day Greeks at a practical level. Gladstone's *Studies on Homer and the Homeric Age* appeared in three volumes in 1858, right before his trip to the Ionian Islands; two more books appeared in 1876, at the time of the Bulgarian agitation.[19]

Gladstone's interest in Homer combined with another influence—

his sympathy with the Greek Orthodox religion—to shape his perceptions of contemporary Greece. Raised as an Evangelical, Gladstone had become increasingly attracted in the 1830s and 1840s to the High Church wing of the Anglican church. He tended to idealize Christianity as based on a single historic tradition, which transcended the quarrels of individual sects. He was horrified, however, when many friends went over to Rome, and he regarded the Papacy with fascinated aversion. These attitudes predisposed him toward the Greek Orthodox, who seemed to combine authentic Christian tradition with rejection of the Vatican.[20]

Primed with these different and even conflicting associations with Greece, Gladstone set out for his new assignment in the Ionian Islands at the end of 1858.[21] From the start, he was horrified at what he found. "Nothing less than an army of Cherubim and Seraphim," he wrote Lytton, the colonial secretary, "can make anything tolerable out of the present system." The difficulties were compounded by bad luck. While Gladstone was on the way to Corfu, the *Daily News* published a letter suggesting that Corfu and Paxos, the islands which were most accommodating to Britain and had the greatest strategic value, be annexed directly as colonies, while the other islands be returned to Greece. The Ionians assumed that Gladstone had been sent to implement this program. Naturally, the residents of Corfu and Paxos now became quite as obstructionist as the inhabitants of the other islands, and Gladstone's mission never recovered.[22] To make matters worse, it soon became clear in London that Gladstone, who had agreed to take the title of Lord High Commissioner, would lose his seat in the House of Commons, since he would be ineligible in his new post to stand in the elections unexpectedly scheduled for February 1859. A replacement was quickly arranged for Ionia, but the parliamentary background was not understood in the Islands, and confusion resulted. He spent only about three months in the East, too short a time to do much more than gain impressions.[23]

Gladstone had tackled a difficult mission. Boldly he suggested that the Assembly be given even more control, but even this was not enough for the Ionians. When the Assembly met in January 1859, they resolved with no dissenting voices to accept a petition expressing the unanimous desire of all the islands to join Greece and shortly afterward expressly rejected Gladstone's plan.[24] In retrospect, it seems clear that Gladstone underrated the force of the Ionian protest, a revolutionary movement springing from a totally different and conflicting perception of the source of the government's legitimacy.[25] The Ionian movement was similar to the later revolts in the Ottoman Empire in Crete and Bulgaria; and it was probably lucky for Gladstone's reputation, as Shannon suggests, that his stillborn recommendations to the Colonial Office remained secret.[26]

Undoubtedly the most lasting feature of the trip was its impact on Gladstone himself and on his perceptions of politics in the eastern Mediterranean. Gladstone's efforts to meet the Greeks on their own ground were unusual for a Briton abroad, but were not, for all that, an unqualified success. Sir James Lacaita, Gladstone's secretary, describes one of Gladstone's addresses to the Assembly, which the statesman proudly gave in Greek. Lacaita, who did not understand Greek, turned to an Ionian magnate near him after the speech and asked his opinion. The reply: "Oh, magnificent, magnificent! But I don't know what it was about, for you see I know no English." So much for the utility of classical Greek in Corfu![27] More satisfactory was his brief visit to Athens at Christmas, where he did some touring (he saw the Acropolis for the first time), consulted with other English diplomatic representatives and philhellenes, such as Sir Thomas Wyse, General Church, and Finlay, and talked with the King and Queen. These experiences, while they confirmed his enthusiasm for the Greek heritage, also reinforced his skepticism about extreme Ionian demands.[28]

Back in London, Gladstone's defense of British rule was not perfunctory. Placing the Ionian problem in the context of Near Eastern politics as a whole, he justified maintaining British rule by the implications for Ottoman control of the adjacent Greek coasts. He concluded that "this small question is the narrow corner of a very great question, one no less, in all likelihood, than the reconstruction of all political society in southeastern Europe."[29]

It did not follow that Gladstone's experiences improved his view of the Turks. He visited the neighboring Albanian coast and was invited by the mother of a local official to a lavish dinner ending with the ritual water pipe. He considered the facilities primitive and the food heavy and indigestible. As for the water pipe, never again! Perhaps it had been spiked with hashish, though in any case, Gladstone never liked smoking.[30] To make matters worse, his hostess asked Gladstone to recommend her son for a governorship, a normal enough request in Ottoman circles, but one which could only confirm suspicions of Turkish corruption.[31] Gladstone may have come away from the Islands "thoroughly disgusted with the Greeks," but this was a mere lover's quarrel compared with his hostility to Turks.[32]

Nonetheless, after 1859 Gladstone for a number of years moderated his "former intense criticism of the Crimean policy." Travel to the eastern Mediterranean seems to have been sobering; whatever his private misgivings, he recognized the enormous complexity of the problem. On the very few occasions when he absolutely could not avoid speaking out, he supported the accepted wisdom of continued accommodation with the Ottoman Empire.[33] Things changed in 1862–63, when a new and supposedly more responsible government came to power in Greece. Inevitably, Gladstone was drawn into the parliamentary debate on Ottoman rule over Christians in general. He "spoke on the Turkish question: reluctantly"[34]; once again, he felt constrained to defend Britain's traditional pro-Ottoman policy. If Britain was not prepared "to encourage a general crusade," her cue was to renounce an exposé of abuses and take the more sensible path of encouraging the Turks to reform while recognizing that Muslim subjects of the Porte as well as Christians suffered from misrule.[35] Gladstone was not, evidently, a mover in the idea of giving back the islands to Greece, although when this plan was proposed by Palmerston and Lord John Russell, he agreed. Among other things, "there were sensible economies to be made." However, since Gladstone's reports from the Islands had never been published, the public believed that he had been a backstage advocate of Greek nationalism all along. Indeed, some Ionians planned to make Gladstone King of Greece, and Gladstone's family was not unsupportive. "Catherine reported that little Herbert was quite taken with the idea: she would be a queen and he a prince."[36] Gladstone was aware of the Ionians' feelings. Three years later in Rome, discussing the return of the Islands with the Pope, he said that "the occasion was perhaps not very good; but the spirit of the people was Hellenic: & we had no interest or plea which would justify us in disregarding in their case the principle of nationality, which within certain limits was a good principle."[37]

Shortly thereafter, a new Mediterranean crisis, the civil war between ethnic Greeks and their Ottoman overlords in Crete, occupied Gladstone's attention.[38] He expressed himself in Parliament with disillusionment. The Porte's apparent failure to live up to the promises made in 1856 of a better life for Christian subjects constituted a breach of "moral faith." And he pointed again to Moldavia and Walachia, two Ottoman provinces already granted autonomy, as the eventual model for southeastern Europe.[39]

Later, as prime minister (1868–1874), Gladstone had to deal with the final stages of the war in Crete. When the Greek government in Athens tried to sabotage an internal Ottoman settlement of the disturbances, Greece and the Porte reached the brink of war. The situation was resolved by an international conference in Paris;[40] Gladstone was obliged to consider how far Britain should go in forcing the Porte to meet the rebels' demands. Since the situation in Crete closely paralleled that which later developed in Bulgaria, this might have been an early opportunity for Gladstone to have denounced Turkish rule entirely. Instead, he tried to limit the disruption caused by the crisis, and, whatever his impulses may have been, he avoided inflammatory public statements. He clearly approved of arrangements which would grant autonomy to Ottoman provinces; he preferred such arrangements to the administrative centralization of the mid-century Tanzimat movement, on which British statesmen such as Palmerston had rested their hopes for regeneration of the Ottoman Empire. Consequently, Ottoman readiness to grant a significant degree of self-rule to Crete must have been critical in enabling him to support Constantinople at this juncture. Early in 1869, he wrote to Clarendon: "As to the local autonomy under Suzerainty & tribute, my opinion has long been that this is by much the best arrangement *in itself* for Turkey & for the parties."[41] Gladstone did not accept the basic assumption of the Tanzimat reform, namely that westernization could be most effectively implemented when power was placed in the hands of a few individuals in Constantinople. He did support the Empire's continued existence (as he did later, in 1876) and recognized that trouble would come if the Porte was obliged to loosen the bonds of empire indefinitely. Later in 1869 he wrote Clarendon: "As to Turkey, would not a federal system, or rather a quasi-federal one, be more practicable & hopeful than the one of purely unitarian centralization?"[42]

Gladstone further elaborated his thinking in 1870. At the time of the Crimean War and in the years thereafter, the Ottoman Empire had existed in a context of support from the European powers. By 1870, this context had changed drastically and the Ottomans had to understand that they faced Russia alone, "if we take as I suppose we must, the *malveillance* of Russia for granted." Even "in this country the whole policy of the Crimean war is now almost universally, & very unduly depreciated; and the idea of another armed intervention on behalf of Turkey, whether sole or with allies, is ridiculed." Turkey must count on her own resources, and rather than looking to foreign aid for survival, must cultivate "the attachment of her own subjects."[43] For Gladstone the most likely method for increasing the European provinces' loyalty to the Porte was the paradoxical one of giving them greater freedom. This solution was not dissimilar in substance to what he was still advocating in 1876, although his methods and tone changed greatly. On Febuary 8, 1876, for example, Gladstone, speaking in Parliament, justified Britain's sympathy for the Porte's Christian subjects, but once again assumed support for the Empire's continued existence: the "integrity and independence of the Turkish Empire . . . can never be effectually maintained unless it can be proved to the world that . . . the Government of Turkey has the power to administer a fair measure of justice to all its subjects alike, whether Christian or Mahomedan."[44]

The corollary, which Gladstone carefully did not draw, was that if the Porte showed itself incapable of providing social justice, the Empire's existence was forfeit. In the next few months, considerable evidence reached Gladstone that this might now be the case and that abuse might have attained proportions impossible to condone. To begin with, there was the troubling issue of the Ottoman default on loans contracted in the West. The Porte's partial failure to meet its obligations does not seem to have touched off a backlash against the Empire in England; most of the bondholders represented big money, rather than clergy, widows, and spinsters.[45] Nonetheless, Gladstone's reaction to the default prefigures his later reaction to the Bulgarian atrocities. He became involved in helping Clara Mockler of Teignmouth, one of the victims,[46] and made a speech on the subject in the Commons on July 21. He pointed out that investors in the 1854 loan (the one to which Clara Mockler had subscribed) had put out their money because the loan was guaranteed by the British and French governments; by defaulting, the Ottomans had made Britain an accomplice in defrauding its own subjects.[47] Gladstone's confidence in fiscal matters, based on long and successful experience, precluded hesitations in judging the rights and wrongs of this issue. It took him somewhat longer to sort out the ambiguities presented by Ottoman political misgovernment, in which the requirements of humanity conflicted with the moral sanctity of treaties and the practical benefits of preserving order in the area.

Despite Gladstone's general avoidance of the Eastern Question, his stature as a champion of Christian beliefs and humanitarian values ensured that he would be one of the first to be told about the unfolding story of massacre in Bulgaria. On May 26, in immediate response to an unexpected and alarming note from Lord Stratford de Redcliffe, Gladstone visited the aging diplomat and apparently received an extended briefing on the state of affairs in the East. Stratford and Gladstone stayed in touch as Stratford's original information was amplified by publication in the *Daily News* on June 23 of Pears's first full description of the facts as they were known in Constantinople. Gladstone recognized that the cabinet was hedging to fend off Liberal attempts to bring whatever information the Foreign Office might have into the open. He attended the House of Commons on June 9, when Hartington tried to extract details from Disraeli, and was disgusted by Disraeli's slipperiness. Gladstone was no better pleased on July 26, when the Liberal leaders agreed to go along with a motion of support for the government offered by T. C. Bruce, the Conservative member for Portsmouth (who was, not coincidentally, chairman of the Imperial Ottoman Bank).[48]

Suspicion of the Turks dovetailed with many of Gladstone's current concerns and prejudices. His friend, the Catholic eccentric Ambrose Phillips de Lisle, reminded Gladstone later that when they had breakfasted early in the summer, Gladstone had handed him a copy of a book by Fleming which prophesied the end of the Ottoman Empire; this provoked a discussion of de Lisle's own book, published in 1855, which asserted that Muhammad was the Antichrist. In de Lisle's mind, the collapse of Islam was associated with the second coming of Christ and the reunion of the eastern and western halves of the Christian church.[49] This reunion had long occupied Gladstone and many of his ecclesiastical friends, especially since the Vatican Council and the promulgation of the dogma of Papal Infallibility. Quite apart from these religious concerns, friends were already subjecting him to political pressure. The polemicist Malcolm MacColl, angry at Disraeli (whom he considered "one of the 'most inveterate liars in Christendom'"), was begging Gladstone to "tear away the mask from the fanciful pictures of Turkey [which] the Government & a portion of the press have presented to the public." MacColl urged Gladstone "to speak on the Eastern question."[50]

But Gladstone did not make up his mind lightheartedly. He immersed himself "for many hours" in the Blue Book recently published on the Eastern Question and attended two meetings at Lord Granville's to discuss appropriate Parliamentary tactics. Stress took its toll; on July 27, he noted in his diary that he had been ill with diarrhea during the night. Only after last-minute cramming did he rise in the House on July 31 to hold forth at length on what he rightly regarded as an unusually tricky and complex subject.[51] His conclusions, once again, were moderate. "The real question," he declared, "is not whether the supremacy of the Porte can be established in its ancient form . . . but whether its political supremacy in some improved form can be—as I hope it may be—still maintained." He concluded, "I say, without the least hesitation, it must [include] . . . measures conceived in the spirit and advancing in the direction of self-government."[52] Once again, Gladstone's preference for autonomy and concern for social justice were anchored firmly within the context of support for the Empire's continued existence; his failure to take special note of the situation in Bulgaria was a clear setback for the nascent agitation.

In the next month, information from the East continued to be confusing. A new letter from Pears, published in the *Daily News,* and a letter from the British emissary Baring, communicated to the House of Commons, made Gladstone think that he had not given sufficient weight to events in Bulgaria.[53] The editor of the *Journal Stamboul,* J. Laffan Hanley, who had been highly critical of the atrocities and of the response of the British ambassador, Sir Henry Elliot, sent information directly to Gladstone, including copies of his articles.[54] But Elliot was quite capable of coming to his own defense: writing Gladstone about another matter on August 5, he remarked: "I see from what you say that you are rather an advocate for autonomy in the Insurgent Turkish Provinces." Elliot pointed out: "I do not think that those who brought forward that view have properly viewed the practical difficulties . . . the populations are divided into several hostile sects, likely to lead to a perfect state of anarchy."[55] The same presuppositions underlay the report of Edib Efendi (the official Ottoman account of events in Bulgaria), which Gladstone read on August 18.[56] He was not persuaded, however; the report, he wrote to Granville, was "a sheer & gross mockery."[57]

Meanwhile many of Gladstone's friends poured out their frustration to him. His old associate, Argyll, confided his disgust upon reading the Blue Book of August 10.[58] MacColl, about to set out on a fact-finding tour of the East with Canon Liddon, wrote to ask for introductions (and incidentally dashed off a charitable hope for Disraeli: "I wish he was a prisoner in the hands of the Bashi-Bazouks").[59] MacColl was still adamant that Gladstone speak out. "I must apologize for troubling you at such length," he wrote on the 26th. "But do, please, raise your powerful voice against the bestial government of Turkey and the degrading policy of our own government."[60] On September 1, returning to the theme, he begged: "I do hope you will make a speech on the Eastern question. The country is evidently thoroughly roused; but it wants guidance." MacColl again let slip his own highly mixed motives by adding: "I think immense capital might be made against Dizzy just now."[61] Other requests continued to pile up. Rev. William Denton and journalist W. T. Stead pleaded with Gladstone to act.[62] And Madame Novikov, the Russian propagandist and Slavophile, wrote to Gladstone, as well as virtually everyone else of importance whom she knew in England, about the death of her brother, Alexander Kireev, as a volunteer in the Serbian campaign on behalf of the Bulgarians. She laid his loss squarely at the feet of the Conservative British government and did not shrink from emotional blackmail: "If Mr. Gladstone had been in power, then had my brother not died."[63]

Examples of the pressure put upon Gladstone can be multiplied; how did he himself assess the situation? None of these pleas seems to have made a difference. To Stead he replied curtly on September 2, thanking him for his letter and briefly praising his stand in Darlington.[64] To Madame Novikov, whose enthusiasm for him had earlier been something of an embarrassment, he did not reply at all, but prudently left the assignment to Mrs. Gladstone (much to Madame Novikov's chagrin).[65]

A much less exotic appeal finally brought Gladstone's frustration to the breaking point. Alfred Days, secretary of the Workmen's Hyde Park Demonstration Committee from Hackney, wrote Gladstone asking for assistance with a demonstration being planned in London against the atrocities. Gladstone, after toying with various means of support, responded with a token subscription and a letter, which was read to the meeting in Hackney.[66] Later, Gladstone filed the communication from Days with the notation, "Pēgē" ("fountain"); and he told Henry Broadhurst that it was Days who had convinced him "that the iron was hot and that the time to strike had arrived."[67] The question he now turned over in his mind was how to act; he concluded, as he wrote Granville with possibly assumed tentativeness, "I am in half, perhaps a little more than half, a mind to write a pamphlet: mainly on the ground that Parliamentary action was all but ousted. Does this shock you?"[68]

Why was it that the decisive contact among so many came from someone outside Gladstone's usual circle? Shannon reasonably concludes that Gladstone recognized that the Bulgarian atrocities had sparked a popular reaction which could be turned to his own political advantage.[69] Yet, in light of all we now know about the religious wellsprings of Gladstone's inner life, it seems fair to say that there was more to it than that. Gladstone's thinking about the Ottoman Empire had been consistent mainly in its ambivalence. It was a situation maddening to his personal desire for logic and rationality, but it was one in which he not infrequently found himself. On the one hand, Gladstone subscribed to the conventional wisdom shared by most Victorian Britons regarding the politics of the eastern Mediterranean. He was willing and able to pay the price of supporting the Ottoman Empire. Although he was never susceptible, unlike many of his contemporaries, to exaggerated expectations of smooth and speedy westernization of Ottoman society, he accepted the arguments that maintaining the Ottoman Porte was necessary for the stability of the eastern Mediterranean and hence a high priority for Britain. It was this set of beliefs which motivated Gladstone in his support of the Empire during the Crimean War; in his efforts to resolve the Ionian question in a way which would not encourage Greek irredentism, one of the major threats to Ottoman authority; and in his readiness to join with other European governments in limiting the damage to the Empire from the Cretan revolt. He implied (in connection with the Ionian Islands) that Ottoman rule in the northern Greek provinces, though internationally sanctioned, was far from ideal; but he added that the British could not indulge in the luxury of criticism as long as they were not prepared to shoulder the burden of helping to restructure the entire political system of the eastern Mediterranean.

Such arguments show Gladstone as a pillar of the Victorian establishment and "a superb political operator."[70] But there was another side. As early as the 1850s, when he was first called upon to take a major public position on the Ottoman Empire, Gladstone, believing that the Turks were corrupt, inefficient, and intolerant, worried that support of their rule over Christians meant a denial of that mystical religious community within which he, like other true Britons, found his identity and his spiritual existence. Allusions to the stability of the eastern Mediterranean seemed irrelevant; better to seize upon the course which was morally right and sort out other aspects later. Predictions of a Russian sweep to Constantinople were too deterministic; surely the Russians would come to grief amidst the ethnic complexities of the Balkans just as other powers had before them. There might be troubles in newly autonomous or independent provinces, but at a certain point, these difficulties must be faced head-on, not used as an excuse for shoring up the status quo. Implied in this position was the belief that doing right was good for its own sake; one might construct political arguments to convince the waverers, but the real justification rested on a set of asssumptions about God's purpose in the world and his power to save those who acted in conformity with his moral imperatives. It was this simple, normative conviction which lay behind Gladstone's apparent uneasiness over his participation in the Crimean coalition, his championing of the Romanians' cause in 1858, his sympathy for the Greeks and distaste for the Turks during the Ionian mission, and his reservations about Ottoman attempts to maintain their power in Crete. While one line of thinking made it possible for Gladstone to be "responsible" and "play the game," another line urged him to break out and follow his moral convictions.

It was a dilemma which Gladstone faced more than once in his life and its resolution was always painful. The young man who apparently tried to defy his family by rejecting the political career for which he had been so expensively educated and personally groomed in favor of entry into Holy Orders and a renunciation of worldly ambitions; the young minister and protégé of Sir Robert Peel who had given up his post over the Maynooth grant, rather than participate in a government which affronted his convictions about the correct relations between church and state; the mature leader who compounded his confused religious image by trying belatedly to lead resistance to the Vatican decrees concerning Papal Infallibility—all were psychologically related to the elder statesman who cherished the political power he had won in part as a leader conforming to traditional, "responsible," pro-Ottoman British policy, but who felt compelled to risk it all in favor of a crusade on behalf of Christian solidarity. The necessity to break out, at least temporarily, to make a gesture, overwhelmed Gladstone from time to time when his careerist instincts and his moral convictions moved too far apart.

In this context, it is not hard to imagine why the appeal from Days was decisive. The working men of Hackney did not share the compromises and rationalizations which formed the common intellectual furniture of the political establishment. Gladstone was in the position of a parent talking to a child, or a teacher talking to young students. Certain easy assumptions about the validity of supporting the Ottoman Empire, which would have been allowed even if they were controverted by other members of the political elite, simply made no sense to outsiders such as the Hackney working men. To have rested his case on the familiar strategic arguments despite the strong evidence of Ottoman brutality would have revealed Gladstone as inconsistent or uncaring or both. He was shamed into taking a position which, when he explained it in the famous pamphlet, was much more radical in tone than anything he had said previously. Indeed, it seems likely that guilt over the narrowness of his escape from condoning Ottoman "crimes" in Bulgaria actually inflamed his attacks. It is true that, in this instance, the moral high ground coincided with the politically astute move, but this had not always been the case. Gladstone was capable of taking a dramatic stand even when, as with his ambivalence over entering Parliament or his resignation over the Maynooth grant, his actions appeared to hurt his career. But some instinct always pulled him back from the brink before he carried principle to the point of disaster; hypocritical he was not, but he was not self-destructive either. In the Bulgarian agitation, the political moment and the psychological breaking-point coincided for once, and Gladstone stood defenseless before the temptation to demagoguery.

6 • The First Stirrings of Protest

By the summer of 1876 the factors necessary for a social protest movement centered on events in Bulgaria were in place. The news of the Bulgarian massacres, which filtered and then flooded into the British newspapers, acted as a precipitating factor. For the politically aware, this crisis accentuated a situation of strain which could no longer be resolved by familiar rationalizations, such as the necessity for imperial governments to take unpopular or harsh actions in certain circumstances, or the notion that any alternative political organization of the eastern Mediterranean would present worse problems. Britain's condition throughout the mid-nineteenth century was structurally conducive to the spectrum of collective behavior often referred to as "pressure from without." More particularly, the background for the protest movement which became known as the Bulgarian agitation went back to the 1867 franchise reform, which gave a voice to a large body of new voters, most of them distinct in regional background, class, and religious affiliation, without providing the means for integrating them into the mainstream of political decision making. It was also related to the serious disarray of the Liberal party, which traditionally spoke to the concerns of the industrial North, the middle classes, Evangelicals, and Nonconformists—a disarray which had arisen from, among other things, profound disagreements over the place of religion in the state. Finally, Gladstone, after many years of balancing his deeply held distrust of the Ottomans with his general adherence to the conventional wisdom about British interests and obligations, had reached the breaking point in August 1876. Presented with the request of the Workmen's Hyde Park Demonstration Committee to explain official British policy in the face of the Bulgarian massacres, Gladstone found that to this naively logical audience he could no longer rationalize Christian Britain's support of murder.

During the summer, autumn, and winter of 1876 the protest movement erupted. Smelser suggests that such a movement, dedicated to bringing conduct into conformity with some hypothetical norm, "may be divided into three temporal phases—the incipient phase, the phase of enthusiastic mobilization, and the period of institutionalization and organization. The movement begins with slow, searching behavior; accelerates into a period of super-charged activity; then settles gradually into . . . routine, day-by-day activity."[1] The summer of 1876 marked the incipient phase, concluding with Gladstone's resounding statement of the generalized beliefs of the movement through his pamphlet and a speech to his constituents at Blackheath on September 9. The burst of activity which followed in September marked acceleration into the enthusiastic phase. Impressive as this phase was, the organizers realized that the pace could not be sustained; before the end of September they were considering strategies for keeping the movement alive once local meetings became repetitious. The national St. James's Hall Conference and the founding of the Eastern Question Association in December solved the problem and pushed the movement into the institutionalized phase, which continued through 1877 and 1878.

At each stage, the reactions of the party in power also served to shape the movement. Largely unconscious and uncoordinated, to be sure, such responses rested upon a fundamental misunderstanding and underestimation of the movement which only began to change in 1878. In discounting the protesters' mood of moral earnestness, some Conservatives, especially Disraeli, offended their critics and exacerbated the protesters' suspicions of the government. To make matters worse, the Ottomans and the Russians acted to suit their own convenience, not the cabinet's. There were moments when the crisis seemed about to die away, only to be revived by events abroad.

Smelser suggests that the leadership of a protest movement is differentiated and performs several functions. The basic division is "between two kinds of leadership—leadership in formulating the beliefs and leadership in mobilizing participants for action." Over time, the nature of the leadership or the relative importance of different types of leadership will change. Leaders such as W. T. Stead, the newspaper editor who launched the protest meetings through calls in the *Northern Echo* of Darlington, and Malcolm MacColl, who originally urged Gladstone to head the movement, were promoters (mobilizers), whereas

Gladstone, whose pamphlet and speeches proclaimed the ideology of the movement, was a formulator.[2]

Not surprisingly, Stead's work organizing a group of concerned individuals at the grass roots preceded Gladstone's mass appeals. Shannon's charge that Gladstone revealed his insincerity by climbing on the bandwagon belatedly and reluctantly seems to rest at least partly on exaggerated expectations.[3] The detailed, demanding work of promoting meetings in different towns and cities across England was not an activity Gladstone ever considered part of his task; whether the work was carried on officially, as during election campaigns, or extra-officially, as in this case, it was always done by subordinates. At the same time, Gladstone's ringing appeals depended for their effect on the attention of a large and receptive audience. Gladstone was the star who came on when the performance had been arranged; he did not hire the room or hawk the tickets. What is remarkable is how deeply Gladstone eventually became involved behind the scenes in advising and guiding those who did organize the protest. But this was a gradual development which broke new ground in connecting so-called "faddists" with revered members of the political establishment.[4] Probably Gladstone himself would have been unnerved if he could have foreseen at the outset how far down an unaccustomed road his principles would take him.

The first accounts of the massacres were published in the *Daily News*, beginning on June 23. As we have seen, such stories were not unprecedented (and the massacres themselves could be compared to other recent episodes in the Ottoman Empire), but the nauseating profusion of detail was new, and the fact that such reports reached Britain at all demonstrated the maturity of different routes of communication. Crete and Lebanon both have extensive seacoasts visited by the British navy; it was easy and natural for the British to gather information about events there. Bulgaria, like other parts of the Balkans, was less accessible by sea and historically the British, with a few outstanding exceptions, had been less interested in this whole range of territory. The reports furnished by British consuls went largely unchallenged, although they were often biased in favor of the Ottomans (in part because the resident Britons had few contacts other than official ones, and in part because London exerted none-too-subtle pressure toward optimism).[5] This dearth of information was alleviated primarily through the activities of missionaries; the groundbreaking work of G. Muir Mackenzie and A. P. Irby on Serbia and its environs, first published in 1867, was a case in point.[6] By the 1870s, Protestant missionaries were well organized and quite capable of playing the role that Catholic priests from Lebanon and Syria, on the scene earlier and in force, had played in raising opinion in Ireland in 1860.

The first reports to reach the European community in Constantinople from the Bulgarian side were contained in letters to Dr. Albert Long, a former missionary in Bulgaria who had become vice president of Robert College. Founded in 1863 by American missionaries, this institution was forbidden by Ottoman law to educate Muslims, and therefore enrolled only Christians, including a large contingent from Bulgaria, many of whom were personally recruited by Dr. Long. The college community contrasted markedly in attitude with the foreign community in general, for most European residents scorned native Christians; the English in particular were nostalgic for the pro-Turkish heyday of the Crimean War when many had made fortunes in war contracting. This general mood was all too apparent when Long and the president of Robert College, George Washburn, tried to bring their version of events in Bulgaria to the attention of the British ambassador, Sir Henry Elliot. Elliot, who was known for his commitment to the Porte, brushed aside the unwelcome information. Long and Washburn received a better hearing from the British consul general, Sir Philip Francis, who suggested that they write a memo to Elliot giving full documentation. They did so, and took the precaution of supplying copies to two British newspaper correspondents, Galenga of the *Times*, and Sir Edwin Pears of the *Daily News*. Both journalists scented a story and both filed reports on June 16. Galenga's report was held by the *Times*; but Frank Hill of the *Daily News* decided that Pears's report was usable and published it on June 23.[7]

The story was too sensational to be overlooked, but it clashed with other accounts, including the cabinet's dismissive response to questions in Parliament.[8] The *Daily News* telegraphed Pears for more details. Encouraged, Pears obtained translations from Long and Washburn of much of their correspondence. Based on these sources, he wrote another, blistering article, which appeared in the *Daily News* on June 30. By now, the *Daily News* was hot on the scent, and challenged Pears to produce still more corroboration. Pears, sensing that his credibility was at stake, suggested an investigation by some sort of official commission. This was the origin of the famous mission of MacGahan and Schuyler. Grisly "eyewitness" accounts commenced in the *Daily News* on August 7 with a particularly grim (though brief) description of slaughter at Batak, which Pears telegraphed to the *Daily News* through Bucharest to escape Ottoman censorship.[9]

But as Shannon points out, "atrocity reports were not enough, even when supported by strong exhortation in general terms, to provoke in themselves a consistent campaign of public manifestations against the government's policy." Much hortatory discussion of the massacres issued from widely respected figures: there were two deputations to Derby on July 14, the Willis's Rooms meeting on July 27, Bishop Fraser's meeting at Manchester on August 9, and Canon Liddon's "sensational sermon" preached at St. Paul's on August 13.[10] None of this was effective in rousing the ordinary British subject outside the charmed circle of the political and intellectual elite. What was important, however, was the fact that the government did not feel obliged (nor in fact would it have been able) to take decisive action calculated to alter the course of events in the eastern Mediterranean.

As the crisis developed, the logical arena to ask questions and to express opinions was Parliament. Britain's role in the East had seemed to be staunchly pro-Ottoman after the dispatch of the fleet to Besika Bay in May 1876. Opponents of the government voiced criticism; the opportunity to reply and to explain gave the government a chance to defuse the discontent. But the ministers clearly misused their opportunity, and the mishandling of the initial questions, particularly by Disraeli, fanned the incipient agitation.

After some initial questions during June, the call for papers came from Edward Jenkins, Liberal M.P. for Dundee, on July 3. The goverment made difficulties about producing the correspondence and the papers were not actually laid before the House until July 21.[11] In the meantime, Disraeli made a brief statement on July 10 in response to a question from W. E. Forster, followed by a longer statement on the seventeenth. On the tenth, Disraeli made a damaging admission: "that there have been proceedings of an atrocious character in Bulgaria I never for a moment doubted." (He had by then presumably received an account from "a Bulgarian of sterling character" on the faculty of Robert College, transmitted by Viscount Strangford.[12]) But Disraeli then suggested that many of the reports were exaggerated. He theorized that there probably was not room in Ottoman prisons for the ten thousand people supposedly jailed, and as to reports of torture, he suggested that the Turks are "an Oriental people who seldom, I believe, resort to torture, but generally terminate their connection with culprits in a more expeditious manner."[13] Disraeli won a laugh, but his flippancy was interpreted as callousness. He apparently had not been fully informed through official sources of events in the East. Four days later he saw a dispatch from Reade, the British consul at Ruse (Ruschuk), which seemed to bear out the stories of massacres, and was reportedly furious that he had not been briefed before his remarks to the Commons.[14] Thus sobered, his words on the seventeenth were more neutral, but again he seemed wide of the mark to many concerned members when he emphasized the political character of the struggle. He declared, "I cannot trace in any manner that the feeling of religious animosity . . . has prompted the general conduct of the masses of the population on either side."[15]

On July 31, T. C. Bruce (member from Portsmouth and chairman of the Imperial Ottoman Bank) brought in a motion supporting the government's policy. In the ensuing debate, Disraeli again went to great lengths to defend his actions and to explain his reservations about accepting reports of the atrocities at face value. He stated, "I was not justified for a moment to adopt that coffee-house babble brought by an anonymous Bulgarian to a Consul as at all furnishing a basis of belief that the account subsequently received had any justification."[16] Although Disraeli's brief statement at the end of the session seemed to show more concern, suspicions were not entirely allayed. Gladstone, writing to Argyll, admitted that Disraeli "is not . . . such a Turk as I had thought" but guessed that Disraeli's motive in supporting the Ottoman Empire was a form of temporizing, based on the calculation that "if vital improvements can be averted, it must break down." In that case, Gladstone suggested Disraeli hoped "to lay hold of Egypt as his share. So he may end as the Duke of Memphis yet."[17] Even more damaging than such suspicions, the characterization of the atrocity reports as "coffee-house babble" was a slip Disraeli would not live down.

Why was Disraeli so inept at handling the reaction to the atrocities? As Blake notices, "personally he seems to have felt little of the indignation which the massacres inspired in most Englishmen of whatever political color."[18] Many observers at the time attributed Disraeli's failure to react to his Jewish background. Yet the relevance of his Jewishness to the crisis was more complex than contemporary anti-Semitic detractors suggested. Disraeli was certainly not a Jew in a religious sense. His father had quarreled with the synagogue when Disraeli was a young teenager and after several years of inactivity had formally resigned. Apparently motivated by the pleas of a friend and a vague sense that children should be brought up in some sort of creed, Isaac D'Israeli had had Benjamin baptized in the Church of England at the age of thirteen.[19] Disraeli remained a practicing member in good standing of his adopted church, although his Jewish heritage was something he had to come to terms with as a young adult. In his late twenties, after various financial and political reverses, he suffered what might now be called an identity crisis. In the hope of reviving his energies and curing his chronic headaches, the family assented to a Mediterranean tour in 1830–31. During this trip, Disraeli redefined Judaism for himself in secularized cultural terms which permitted him to maintain a psychological link despite his lapse from religious faith. His conception of the Jews as a chosen people with a unique message for all mankind would inform later novels, such as *Tancred*.

In the course of his travels Disraeli visited the Ottoman Empire. Since he never differentiated clearly between Jews and Muslims, he found parallels between Jews and Turks which seem surprising to a later generation. As the editors of his letters put it, "he saw the Porte as the last bulwark of a civilization to which he seemed instinctively to respond."[20] Ironically, Disraeli visited the same area of Albania which Gladstone would see nearly thirty years later; whereas Gladstone felt foolish and ill at ease, Disraeli welcomed the experience with high glee. His original intention of volunteering for the Ottoman army in order to help put down a local rebellion was frustrated by the prompt repression of the disturbances; but Disraeli had a capital time when he "turned . . . [his] military trip into a visit of congratulation at headquarters."[21] Like Gladstone, he spent an evening with the locals. Again, conversation was difficult at first, but Disraeli and his madcap companion solved the problem by producing a bottle of brandy. Eventually their host called for "a most capital supper . . . accompanied to our great horror by—wine. We ate—we drank—we eat with our fingers—we drank in a manner I never recollect—the wine was not bad, but if it had been poison, we must drink, it was such a compliment for a Moslemin, we quaffed it in rivers."[22] Life in Constantinople was less exciting, but most agreeable; Disraeli recorded his conviction that "the habits of this calm and luxurious people entirely agree with my own preconceived opinions of propriety and enjoyment."[23]

Disraeli thus felt a significant cultural affinity for the Ottoman Turks. In addition, it was historically demonstrated that the Ottoman Porte, whatever its deficiencies in administration, was more tolerant than the successor Christian governments in the Balkans.[24] Yet it is implausible that Disraeli, whose championship of Jewish rights was always cautious, and whose policy was pragmatic to a fault, would have slavishly or even systematically followed sentiment or sought hypothetical benefits for a group with which he only partially identified. The real impact of Jewish perceptions upon Disraeli's foreign policy can best be understood if he is placed in the context of Jewish views of the crisis. Disraeli had many Jewish friends, most notably the Rothschilds, and he dined with Lionel Rothschild frequently. Indeed, in the words of Richard Davis, "after the death of his own, the Rothschilds were the nearest Disraeli had to family."[25] It seems to follow that he must have been well aware of Jewish perceptions of events in the Near East.

A major concern for nearly ten years had been the savage persecution of Jews in Romania. Conditions were not much better in Serbia. Contemporary Jews had learned the bitter lesson that persecutions, however tragic, were not the end of the story. Far worse massacres had been perpetrated against Jews than the massacres in Bulgaria, yet times had changed and Christian rulers had improved their treatment of Jews; why should not the Turks improve their treatment of Christians?[26] Pogroms of Jews in Russia were already searing news in the West; Jews did not believe that they would be followed by the dissolution of the Tsarist regime. To Jews, the protesters had therefore made a "fatal mistake of confounding two questions totally distinct—the Bulgarian atrocities and the Eastern Question."[27] It seems likely that Disraeli shared this lack of astonishment or shock at the troubles of the Christians and in similar fashion separated sentiment from strategic judgment. But there is no doubt that his response isolated him from most of his colleagues and made him an easy target for the gibes of the press. At the end of September, Stead, referring to Disraeli's recent controversial elevation to the peerage as Earl of Beaconsfield, sneered, "He, whom she [England] had placed in his high position, this new made Earl—so proud of his gaudy coronet, that he has not a word to say about the sufferings in Bulgaria—listens to the entreaties, the sobs, and the prayers of his country, only to reply with flippant scorn and defiant braggadocio."[28] Yet even Disraeli's unsatisfactory discussion was better than nothing. Parliament adjourned for the rest of the autumn and winter on August 15, inevitably fueling agitation.[29] The usual forum for airing grievances was not available, while the heated letters written to the newspapers by members during the recess concerning the shame of the Bulgarian atrocities probably inflamed popular feeling further by seeming to give official sanction to the agitation.

The spectacle of members of the House of Commons hanging back while ministers stuttered through seemingly lame and self-serving justifications was notable, and it was exploited to the full by W. T. Stead of the *Northern Echo* of Darlington, the individual who was first able to bring the question to the masses. Indeed, he was so successful that later in the crisis, Gladstone suggested that the *Daily News* should copy the *Northern Echo's* performance. According to a recent authority, "under Stead until 1880, the *Echo* was probably the most impressive provincial newspaper in the country." It was one of the earliest examples of what came to be called New Journalism—that is, "Nonconformist morality" presented "in an indisputably sensational and often prurient manner" so as to accomplish the goals of spreading the word of God and making "a commercial success."[30]

This New Journalism was in many ways Stead's personal creation, and the Bulgarian agitation was his first campaign. He was helped by the fact that the paper's owner had gone off on vacation to Switzerland, leaving him a more or less free hand. He had always cherished a lofty view of his function: "to think, write and speak for . . . thousands . . . It is the position of a Viceroy . . . God calls . . . and now points . . . to *the only true throne in England, the Editor's chair, and offers me the real sceptre.*" Now, as he put it, in the crisis in Bulgaria, "I felt the clear call of God's voice: 'Arouse the nation or be damned.'" Stead's intention was to bring popular views (as he interpreted them) to bear on the political process; "he wanted the press to act as an extraparliamentary pressure group of enlightened journalists interpreting the will of the people."[31] His methods went well beyond the traditional writing of leaders and editorials. Early in July, he published the first call for public meetings to protest the government's policy by petitions to Parliament.[32] These calls were accompanied by information about the massacres and by appeals to the North Country to act according to its own ethical code in a situation which ultimately posed a question of morality. A few days later, on July 14, the newspaper published a detailed description of the meeting called by the mayor in Stockton.[33] Calls to meet and reports on meetings continued during July and August until, by the end of August, Stead was appealing in an editorial for mass meetings throughout the counties of Durham, Northumberland, and Yorkshire.[34]

Several things distinguish these appeals. One is the detailed knowledge of and attention to all the small localities of that section of northern England. A second is the sensational quality of the reporting. As "eyewitness" reports became available, Stead reproduced them and then milked them for all they were worth in his commentary.[35]

Finally, Stead's appeal was buttressed by a call carefully tailored to his audience. He spoke to the newly enfranchised, roused them against the rich establishment of London, and gave expression to their routinized religious bigotry, a radical tradition which reached back to the seventeenth century. For example, the *Northern Echo* printed a letter from a correspondent in Stockton who discussed the predictions of Robert Fleming, an eighteenth-century Presbyterian minister whose anti-Muslim writings even reached Gladstone himself. Fleming had predicted, "The sixth vial will be poured out upon the Mahometan Antichrist," and Armageddon was confidently set for 1970 or 1980.[36] This linkage of the movement with existing religious prejudices undoubtedly appealed to the spectrum of the major Nonconformist sects. But, taken as a whole, Stead's tone was too Puritanical, too redolent of the atmosphere of chapel and mill, to recruit adherents from the broader milieu necessary if the movement were to gather the numbers required to impress the government on an issue concerning which the protesters themselves had little specialized knowledge or control. What was needed was a more sophisticated and inclusive set of beliefs.

This was provided by Gladstone. It was exactly what Stead had hoped for when he wrote Gladstone on August 26, giving full and glowing accounts of his work toward raising the North Country "as a man."[37] Gladstone's reply was tepid.[38] Probably Shannon is right when he concludes that it was Stead's "tactless" insistence that Gladstone return to leadership of the Liberal party which more than anything else nettled Gladstone.[39] Only after his struggle with a response to the Hackney working men did Gladstone turn his attention to Stead's request. On August 28 he began work on "a possible pamphlet on the Turkish question." The subject was probably stressful, though he attributed a bout of lumbago to "physical exertion." He felt no better the next day, and was forced to spend a good part of it in bed; he complained that trying to write made matters worse. On August 30, he disciplined himself not to write at all and nursed his ailment; but by the thirty-first, he discovered that he could prop paper against his knees in bed, and "made tolerable play" with the pamphlet. By the first, he was able to dispatch the longest section to the printers. He also realized that his indignation needed additional factual support beyond the Blue Book he had at hand. Accordingly, he wrote Frank Hill at the *Daily News*, asking him to supply any information the newspaper might have. On the second he completed the text, again writing much of it more or less prostrate. His relief was evident; although he did not get up until four o'clock and required two hot baths, he claimed to feel considerably better. On September 4, he went up to London and "in six or seven hours, principally at the B. Museum" added what was necessary based on additional reading. On the fifth, he finished correcting the proofs, went over the text with his friend and former Foreign Secretary, Lord Granville, and by seven o'clock "received complete copies." By the end of the evening, he "sent off copies in various directions."[40] It is probably not fanciful to suspect a connection between the vitriolic tone of the pamphlet and the pain that Gladstone was suffering. But the pamphlet undoubtedly owed as much to Gladstone's own indignation and to his instinctive perception of the mood of the country. Whatever the cause, he certainly expressed a widely felt reaction. The first forty thousand copies of the pamphlet sold out in three to four days after printing; two hundred thousand went in the first month.[41] Many shared Stead's perception: "You have once more taken your proper place as the spokesman of the national conscience."[42]

The message of the pamphlet was an extraordinary blend of personal concerns, appealing generalizations, and typically Gladstonian ambiguity, climaxing in the "revivalist" rhetoric his readers awaited.[43] What precise set of beliefs Gladstone thought he was enunciating it is hard to say; as always when in his demagogic vein, he said more than he intended and implied more than he said. Certainly the changes rung chimed perfectly with the anxieties, exasperations, and secret wishes of his audience. The message assumed a life of its own. In ways that Gladstone could not have foreseen, and would have distrusted if he had, the pamphlet sketched the symbolism which connected events in the East to events in England and linked both to the grievances of the disparate groups which made up the agitation. The pamphlet provided a program, at once galvanizing and vicarious, for groups who would never have been able to agree upon a specific direct remedy for their malaise.

Simplest of all, Gladstone could finally share his sense of liability for supporting the Ottomans during the Crimean War. He divulged his reluctance to speak out as long as there was any possible doubt about the facts concerning Bulgaria. But, he declared, given the reports from Schuyler, MacGahan, and Baring, "the responsibility of silence, at least for one who was among the authors of the Crimean War, [was] too great to be borne." However, the pamphlet was far more than a personal confession; Gladstone generalized his sense of guilt to include the English people. "We have been involved," he declared, "in . . . moral complicity with the basest and blackest outrages upon record within the present century, if not within the memory of man."

All this had come about because the English people had been too trusting, too deferential, toward their leaders. "The people of this country have shown a just, but a very remarkable, disposition to repose confidence in the Government of the day; and the Government of the day has availed itself to the uttermost of that disposition." The consequence was that the people of England had been tricked. (Just as they had been tricked with regard to the promises of the Second Reform Act.) Now they were waking up. "The working men of the country . . . have . . . shown that the great heart of England has not ceased to beat." But a difficult task, demanding the role reversal implied in the transition to a more democratic system, lay ahead: "the nation . . . must . . . teach its Government, almost as it would teach a lisping child, what to say."

So far, Gladstone had laid out, in relatively straightforward terms, the failure of the British government to respond to the moral concerns of newly enfranchised working-class voters. Once he had established the trickiness of the government, symbolic connections followed. The Porte, too, was castigated for trickiness and unresponsiveness. The crisis in the East arose from "the total failure of the Porte to fulfil the engagements, which she had contracted under circumstances peculiarly binding on interest, on honour, and on gratitude." The Porte, too, had failed to live up to its obligations; "a lurid glare is thrown over the whole case by the Bulgarian horrors." The seeming similarity between the procedures of the British government and those of the Ottomans was locked into place by the fact that in the present crisis they were co-conspirators. "They [Disraeli and his colleagues] have not understood the rights and duties, in regard to the subjects, and particularly the Christian subjects, of Turkey, which inseparably attach to this country in consequence of the Crimean War, and of the Treaty of Paris in 1856."[44] Like the British government in the Education Act and the Public Worship Regulation Act, the Ottomans had conspired against their Christian subjects.[45] This suspicion was confirmed by the British government's unhesitating willingness to become an accomplice in the Bulgarian massacres.

In addition to their deceitfulness and their intolerance, Gladstone blamed the Turks for their "elaborate and refined cruelty"; their "relentless fatalism"; their "abominable and bestial lust"; and their "utter and violent lawlessness." It was a picture of an oppressive ruling class which had many symbolic associations for Britons, at a time when the luxury, corruption, and immorality of the "Upper Ten Thousand" were a standing grievance with the Nonconformist middle and working classes. The repelled yet fascinated prurience on which Gladstone drew, and which also attracted readers to newspaper accounts of the massacres, was not unrelated to the titillated revulsion which greeted tales of sexual misdemeanors in high places in England. Furthermore, the racial gulf between persecutors and victims, brought out by quoting Disraeli's own evasive and misleading words, might well have reminded British religious leaders of Disraeli's distance from them as a born Jew, a member of a group racially identified with the Ottomans by many at that time, including Disraeli himself.[46] It is noteworthy that twice during the autumn of 1876, *Punch* portrayed Disraeli in a Turkish guise.[47]

Finally, Gladstone addressed himself to the "burden of empire" arguments used to justify the Porte's actions. He was thoroughly impatient with these rationalizations. In response to predictions that Christian Bulgarians and Muslims would never live peacefully together under Christian rule, he cited proclamations from the rebels calling for brotherhood with those Muslims who were willing to rally to the new regime. And the familiar arguments from expediency, in Gladstone's view, were simply elaborate means of getting around uncomfortable truths. It was no accident, he declared, that Schuyler, whose detailed reports from the scene had alerted the West to what had happened, was an American, for America was disinterested. "She enters into this matter simply on the ground of its broad human character and moment; she has no 'American interests' to tempt her from her integrity, and to vitiate her aims." Gladstone also warned against the readiness to believe Ottoman promises. "What we have to guard against is imposture." He predicted that with a new Sultan on the throne, there might be "new constitutions; firmans of reforms; proclamations . . . enjoining extra humanity. All of these should be quietly set down as equal to zero." In his embitterment, Gladstone was not willing to accept any pledges of Ottoman reformation. He finally turned the "burden of empire" argument squarely on its head. Noting suggestions that the different components of the crisis might be dealt with separately, he insisted: "It would have been as reasonable for the Thirteen Colonies of America in 1782, to negotiate separately for peace with Great Britain, as it would be for Europe in 1876 to allow that, in a settlement with Turkey, the five cases of Servia, Bosnia, Herzogovina,

Montenegro, and Bulgaria, should be dealt with otherwise than as the connected limbs of one and the same transaction." Indeed the Ottoman Empire and the British Empire were similar; but the parallel led to one of Britain's least proud hours, and a moment of collapse and redefinition.

For those Nonconformists and High Churchmen who saw the British government as intolerant of their religious preferences and for those new voters who saw the establishment as unwilling to make good on its political commitments, Gladstone had erected an appropriate symbolic scapegoat in the Ottoman Porte, known for its supposed systematic religious discrimination and congenital refusal to implement promises of political reform. Groups which could never have adopted a common program of internal change as a focus for social protest were able to coalesce around a foreign issue about which they knew little and into which they could read whatever their own needs suggested.

What Gladstone himself saw in all of this is far from clear. No sooner had he uttered his denunciation of the Ottoman Empire than he seemed to retract through a characteristic bit of logic chopping. Did he mean to give up the "territorial integrity of Turkey?" No indeed, he replied; but integrity did not mean freedom to do whatever the Sultan chose. Integrity could be reconciled with wide-ranging grants of autonomy to the component parts of the Empire. As long as the "titular sovereignty" of the Porte was maintained, other powers could be excluded from the area and "the wholesale scramble" averted.[48]

It might seem that Gladstone, for all his brave words, had retreated to a position similar to that which he had held for a number of years, and had enunciated most recently when he had declined to go to the Cretans' aid against the Porte. Yet he could not resist a peroration which put all in doubt again and gave comfort to his most radical readers: "Let the Turks now carry away their abuses in the only possible manner, namely by carrying off themselves. Their Zaptiehs and their Mudirs, their Bimbashis and their Yuzbachis, their Kaimakams and their Pashas, one and all, bag and baggage, shall, I hope, clear out from the province they have desolated and profaned."[49] It was incantation, not workaday political statement; and as such it spoke to the yearning for inspiration felt by his readers within the incipient protest movement.

Almost immediately afterward, Gladstone followed up with a major speech at the invitation of his constituents at Greenwich. He delivered the speech at a mammoth public meeting at Blackheath. The plan had been under discussion for a couple of weeks; indeed, Gladstone had at one point thought of the speech as a substitute for a pamphlet.[50] He had originally tried to have the meeting held indoors, but was prevailed upon by the organizers to speak outside on a Saturday (September 9), to a crowd estimated in numbers varying from six or seven up to ten thousand. As he himself implied,[51] it was one of his best performances at what, in moments of depression, he was inclined to consider demagoguery.

The speech, like the pamphlet, replicated Stead's strictures on the Turks and appealed, thanks to Gladstone's unique combination of hair-splitting definition and careless rhetoric, to the whole spectrum of the protest, which ranged from committed pro-Russians to pacifists and neutralists.[52] Both the pamphlet and the speech were calls to action, given their urgency by the grisly background. The pamphlet, after an extended condemnation of the Ottoman Turks and their rule, ended with a ringing denunciation of the Turkish presence in the Balkans. The speech at Blackheath was both more explicit and more ethnocentric. Gladstone addressed the Ottomans: "You shall receive your regular tribute . . . you shall retain your titular sovereignty, your empire shall not be invaded, but never again as the years roll in their course, so far as it is in our power to determine, never again shall the hand of violence be raised by you, never again shall the flood-gates of lust be open to you, never again shall the dire refinements of cruelty be devised by you for the sake of making mankind miserable."[53] The speech was clearer in its prescription for the eastern Mediterranean than was the famous "bag and baggage" statement at the end of the pamphlet. It demonstrates once again that Gladstone had not given up his wish to maintain the Ottoman Empire as a loose federation organizing the Balkan region. Scrutinized closely, it was a more moderate statement than many of his listeners believed they were hearing. However, Gladstone's implicit reaffirmation of Britain's right to dictate events in the eastern Mediterranean, delivered with all the charisma of an Old Testament prophet, was not in any sense disappointing; it was calculated to appeal to Britons, whatever their background. The Blackheath meeting crystallizes the sense of transcendence binding speaker and crowd together which is typical of collective behavior.

Smelser tells us that in small group behavior

> *communication* and *interaction* . . . "[rest] on personal confrontation and [follow] the pattern of a dialogue, with controlled interpretation by each participant of the action of the other." In large groups new forms of

communication and interaction arise, such as . . . the one-way communication of the mass media . . . [Furthermore,] in larger groups new devices such as "incitation, agitation, gaining attention, the development of morale, the manipulation of discontent, the overcoming of apathy and resistance, the fashioning of group images, and the development of strategy" gain precedence.[54]

This contrast describes well the difference between the more rational tone of the early small-town public meetings, where everyone knew everyone else, and a mass experience such as the Blackheath gathering.

Finally, the Blackheath speech and indeed the whole experience of the autumn was noteworthy for its effect on Gladstone, an effect typical of collective behavior. Gladstone later recollected: "I acted under a strong sense of individual duty without a thought of leadership; nevertheless it made me again leader whether I would or no. The nation nobly responded to the call of justice, and recognised the brotherhood of man. But it was the nation, not the classes."[55] Gladstone's sense of being buoyed up by a mass which was no longer identifiable in terms of specific interests or economic backgrounds is typical of collective behavior, since "the group conveys a sense of 'transcending power' which 'serves to support, reinforce, influence, inhibit, or suppress the individual participant in his activity.'"[56] Such emotions, both simpler and more complex than opportunistic calculations, seem to offer a plausible explanation of Gladstone's state of mind as he embarked on leadership of the protest. The commitment of such a charismatic personality to the role of formulator of the beliefs of the movement was decisive. Previous massacres in Lebanon, Damascus, and Crete had offered earlier possible precipitating factors; all had been reported in a context of strain with respect to British purposes in supporting the Ottomans. The "genocide" in Crete occurred at the time a condition of conducivity was created by the passage of the Second Reform Act. Only the Bulgarian "atrocities," however, connected additionally with the failed response unwittingly perpetrated by Disraeli and his cabinet in Parliament during the summer of 1876 and with leadership of the quality of Stead as promoter and Gladstone as formulator of the movement's belief system. This combination of factors ensured that the protest would expand.

7 ◆ The Movement Matures

The next phase of a social protest movement, the enthusiastic phase, is typically "a period of supercharged activity." Many new leaders join and fill new roles, as publicists, polemicists, or bureaucrats. They must advertise the movement more widely and hold the followers already won. These leaders of the maturing movement may come from groups sensing strain; not previously active, they may be converted by the rhetoric of the protest, or they may already lead existing organizations "with similar or related dissatisfactions." They "may be marginal or respectable; they may come from 'nowhere' or they may be permanently established in extremist groups which lie in wait for disturbances and then move in to assume leadership." They bring their supporters with them, if they have some; and these recruits in turn diversify the character of the movement, so that beyond the original hard core of beliefs and the people motivated primarily by them (the "real" aspect), the protest acquires a "derived" aspect from the heterogeneous individuals and subsidiary causes attaching to a movement as it succeeds. During this period of expansiveness, a variety of specific "grievances" will inevitably be gathered under the umbrella of the original belief and a larger "membership" will be attracted, including many who contrast with the original core. Drawing on the resources provided by these differing backgrounds, the protest may adopt standardized "pattern[s] of mobilization" which have been experimented with and perfected by earlier social movements. The repertoire of tactics is fruitfully enlarged; but this advantage is offset by the danger of disagreement and factionalism. The authorities' attempts at containing the protest may force the malcontents closer together; but cooperation may highlight conflicting styles and spark dispute. All these factors affect the course of the movement and its degree of success or failure as it evolves into the final, bureaucratic phase.[1]

At the beginning of September, Gladstone, the great formulator, was acknowledged, at least by others, as the leader. Stead, writing about Gladstone's pamphlet in the *Northern Echo* on September 7, pledged an allegiance rather generally felt: "Mr. Gladstone is more than the High Priest of Humanity, pronouncing Anathemas upon the wretches whose crimes have horrified the world. He is the most powerful of all living Englishmen . . . At this moment, Mr. Gladstone is the real ruler of the land. He has dictated our policy in the East."[2] Consciously or not, Stead highlighted Gladstone's essential contribution. He had not invented nor originated protest meetings over Bulgaria; he had legitimated, even consecrated them. A humbler and less eloquent observer made the point more explicitly in a letter to Gladstone himself:

> I made a special pilgrimage to Blackheath on Saturday; and feel irresistibly impelled to thank you . . . your speech (admirably supplementing and enforcing the pamphlet) has given such a complete resume of the situation conceived in a spirit utterly removed from party considerations, as furnishes me (and doubtless thousands of your fellow-countrymen feel the same)—with the most cogent *reasons* and *justification* for the remarkable outburst of righteous indignation that now emerges from John o' Groats to Lands End.[3]

Right after the meeting, however, Gladstone apparently faltered. He suggested to Granville that the latter take over leadership of the movement.[4] It was a momentary tremor such as Gladstone often experienced when facing portentous activity. He seemed nonetheless to function as leader. In the week after Blackheath, he sent off a flurry of more than a dozen letters and telegrams connected with the subject, plus a more considered statement for the *Daily News* and *The Times*. The result was "strong neuralgia."[5]

The next step might well have been to galvanize protest by appearances at well-chosen local meetings. This Gladstone had no desire to do. Writing Granville early in October, he tried to define his position. "I regard myself as an outside workman, engaged in the preparation of materials which you & the party will probably have to manipulate and then to build into a structure."[6] He was not willing to preclude public appearances; he expressly repudiated a suggestion in the *Daily Telegraph* that he was no longer available to speak.[7] In fact, though, he seems to have been discouraged by Granville's dampening comments and by the volume of "abusive" correspondence he received: "once 'the People's William,'" cackled one correspondent, "but now forever to be known as Bag and Baggage Billy."[8] His decision to keep to a tour of country houses (which must have been planned long in advance) offered a kind of escape; while it allowed him to rally aristocratic support, it removed him, so he hoped, from pressure to speak openly.[9]

If this was Gladstone's plan, it backfired. Wherever he went, public meetings followed him. At the end of September, he visited the Duke of Cleveland at Raby near Darlington and was asked to speak at the nearby town of Staindrop. Gladstone felt besieged. He saw the deputation in a harassed frame of mind, "endeavouring hard to fight off a meeting and speech."[10] Apparently they were not willing to take no for an answer, for they followed up their verbal appeal with a letter, begging now for an interview rather than a speech and offering their "beautiful room" with "no *Reporters.*"[11] Gladstone relented; to the "great pleasure" of the group, he "promised" to meet them[12] during an outing to tour the church. The weather was rainy, and so, as the little group stood awkwardly in the damp, the local member of Parliament suggested that they remove to the public hall. Gladstone had been manipulated, and he admitted it. He did talk, but very unwillingly. Characteristically cautious about inciting people to act beyond their powers, he feared he might be labeled a "rogue and impostor."[13] Essentially the same pursuit went on at Durham, Coldstream, Duns, Berwick, and Alnwick.[14] As Gladstone summarized the trip for Frank Hill, the editor of the *Daily News*, "the feeling in this northern country is extremely strong and I have the utmost difficulty in preventing my round of visits from changing into a tour of propagandism, which under the circumstances would be entirely objectionable."[15]

Arguably Gladstone's trip was all the more effective for his reluctance. The phenomenon of a major statesman heading a popular campaign was still virtually unknown, and Gladstone may have been right in thinking that eagerness on his part would boomerang. As it was, his hesitations were charming. The lucky few who managed to hear a few words from the great man gained a sense of having been chosen that no widely publicized mass rally could have conferred. But quite apart from criticism, Gladstone really did not trust public appearances; his impulse was to continue in the vein which was most familiar—that is, debating through pamphlets, articles, and letters to the editor.

This reluctance to place himself prominently at the head of the emerging movement was not at this stage detrimental to the process of mobilization. Their enthusiasm vindicated by Gladstone's public

confession of belief, men and women all over England set about organizing meetings on an even larger scale than before. In the provincial towns, particularly in the North, and in the more modest sections
of London, protest meetings proliferated, exemplifying that "super-
charged activity" typical of the enthusiastic phase of social protest.

In 1876, protest usually began with essentially spontaneous public
meetings. Seventy percent of the petitions sent to the Foreign Office
originated with such gatherings (see Table 1).[16] They were generally
initiated by requisition to the mayor. Stead, calling for meetings in the
Northern Echo, had urged that concerned individuals should not wait
for local notables to act; in many cases, the original movers were few
in number and modest in position.[17] Another, often overlapping,
source of leadership was the clergy. Nonconformists, as Shannon has
noted, were especially active at the denominational level and many
individuals were also involved, although the heavy participation by
particular chapels came later.[18]

A somewhat different pattern emerged in London, where an especially active role was played by politicians associated with the working
classes, either men of working-class origin or middle-class Radicals.
They brought to the Bulgarian campaign rich experience in "pressure
from without" and an impressive network of connections. Cremer and
Howell had both cut their teeth on the agitation surrounding the great
1859-60 strike in the London building trades, which had led to a lock-
out involving seventy thousand men. Several had been active in the
National Reform League in the 1860s, which had worked for passage
of the Second Reform Act, and Bradlaugh had actually helped lead the
Hyde Park Riots in 1866.[19] In the 1870s, most existed in a fluid zone
between Lib-Lab conventionality and Marxist alienation.[20] Although
by this stage in their lives most were professional agitators, those leaders born into the working classes almost invariably had a solid background as skilled artisans, and hence were members of the so-called
labor aristocracy.[21] Through the Bulgarian agitation, they worked with
middle-class politicians of Liberal sympathies as well as with some
party leaders.[22] Their involvement broadened the movement both in
terms of membership and in terms of strategic experience, but brought
potential disharmony, since they held somewhat different political priorities and, for the most part, were outspokenly secular in outlook.[23]
Furthermore, they brought with them an organized network of working men's clubs and trade societies, which had their own structure
and objectives and their own quarrels with each other.[24]

In the last two weeks of August and the first three weeks of Septem-

Table 1. Groups that produced petitions, 1876–1878 (in percentages). Where more than one number appears, the larger number includes petitions that fit into more than one category.

	1876			1877				1878 — Parliament		
	News-papers	Foreign Office[a]	Parlia-ment	News-papers	Parlia-ment	News-papers	Foreign Office	Jan-Feb	April	May
Unknown	4	3	1	3	1	2	2	0	0	0
Agricultural meetings	2	0	0	0	0	0	0	0	0	0
Conservative/Conservative associations	2	6/7	0	12	5/7	5/7	14	0/1	0	0
Orange Lodges	0	2	0	0	0	0	2	0	0	0
Foreign affairs committees	0	1	0	0	0	0	0	0	0	0
Chambers of commerce	0	0	0	0	0	2	1.5	0	0	0
Eastern Question Association	0	0	0	1	0	0	0	0	0	0
Liberal associations	4.5	0	0	52	36	25	10	2.5	2	4
Members of Parliament	2	0	0	0	0	11/12	0	0	0	0
National bodies	2	1	0	1/6	2	0/4	2	0	0	0
Organizational meetings	2.5	0	0	0	0	2	0	0	0	0
Public meetings	63	70	14	16	24	21	19/20	8	1	13
Petitions—individually signed	0	0	68	0	18.5	0	0	18	39	33.5
Religious bodies	17	15	14	10	11	16	29	68	55	48
Town councils	0	0	0	0	1	3	3	1	0	1
Working men's meetings	2.5/7	5	2.5	5/6/17	3/7	11/14	21/24	1	1	1/1.5
Peace associations	0	0	0	1	0	0	0/2	.5	0	.5
Farmers' associations	0	0	0	0	0	0	0	0	0	.5

[a] R. T. Shannon, *Gladstone and the Bulgarian Agitation, 1876*, 2nd ed. (Hassocks, Eng.: Harvester Press, 1975; originally published 1963), pp. 148–153, 239 n.1.

ber, these leaders created an extraordinary efflorescence of protest.[25] Numerically, the north of England predominated,[26] and feeling there continued to run high even while it was abating elsewhere.[27] If the number of these protests is related to the size of population, though, the picture is somewhat different: the Southwest had the highest ratio of protests per thousand inhabitants, followed by Wales, with the North in third place.[28] Most protest meetings took place in towns, sometimes small ones, and cities; there were virtually no county protest meetings.[29] And the Midlands were relatively less affected (see Figure 1).[30] Possibly because of the prominence of Nonconformists, and certainly because of the humanitarian focus of the movement, women played a large role. A committee for a women's memorial to the Queen was set up and in a mere three weeks gathered 43,845 signatures.[31] Women were especially active in the widespread efforts to raise money and to provide warm clothing.[32]

It is instructive, though tricky, to estimate the numbers participating in the meetings.[33] Despite its later notoriety, the protest was not the autumn's principal attraction. For instance, early in September, Mun-

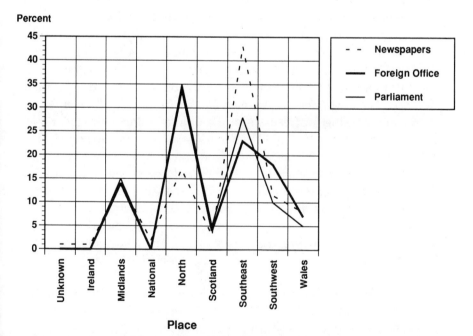

Figure 1. Geographical sources of petitions and meetings, 1876. Foreign Office figures are taken from Shannon, *Bulgarian Agitation*, pp. 149, 239 n. 1.

della drew eight to ten thousand to a Sheffield meeting featuring a general report to his constituents, but only about three thousand for a subsequent meeting devoted specifically to the Eastern Question.[34] Surely most meetings were much smaller.[35] The modest scale is particularly striking when they are compared with demonstrations in 1878, when war seemed imminent, or with Conservative gatherings on other topics in 1876. At the end of September Northcote's visit to Nostell Priory, home of the junior Conservative whip, Sir Rowland Winn, afforded the opportunity for the Union of Conservative Associations to gather 30,000 Conservative voters from all over the West Riding for a day of speeches, singing, and picnicking on the grounds.[36] Apparently the Bulgarian agitation in 1876 appealed to a hard core of dedicated supporters, expanded by Nonconformist and working-class groups who tended to associate themselves with Radical causes. It was not, at this point, either a mass concern or a mass threat.

As the original promoters sought to organize, they adapted a standardized "pattern of mobilization,"[37] similar to those used by the Anti–Corn Law Leaguers and the Chartists. The meetings were called by requisition and announced in the local press, and attended by individuals particularly stirred by reports of disaster or simply seeking entertainment. Local dignitaries such as members of Parliament and respected ministers and clergymen also attended, and many were put on display on the platform. Each group considered a series of resolutions, including a central one stating support for British noninvolvement in Bulgaria.[38] Models for the resolutions were provided by the *Northern Echo* and later by Freeman in the *Daily News*.[39] Freeman's formulation, calling for freedom for the Ottoman provinces, went far beyond Gladstone's plea at Blackheath for mere autonomy, and his more extreme wording was frequently adopted. After the resolutions, local dignitaries made favorable speeches and read letters from prominent Londoners. A debate and a vote followed, although often assent was simply declared unanimous. Sometimes amendments were offered, but they were usually voted down. Then the resolutions were forwarded to the Foreign Office as a petition. The whole affair would be written up in the newspaper next day, coupled with calls to other localities.[40]

It is hard to exaggerate the contribution made by newspapers such as the *Northern Echo* and the *Daily News*. Almost singlehandedly, they created an atmosphere in which communities that did not hold meetings were considered heartless. The press was usually better organized than the parties, and party whips often founded or coopted newspapers to target segments of the public. As a result, certain tasks of mobilization, which might in the twentieth century have been accomplished through the parties, were performed instead by the newspapers.[41]

For those who questioned the wisdom of the meetings (for example, upper-class politicians), attending and speaking out was not necessarily the most productive course. Instead, they used their aristocratic and gentlemanly connections to advance the interests of the sitting cabinet through all the techniques of pressure, backroom politics, and shady business which had made the electoral system "work" time out of mind.

The Earl of Derby, Disraeli's foreign secretary, with his impressive connections, was a natural person to turn to if questions arose about the extent and direction of such activities; but Disraeli received his share of confidences as well. As the Earl of Denbigh recounted to Disraeli's secretary, Montagu Corry:

> I must say that Mr. Gladstone's conduct is simply *vile*, because he well knows the state of the question, the almost insuperable difficulties, the Govt has to contend with and which for mere personal motives, he goes about stumping the Country, like a Yankee Presidential agent, and exciting rogues and fools to chatter about what they know nothing . . . I must confess, it makes me sick to read the trash which is uttered as I told two *Gents* who called upon me to have my name put down on one of their Committees, that I knew a great deal more of the question than they did having been attached for six years to Lord Ponsonby's Embassy at Constantinople, and that I could find plenty to do, as they might, with any spare money by giving it to our own distressed countrymen and women.[42]

H. Drummond Wolff took an even more decided part. He wrote Disraeli in a high good humor about the goings-on at Bournemouth: "Auberon Herbert & his friends tried to steal a march upon me & to get up a meeting at Christchurch to entrap me into being present & to pass votes of censure on the government. The trustees of Christchurch & Bournemouth were however too much for them. Drags and coaches for Conservatism drove over from Bournemouth." The Conservatives' resolution was passed by a wide margin. Drummond Wolff concluded cheerfully, "This corner of the kingdom has done its duty."[43]

But oligarchic control of opinion was not as easy as it had been, as was demonstrated by the Crawshays' experience in the Newcastle area. Sidney and George Crawshay came of a family which had made money in iron mines in Wales and had extended to the north, with a large factory at Gateshead. A relative earlier in the nineteenth century had left an estate of close to two million pounds sterling.[44] George Crawshay was attracted by the ideas of David Urquhart and became an ardent admirer of the Ottoman Porte. One of the most active of Urquhart's Foreign Affairs committees was organized at Newcastle. Crawshay also became involved in business ventures in the Middle East and invested heavily in Ottoman bonds.[45] Then came the Ottoman default in 1875–76 and the prospect of substantial losses.[46] Both Sidney and George and their close associate, Charles Frederick Hamond, M.P. for Newcastle, were extremely active through the local Foreign Affairs Committee, which seconded Hamond's activities in London. They tried to win a more advantageous settlement of these loan obligations than the Porte was initially willing to offer, but all three, like most of the bondholders, continued to support the Ottoman government, which was in fact the likeliest source for repayment.[47] When protest meetings were held in 1876 in Newcastle and neighboring Gateshead, they were less unanimous than meetings in most other northern towns.[48] At Merthyr Tydvil, however, in the area where the Crawshays had shut down their iron works in response to declining prices and a union movement among the men, opposition to the progovernment position held by the Crawshays was fierce, and Henry Richard, M.P. and leader of the Peace Society, was cheered repeatedly during a stirring pro-Gladstonian speech.[49] The power of local magnates to control political developments wherever they were major employers was passing.[50]

One striking feature of the 1876 meetings was the virtual absence of disruption or counteragitation. Those who disagreed with the views of the protest most often did not take the protesters seriously; the movement seemed to be just another ripple on the radical fringe. Those who did notice it as something more were typically annoyed or outraged, but not unnerved; they believed that after a short outburst, this aberration would vanish, most probably to be replaced by diametrically opposite opinions.

As a result, attempts to sway or break up agitation meetings or to mount progovernment rallies were virtually nonexistent.[51] The principal challenges to the movement came from within. Would a proliferation of local meetings, mostly small, carry weight? If not, could the diverse groups work together to break through the numerical limits of local participation? Or would they fall prey to the factionalism endemic in social movements? Could they continue to engage leaders of national stature, like Gladstone, or would they fall back into marginality—like previous pressure campaigns, dependent on unknowns for leadership, or worse yet, on suspect professional agitators? The meetings held in London in September and October 1876 illustrate these difficulties and the initial attempts made to surmount them.

The early protest efforts were primarily isolated initiatives. In mid-August, for example, a "committee of representative working men" met under the presidency of Thomas Mottershead. The original objective of this committee, the group that first contacted Gladstone, was to arrange a mass meeting against the atrocities in Hyde Park.[52] Discouraged by the historian Edward A. Freeman, not usually noted for moderation,[53] they opted instead for a meeting on the grounds of the Hackney Working Men's Club and Institute on August 29.[54] Other early examples include deputations to the Foreign Office, organized by the trade societies through Edward Levy Lawson, editor of the *Daily Telegraph*,[55] and by the Workmen's Peace Association, always concerned about potential war.[56] After an unsuccessful effort to bring the two together, they met with Derby successively on September 11.[57]

More important for the development of the agitation were two parallel efforts to organize major indoor rallies, one mounted by financial magnates in the City, the other by working men. The City magnates moved ahead early in September with a protest meeting similar to those being held around the country, but more ambitious. Their task was not easy, for most City men apparently favored Disraeli. The Rothschilds, although Liberals, were squarely in his camp. The financial world of the City included major Turkish bondholders, like Edward Howley Palmer of the Bank of England, who was said to have been involved to the tune of six or seven hundred million pounds.[58] London's financial magnates had huge investments in Russia as well,[59] investments which were threatened by war since the fragile Russian economy seemed unlikely to withstand such pressure without bankruptcy.

A substantial group of men in the City, however, including but not limited to Liberals, supported the agitation—men like Josiah J. Merriman, a Radical barrister who had belonged to Marx's First International and had flirted with extremist groups as early as the days of the National Reform League,[60] or Samuel Morley, the great textile manufacturer. Early in September, this group organized a requisition to the lord mayor which attracted eight hundred signatures and justified an organizational meeting at the Cannon Street Hotel on September 8. Merriman, who chaired, held out hopes that Gladstone would speak.[61] Immediately after the organizational meeting, the group sent a telegram designed to whet Gladstone's interest about the upcoming rally.[62] A formal invitation followed on September 11.[63] As anyone who knew Gladstone could have guessed, persuading him to accept was not easy. Despite Gladstone's attempt to head them off with a telegram refusing to participate,[64] Merriman insisted on leading a deputation to Hawarden.[65] Such a personal appeal would later work at Staindrop; but in London Gladstone was afraid of turning the occasion into a party rally,[66] and he "persisted in saying no." Although the delegation went away empty-handed, they did impress Gladstone. He had been delighted to see them and reflected in his diary: "This journey is a remarkable indication of the state of public feeling . . . All goes well. Oh what shd be our gratitude!"[67]

Despite this setback, planning went ahead for the City meeting. It was eventually held on the evening of September 18. An especially impressive roster of dignitaries sat on the platform and a very large crowd attended, including a number of ladies active in the relief effort for whom seats had been especially reserved.[68] Admission was by ticket and a substantial number were unable to get in, so an overflow demonstration took place outside. Resolutions were presented against the atrocities, in favor of the Bulgarians, and for the independence of the Slavic provinces of Turkey. There was some heckling, but an amendment supporting the government met "with derision" and was quickly declared to have lost.[69]

Meanwhile the working men, organized by the Mottershead committee, had been arranging a meeting in Exeter Hall.[70] Working men's associations all over the metropolis were asked to participate, and a handbill announcing the meeting "circulated amongst the workshops and clubs."[71] On Saturday night, September 9, the local committees in Lambeth, Southwark, Finsbury, Marylebone, Chelsea, Hackney, and Tower Hamlets met to plan their contributions. In Southwark "several lodges of the Labourers' Union" decided to meet at the obelisk on Blackfriars Road and then march as a body to Exeter Hall.[72] Since not all who wished to attend would be able to get in, plans were made for a torchlight rally outside in Trafalgar Square.[73] A particularly large accession of support came from a meeting of the Labour Protection League held in the Minories. This group, organized in the early 1870s to advocate the demands of the dockers,[74] represented "ten thousand members." They determined to meet on Clerkenwell Green, scene of many radical assemblies, and to march in procession to Exeter Hall and Trafalgar Square.[75] Final touches were put on the arrangements and drafts of the resolutions were displayed at more than twenty local gatherings on Saturday evening, September 16.[76]

The meeting was a success. The platform guests included a roster of working men, as well as middle-class M.P.s. Henry Fawcett, the blind Cambridge economist and radical M.P., in opening the deliberations, stated that this was an opportunity for working men to use their newly acquired political power to call for Parliament to meet and to act on behalf of the Bulgarians. Working men would be able to show how responsible they were. Other speakers were not so conciliatory. P. A. Taylor referred sardonically to "a system which needed the perpetual recurrence of something like a revolution in order to bring the Government into harmony with the best aspirations and feelings of the people," while Bradlaugh, the secularist agitator, frankly called upon working men to follow the example of the great days of the Hyde Park riots and to hold meetings all over the country until Disraeli was driven from office.[77]

The protesters undoubtedly hoped that these well-attended and eloquent meetings would suffice to make the cabinet modify its position. Theoretically, the movement should have marked time while the resolutions were presented and the ministers were given an opportunity to react. The agitation, however, did not take place in a vacuum, and it was now overwhelmed by outside events. On the evening of September 19, Baring's report on the massacres was belatedly published in the London Gazette. It was supposed to justify the Turks, but unintentionally seemed to lend support to the agitators.[78] Disraeli and Derby reacted in opposite ways to this new information. Derby appears to have been horrorstruck. On September 21, he sent new instructions to Elliot, which were immediately made public. In them Derby took note of the "just indignation" of the "people of Great Britain." Characterizing the Bulgarian "crimes" as "the most heinous that have stained the history of the present century," he ordered Elliot to seek a personal interview with the Sultan and to demand that the Porte take steps to rectify the damage.[79]

Disraeli, on the other hand, was not ready to admit, at least not publicly, that the agitators might have been right. He gave his interpretation of what had happened in Bulgaria in a speech at Aylesbury at the annual dinner of the Royal and Central Bucks Agricultural Association. It was a critical moment and a test case, for he was supporting the Conservative candidate in the by-election for the seat he had vacated upon his recent elevation to the peerage. The Liberals had turned this contest into an informal referendum on the protest. Disraeli, conscious of this agenda, roundly denounced the Bulgarian revolt as the work of outsiders,[80] much to the dismay of the agitators. Indeed, Stead wrote Gladstone: "Is it possible that the Aylesbury speech was delivered under the influence of strong drink? It would be charitable to think so."[81] For the committees at work in London, this rather clumsy attempt to influence opinion was a red flag, which, at least for the moment, diverted attention almost completely from Derby's more measured response.[82] The committees' increasing radicalization was shared around the country.[83]

There were two obvious routes to expand the agitation. One was to try again to involve Gladstone. The other was for working men and City magnates to cooperate more closely. The Exeter Hall meeting of working men had gathered some five thousand people; according to Merriman, the Guildhall meeting called out four thousand.[84] A joint effort would have had double the impact.

The working men pinned their hopes on Gladstone. Under the shock of the Aylesbury speech, the Mottershead committee immediately decided to organize another meeting, to be held in St. James's Hall,[85] and the secretary, J. Alfred Giles, alerted Gladstone. Declaring that "the present agitation should not cease until a change of policy or a change of ministers is effected," he asked Gladstone to reply to Disraeli's attack at Aylesbury by presiding at the projected meeting.[86] Gladstone again refused. The committee did not give up, however, and in a second appeal Giles begged him at least to be present. This was not to be just another London meeting, he declared; what was needed now was a meeting with national significance, and Gladstone's presence in the chair would have conferred that distinction. But, Giles admitted, the committee had given itself an additional assignment. In the present crisis, Gladstone ought to be prime minister. If Gladstone were present at St. James's Hall, they would be able to make him understand that his return was, they firmly believed, the national wish.[87]

It must have been, from Gladstone's perspective, a communication more embarrassing than gratifying; but with evident agony, and apologies to Granville, he decided to compose a reply, which would be read at the meeting.[88] In his strongest public statement yet, Gladstone went so far as to suggest that the cabinet was violating accepted constitutional practice by refusing to consult the people, either by dissolving Parliament and holding elections or, at minimum, by convening an autumn session.[89]

Meanwhile the agitators in the City were giving their attention to the possibilities of enhancing their numbers by cooperating with the working men. The situation was complicated by the fact that there were now two rival committees organizing working men's demonstrations. In addition to the Mottershead committee, Dr. Baxter Langley, a journalist with a long career in the working men's press, was trying to arrange a mass rally in Hyde Park on a Sunday, when most working men would be free.[90] J. J. Merriman wanted to join forces with the latter group. On September 28, Merriman in effect offered a bargain. He would bring the working men "the countenance and support of the wealthy and influential men of the City," on condition that the Hyde Park meeting was orderly.[91] Next day, he came back with new conditions. The City committee worked closely with Nonconformist and High Church agitators who were adamantly opposed to political meetings on Sunday. The Hyde Park Demonstration Committee's objection to moving the meeting to Monday was cogent: working men would not be able to come on a workday. Merriman hinted that some leading ministers might announce the meeting during their services if it were not held on Sunday; he suggested that some ministers might attend; and as a final incentive, he held out the hope that some employers might grant a half holiday. The Hyde Park Committee greeted the new plan with suspicion. They did agree to meet on Monday, October 9, but went on record that "this Committee hopes this concession will secure from the middle classes co-operation in a movement which had its origin amongst the working classes, to whom the most convenient day of meeting is Sunday."[92]

Planning continued through early October, but even before the meeting took place, the City committee, apparently divided, thought better of their cooperation and decided to turn their efforts to a different project altogether. Merriman loyally attended, but, despite early assurances,[93] few men of the cloth appeared. Dr. Parker, of the City Temple, and the reformer Newman Hall were the principal representatives. The weather was "threatening and disagreeable." Plans had been made to mount three platforms, but only one operated effectively and the total audience was said to have amounted to about a thousand. Langley did secure what he took to be unanimous passage of resolutions calling for Gladstone's return to leadership, but the participants seemed rather chastened, and the rally ended abruptly and a bit ingloriously in a "sharp shower of rain."[94]

The experiences in London, viewed in perspective, were not encouraging. It seemed clear that Disraeli at least would not be influenced by the protest as it had developed thus far. Meetings limited to recognizable groups or specific localities, even if large and enthusiastic, were not enough to impress the prime minister; nor, for that matter, to involve Gladstone. Yet attempts to break out of this mold were blocked by the jealousies and suspicions dividing City magnates from working men, Nonconformists from nonbelievers. Problems had surfaced around the country as well. How could leaders keep up enthusiasm once the initial excitement had peaked? As Stead ruminated in a letter to Gladstone, they couldn't go on indefinitely holding one round of protest meetings after another and expect people to continue to attend.[95] However, there were precedents for something more ambitious: both the Anti-Slavery movement and the Anti–Corn Law League had successfully mounted national conferences. It was apparently Robert Leader of Sheffield who thought of adopting this example.[96] It was this more elaborate proposal which would draw the different individuals and organized groups into a national campaign and in the process convince Gladstone that his participation was mandatory. Involved at first behind the scenes, teased out of his reserve by flattering requests for advice, Gladstone at last came to see the public assumption of leadership as a moral imperative. He moved from speaking out through the "occasional" pamphlet or speech in September, a role particularly well suited to his self-chosen semiretirement, to the riskier part of putting himself consciously at the head of an organized, countrywide protest movement.

The new developments originated with the efforts of local Radical organizers in the industrial North. Robert Leader and Henry Joseph Wilson, leaders of the Sheffield Liberal Association and proprietors of the Sheffield *Independent*, initially sent invitations for a planning session to neighboring Liberal Associations. Representatives from Manchester, Leeds, Darlington, and Sheffield gathered in Sheffield on September 30. The group at Birmingham sent an "encouraging" letter; a similar communication came from Liverpool. After lengthy discussion, the organizers adopted the project of a national meeting and made plans to set up a subcommittee and to contact the major Nonconformist organizations as well as additional Liberal associations and Samuel Morley of the *Daily News*.[97]

Leader did not delay in following up this promising beginning; he wrote immediately to Morley and also to J. J. Merriman of the City committee. For Merriman, the invitation came just in time to save him from serious embarrassment. He had aggressively pursued the strategy of combining efforts with the working men during the last part of September, but it was far from an unqualified success. Disagreements over technical details like meeting times masked profound differences in outlook. Now holding another card, he was able to state at the City committee's October 4 meeting that "he thought it was only right that a minority, however small, (even if limited to one person) should not be committed to an altered and extended agitation." He accordingly proposed that they dissolve their committee, "as having carried out the objects of the requisitionists their functions had ceased," and reorganize to cooperate with the people at Sheffield. It seems likely that Merriman's unnamed opponent was Samuel Morley.[98]

At this point, apparently telling no one but Wilson,[99] Leader took another, critical step. He had, in the past, communicated from time to time with Gladstone through Mundella. Now, using the excuse that Mundella was on holiday, Leader wrote Gladstone directly. The matter, he hinted, "may be kept entirely private." He outlined the meeting with the northern Liberals and explained that he had already written to Merriman and Morley; if they were prepared to join the conference, it would be possible to move to technical issues such as "time and place." He admitted that he had concluded on his own that Gladstone should have advance warning of what was afoot and be asked for his blessing. If he responded favorably, they could then ask Gladstone formally about the plan and he could endorse it in any way he chose for publication.[100]

The hollowness of Leader's insinuation to Gladstone that Mundella was unavailable is revealed by the fact that he apparently brought Mundella up to date on the planning too. Mundella, predictably, was enthusiastic; he wrote on October 4: "I think your idea of a great national Conference on the Eastern [sic] a very good one. Meetings seem to have done all that could be expected of them and further efforts ought to take the new form you have wisely indicated. A large representative Conference to be held in London or in some central place in the country could speak *once* for all, and speak unanimously. I shall be glad to hear what you have done in the matter."[101]

Initially, everything seemed to go swimmingly for Leader and Wilson. The plan was given a preliminary airing in the *Daily News* and, next day, in the Sheffield *Independent*.[102] Merriman and Morley were cooperative, and overtures were even received from the Mottershead committee based on the assumption that this was to be a "large conference of working men representatives." Leader may have been a trifle put off by their offer of support, for he replied a bit frostily that "we had not thought of a conference of any particular class of society, but of such delegates as the cities and towns throughout the kingdom may send."[103]

Mundella had also risen to the bait; he already saw himself playing a very large role.[104] The child of Italian immigrants, Mundella worked in the mills as a young boy and became first the foreman and later the proprietor of a successful hosiery mill. He was elected M.P. for Sheffield in 1868 in a bitter three-way contest with Roebuck, in which carefully organized working-class support had been decisive. Mundella differed from other working-class leaders who were elected to Parliament, such as Thomas Burt in 1874 or Henry Broadhurst in 1880. By the time he entered Parliament Mundella had already made the transition, through what has been called "brass-voiced cunning," to the ranks of rich middle-class industrialists. In this respect he was like John Bright or Samuel Morley, and only removed by a generation from his hero, Gladstone.[105] His leadership in the national conference exemplified both his ability to appropriate the ideas of subordinates and his commitment, as a Radical with ambitions, to bringing cooperation between both ends of the socioeconomic scale and all elements of the Liberal party. One of his first efforts, upon learning of the conference plans, was to try to contact the working men in London, not a simple task. He complained to Leader that he wasted an entire afternoon trying to see Broadhurst and Howell.[106] Eventually, his efforts paid off, and protected by a shell of conceit, he was only slightly dampened by the discovery that Broadhurst and his friends were already in touch "with our indefatigable friend Mr. H. J. Wilson and were at work on a movement of their own."[107]

In fact, as the leaders rushed forward, considerable differences of opinion developed, and there was a real danger that the promising initiative might fall victim to the factionalism that had plagued efforts in London. One major issue was exactly what form the conference should take. Everyone agreed that it should be a representative gathering, impressive for the credentials of the participants and the evidence of groups behind them, rather than, as had been the case in the last few weeks, for the sheer number present. There agreement stopped. Stead, the most idealistic, held himself largely aloof from the planning. He favored "an informal Parliament," "a self-consciously substitute parliament, or National Convention" rather than "a party demonstration," held in a provincial center such as Darlington.[108] The Sheffield group favored a meeting in London and recognized that the gathering must be more or less political, though, as Mundella cautioned later, "it must not appear to be a *strictly party* conference, but must include all those who in the interests of civilization and humanity, desire the extinction of Turkish rule."[109] Still a third point of view, the most unabashedly partisan, was aired in Birmingham. Joseph Chamberlain, who had made the Birmingham Liberal Association into a self-proclaimed model, was willing to have a meeting at Sheffield, but wanted it to be explicitly grounded in existing Liberal associations and other Liberal groups and to include all Liberal M.P.s.[110]

The Birmingham people were a force to be reckoned with. For a moment, it seemed that the entire plan would fail, sabotaged by the savage jealousies between towns. A planning conference was organized for October 12 at Birmingham. Apparently even before the meeting, Leader realized that the various factions would not cooperate, and that the burgeoning plans must be frozen. He sent word by telegram to Mundella, interrupting him in a flurry of activity in London where he had "altogether laid . . . [himself] out for a bit of judicious agitation." Leader, sensing the problems, had undertaken a preliminary "mission to Birmingham"; the results were not encouraging.[111] The discussions on October 12 apparently did not help. Chamberlain was still unwilling to participate in a national conference on the terms outlined by the Sheffield people.[112] Probably Mundella was right in suspecting envy; with some bitterness he wrote Leader, "nothing seems to go down with Birmingham that is not of *home manufacture*."[113] But there was a philosophical issue as well. Should the Bulgarian protest develop through another special interest group, on the periphery of the two political parties, yet influencing both? This was the implication of the Sheffield position. Or should it be exploited to galvanize the Liberal party and dramatize the need for reorganization, as Chamberlain wished?

Fortunately, at this apparent impasse, Leader's approach to Gladstone paid dividends. Leader received a letter from Gladstone written on October 19,[114] which granted him and presumably Wilson as well an interview in London the following Tuesday (October 24). In some confusion, Leader wrote back revealing the debacle at Birmingham and protesting, somewhat disingenuously, "I should have written you the result of our Birmingham consultation but did not know where to address you." He also mentioned that he had told Mundella about the plans for a meeting and had asked for his blessing.[115] The favor aroused high excitement in the Sheffield contingent, as is evident from Mundella's warning to Leader. He advised: "It seems to me that it must above all things be preserved *a dead secret*. If it were once suspected that Mr. Gladstone had done anything to encourage agitation, all the Tory and semi-scandalous press would heap insult and obloquy on him . . . If therefore Birmingham is taken into counsel it should be only the Chairman I think, and not a number of people."[116]

The need for action now seemed more and more pressing, for Mundella had just been bombarded by worries from another source. As he was writing Leader, he received a telegram from Auberon Herbert, whose brother, the Earl of Carnarvon, was a member of Disraeli's cabinet.[117] In great excitement Herbert telegraphed: "matters most serious shall I come to you for two days agitation should not cease now day or night."[118] Mundella and Herbert were good friends, but Mundella had no illusions about Herbert's character, which he correctly judged "impulsive, and sometimes rash."[119] Herbert soon recognized that his alarm had been premature;[120] but his correspondents had been upset. When Mundella met him, they decided there was ample need for the conference.[121]

Just what sort of reaction was obtained from Gladstone when "Mr Leader & conclave" met with him on October 25 is not clear.[122] Gladstone wrote Hartington a characteristically ambiguous letter, which Hartington probably took as proof that Gladstone had nipped meeting plans in the bud, or at least, in Shannon's phrase, "positively discouraged" them; but it seems likely that when Gladstone "advised to hold no meeting unless sure of success, to consider whether meetings would not be better at a later time, to proclaim that what we want is the practical liberation of provinces,"[123] his hearers from Sheffield optimistically concluded that they had simply been exhorted not to fail. They now moved ahead vigorously.

It was natural for the Sheffield leaders to fuse with another group, of which Mundella became the chair.[124] At the end of the last parliamentary session a small committee of members had been put together to watch developments in the East. Auberon Herbert and F. W. Chesson, the working-class organizer, were designated secretaries. On October 31, this group decided to write around the country to ascertain if they could gather "about 200 good and influential names" of persons who would act as conveners for a conference.[125] But Mundella's mood continued to fluctuate;[126] he recognized that arranging such a meeting would be enormously difficult, and he complained of "the total absence of organization here." As he confided to Leader, "our two secretaries are not able to do the work. Chesson is a man full of business, with his living to earn, and too much to do. And Herbert is wanting in business qualities, has too many irons in the fire and is not in London for three days together."[127] What he needed to galvanize the efforts was Gladstone's explicit approval. On November 6, Gladstone finally wrote Mundella: "I regard with much satisfaction the plans upon which you are engaged."[128]

The work of gathering names had been going on apace. Chesson went back to Leader and some of the other organizers in the north and asked them to gather names locally.[129] In addition to well-known political agents, Chesson also contacted religious leaders such as Canon Liddon.[130] By November 17, preliminary planning had proceeded far enough that the Parliamentary committee felt able to commit publicly to calling a national conference.[131] After a short lull, the state of the Eastern Question again seemed ominous. News of the international conference to be held at Constantinople and of the appointment of Salisbury as Britain's plenipotentiary had been relatively reassuring to the agitators.[132] Then the hopes that a solution might be negotiated were dashed by Disraeli's speech at the Guildhall. On November 9, he announced that Britain's ability to fight in a good cause was "inexhaustible,"[133] seemingly a broad hint that Britain was willing to campaign for the Ottomans if necessary.

From the time he gave his formal blessing on November 6, Gladstone was heavily involved in advising Mundella behind the scenes. It was a modest role, played out through a series of friendly letters between colleagues, and it is not hard to imagine why Gladstone put it in a different category from public appearances or extensive involvement with the working men of London. But by it he was drawn ever more deeply into the agitation. On November 6, he gave Mundella detailed instructions concerning a proposed draft for a statement of purpose to recruit conveners.[134] A dispute ensued with Herbert as to whether to specify the provinces of Bosnia, Herzegovina, and Bulgaria by name as the focus of the protest (as Gladstone wished), or to use the more inclusive phrase, "European Turkey."[135] Despite Herbert's backstage intrigues, Gladstone won; Herbert had to report that "the Committee decided yesterday that the words as you originally sent them, should be preserved."[136] In fact, Herbert's instinct to push everything to extremes seems to have condemned him; by the third week in November the parliamentary committee "proceeded to nominate a Conference Committee to carry out the arrangements," and did not retain Herbert as honorary secretary.[137] Later Mundella admitted that his "first business" had been "to extinguish the irrepressibles . . . A. Herbert . . . would have damned the whole thing."[138]

With the gathering of sponsors well under way, the planners turned to the objectives of the meeting. One idea was to provide the means for "diffusing through the country sound information on the various branches of the question."[139] As Gladstone understood it, this would open enormous and profitable fields of activity. On November 22 he wrote Herbert outlining a series of subjects for publications including information from Turkish newspapers not readily available in translation, facts about the Koran, historical details about the reform movement in Turkey since 1839, and more data about conditions in the various Christian provinces.[140] As he summed matters up in another letter: "I cannot but hope there will soon be some machinery of vigilance, and comment, and of communication, in constant action."[141] The summons to the conference, sent out on November 30, proposed "that an Association should be formed, as a result of the Conference, for the purpose of watching events, of giving further expression, if necessary, to public opinion, and diffusing through the country sound information on all branches of the question, by means of publications, lectures, and meetings."[142] This was the origin of the Eastern Question Association.

Meanwhile the organizers of the national conference had been putting the final touches on their list of conveners. Mundella was categoric: "I don't intend that any Radicals shall speak *if I can help it.* I want to fire off the Bishops, the Parsons, the Peers, the Literati etc. not those who have been the Actors heretofore but a *new set.*"[143] Gladstone had been heavily involved in the selection from the start. He counselled keeping the "religious basis broad" and noted that a number of prominent High Churchmen (Liddon, Denton, and MacColl) were "sure." But he also emphasized the importance of seeking out Nonconformists and mentioned especially Samuel Morley and Newman Hall, with whom he was already in close touch.[144] As the planning developed, particular efforts were made to woo Liddon, and this was wise; Liddon had his own network and could encourage waverers.[145] But even at the height of the enthusiasm, it was difficult to float over interdenominational suspicions and doctrinal disagreements. There was evidently some distrust of the Ritualists,[146] and Roman Catholic participation remained limited. Although Mundella specifically asked Gladstone to recruit Catholics,[147] his success was limited. Ambrose Phillips de Lisle joined eagerly, but despite de Lisle's intercession, Cardinal Manning remained hostile to the whole idea of agitation and Newman, asked by Gladstone to become a convener, refused.[148]

The "literati" were approached, quite successfully, by William Morris.[149] The politically powerful were also carefully cultivated. Mundella was eager to capture the Cavendishes, and counted on Gladstone for help.[150] Unfortunately, these prominent Whigs slipped away; after dangling for some days, Frederick Cavendish, as Hartington's brother a major prize, wrote Mundella that "flattered" though he was, he could not join, and although Gladstone promised to talk to him, he did not change his mind.[151]

At the other end of the political spectrum, some working-class Radicals were also specifically courted. Howell, one of the grand figures of the trade union movement, was made a member of the committee.[152] So was Broadhurst, the secretary of the Labour Representation League; the League was later asked to send a delegation.[153] Howell and Broadhurst were the only two working-class speakers at the conference, however. Indeed, Mundella felt obliged to apologize afterwards to his more radical colleague Wilson for the elite tone of the program. Wilson might "laugh" but, so Mundella assured him, it was "a grand 'coup'" that Lord Arthur Russell and the Hon. Frederick Leveson-Gower agreed "to stammer out a few words . . . It let in a host of old Whigs and County notabilities," and as for the great British public, they "will toady the owners of ancestral names."[154] Nonetheless, taken as a whole the conference, gathering about a thousand persons including two to three hundred women,[155] was impressively large and broadly based. Indeed, observers compared it to the old days of the Anti–Corn Law League, and *The Times* claimed never to have seen an assemblage which "obtained support over so large a part of the scale of British society."[156] It testified to the power of the protest to bind together individuals of differing backgrounds and objectives through a focus on common action on a morally exciting but practically remote issue.

It seems fair to say that none of this would have been possible without Gladstone. Repeatedly, men who would not work easily with each other deferred to his authority. He was the star; and it is not surprising that Mundella spent many anxious moments coaxing him to move beyond his backstage role and agree to speak. Gladstone considered speaking to be another matter. From the moment he first approved the gathering, he warned Mundella that "I think it best for the common cause that I should not take part in the Conference."[157] In the organizers' view, this destroyed much of its effectiveness, and Mundella begged Gladstone not only to appear but, even more important, actually to make a speech.[158] Gladstone coyly responded that he preferred to "stand out for a later period" and suggested the Earl of Shaftesbury or the Duke of Argyll instead.[159] Shaftesbury was a logical candidate, and Mundella followed up the idea. This reflexive radical could not say no, but his participation, as chairman,[160] did not lessen the desirability of capturing Gladstone. Mundella appealed again on December 1.[161] Acknowledging Gladstone's fears that the conference, if addressed by him, might seem too political, Mundella assured him on December 2 that "we leave all *political* leaders out, but we cannot play Hamlet and omit the Prince of Denmark."[162] Meanwhile Gladstone was under considerable pressure from Hartington and Granville to decline, and it was only after much agony that he "came to the conclusion . . . that it was desirable . . . to make a further utterance."[163]

By then, the final details were being put into place. A detailed statement of objectives and rules was distributed to the speakers.[164] Instructions for choosing delegates were sent out and selection went forward.[165] The process varied from place to place. In Manchester, the proceedings were elaborate, and replicated the earlier protest meetings. A requisition was directed to the mayor demanding a meeting "to consider the propriety of appointing delegates from the city to the national conference . . . in London." The mayor, Alderman Heywood, duly convened and chaired a formal meeting, complete with a roster of dignitaries on the platform and a series of speeches including some from the floor. Those who favored participation in the conference were a "great majority," but opponents had come and there was "considerable interruption." The mayor actually threatened to call the police, and was only prevented by his dislike of police involvement at political meetings. After considerable discussion and a motion supporting the government (which was voted down), the motion to join the national conference and to accept the prepared list of candidates was adopted with very few dissenting voices. The delegates included prominent local figures who had already distinguished themselves in the agitation, such as the Bishop of Manchester and the M.P. Jacob Bright, John Bright's brother.[166]

In other instances, the process was simpler. In Sheffield, Mundella more or less arbitrarily directed Wilson to assemble a likely group by canvassing "the Nonconformist Churches, the Trades Council, the Liberal Association, the Society of Friends and others."[167] At Oxford, an informal "meeting of persons sympathizing with the objects of the National Conference" was held one afternoon at Exeter College and the participants unanimously picked Liddon as their representative; one of the participants was then instructed to tell Liddon of his good fortune.[168]

These selections crowned a very successful autumn's work. In making the conference representative, Mundella and his friends had ensured that it would transcend the small groups, whether geographically or socioeconomically defined, who had hitherto protested individually, or sought ineffectually to combine as blocks. Even so, their constructive plan might have been destroyed by factional rivalry at the start had not Gladstone been willing to contribute. The extent of Gladstone's involvement in turn depended on two factors, both related to the scope of the scheme: first, given the weeks of planning required, he was able to slip into a major role quite gradually; second, by the time he faced the extent of his responsibility, it was clear that what was at hand was no mere partisan babble but truly a national movement. Gladstone's participation, now proclaimed to the world by his appearance as a major speaker at the conference, again underlined the national character of the agitation. In short, the problems of factionalism and marginality had been—and had to be—solved simultaneously.

The meeting itself took place on December 8, 1876, lasted all day, and was adorned by a bouquet of speeches carefully combined to represent the major issues and figures of the agitation. Besides providing propaganda, it institutionalized the protest by setting up a formal body, the Eastern Question Association. The large and inclusive gathering represented almost all the major groups involved. Along with politicians and members of Parliament, there was broad religious participation: Canon Liddon and E. A. Freeman among High Churchmen; Newman Hall, J. J. Colman, the mustard manufacturer, and Samuel Morley as prominent Nonconformists. There were representatives from many different socioeconomic levels. Industrial magnates were represented by J. S. Wright, along with Colman and Morley. Broadhurst and Howell spoke on behalf of working men, though other leaders identified with working-class agitation were present, such as Probyn, Chesson, and Fawcett. So was Joseph Arch, leader of the National Agricultural Labourers' Union.[169] The group least in evidence was the radical secularist working-class element, since Broadhurst and Howell were both Wesleyans, and Arch was a Primitive Methodist.[170] The leader most sympathetic to these circles was Auberon Herbert, but he hardly qualified as a member of the working class.

There was considerable evidence that the movement had attracted many different existing pressure groups. References cropped up throughout the day to the anti-slavery movement; Sir Thomas Fowell Buxton, one of the grand figures of that crusade, was present and spoke.[171] So did Henry Richard, a prominent Quaker and president of the Peace Society; he emphasized that "he did not want to go to war against Turkey any more than for her; he did not believe in war, and especially a war waged in the interest of philanthropy."[172] John Simon, Reform Jewish Liberal M.P. from Liverpool, remained loyal to his party at a time when many Jews preferred the Conservative position, but he insisted that if new Christian states were set up, Jews must be protected from the persecution which so often followed.[173] The protest was eclectic, in a way that was typical of developing social movements,[174] yet remarkable agreement had been won thus far on the positions to be adopted and the actions to be taken.

Gladstone, who spoke for an hour and a half, outdid all the other speakers and wove everything together.[175] Though he himself judged his performance harshly (the speech, he wrote, had been "far from wholly to my satisfaction"[176]), others were delighted. He addressed most of the major justifications for support of the Ottoman Empire. He anticipated the burden of empire argument by using it for his own purposes. Analyzing the power of the Muslim rulers in the Ottoman Empire, Gladstone admitted that it was comparable to "what was once the position of the Orangemen in Ireland." At that time, Gladstone declared, if "any tolerably clean-handed Power" had been able to intervene and set things right, humanity would have offered thanks. But all this was "100 years ago." England had reformed, the Porte had not; and it was no longer possible to have confidence in the Turks.

True, there were strategic concerns in the Balkans. But the Russians were not so unethical as they were often painted. For example, the

British had emancipated their slaves; they now had "a formidable rival in the field, and that rival [was] the present emperor of Russia." Even so, if the Bulgarians were to be endangered by Russian aggression, they could best resist as free men: "in . . . liberty alone . . . you can find efficient defences for them." It was a phrase reminiscent of his famous speech on behalf of the Romanians almost twenty years before.[177] But Gladstone had learned his lesson on careless statements about the future status of the area. Disagreement had been rife within the protest as to just what sort of arrangements, from limited autonomy to full independence, should be conferred upon the Ottoman provinces in Europe. Backing away from the extremism of his "bag and baggage" phrase in the pamphlet, he outlined a number of possible interim steps along the road to complete freedom, and added, "all these, and many other questions I do not presume to solve." It was an unusually conciliatory stand for a man who, generally speaking, was tortured by ambiguity. In contrast, the most inflammatory rhetoric was pronounced by Edward Freeman, who spoke to the alleged necessity of defending the routes to India through the Middle East. He declaimed: "Let duty come first and interest second. Perish the interests of England, and perish her dominion in India, rather than she should strike one blow on behalf of Turkey."[178] It was a riveting phrase, and one which would return to haunt the protesters.

For the most part, though, the conference was distinguished by its moderation. The most radical suggestion came from Fawcett, who proposed that no taxes be paid for expenses related to war until the country had been consulted through a general election. But this idea was passed over without comment. The central business was proposed by the Marquis of Ailesbury early in the afternoon session: "That, in view of the present state of the Eastern Question, and as a result of this Conference, an association be formed, for the purpose of watching events, of giving further expression to public opinion, and of spreading correct information upon the subject throughout the country."[179] It was a measure on which everyone present could agree (although evidently no formal vote was taken); but it was portentous nonetheless, for by setting up the Eastern Question Association, it institutionalized the protest and gave it a life of its own.

No one was more conscious of the magnitude of what they were about than Gladstone himself. In his speech he rehearsed the cabinet's actions during the summer and autumn and explained how the official response to the crisis had brought him to a turning point. He had been shocked by the levity of Disraeli's speech in the Commons on July 31, when despite growing evidence of massacres, he "deprecated" "interference" in the Ottoman Empire. Thanks to the protest, Gladstone announced, such heedlessness had quickly become impossible. At Aylesbury, the premier had mentioned "great activity . . . but . . . did not tell us what . . . [it] was all about." Then came the Guildhall speech in November, when Disraeli, reversing his stand of the summer before, had finally admitted "that we had duties towards the . . . Christian populations in Turkey," but then had tied these duties to the maintenance of existing arrangements under the totally unsatisfactory Treaty of Paris of 1856. The protest had stimulated progress, but the work was not finished. Derby's dispatch outlining the steps the Porte must take to compensate for the atrocities had been beneficial; but it "has been written for more than two months—no results have followed." Lord Salisbury's appointment as plenipotentiary to the conference at Constantinople to discuss the internal situation of the Ottoman Empire "is an improved and a hopeful feature," but his hands had been tied by Disraeli: "we want to cut him adrift." In fact, what Gladstone described was exactly the sort of response by the cabinet likely to encourage further social protest: they were "appearing to vacillate in the face of pressure."[180]

He himself, despite his hesitations behind the scenes, was willing to become accountable for what the protest might bring, and he explained why.

> Undoubtedly there is not a man among you on whose head that responsibility weighs so heavily as on mine . . . To attempt to regulate the foreign policy of the country by pamphlets and by meetings, to depart from the well-established and happy precedent of leaving the discussion of such questions to those who can consider them continuously, with full information, and with the right of representing England in the face of the world—depend upon it that these are very serious matters . . . By the very fact that it is now proposed to form an association as the result of this Conference you take an exceptional course . . . Now, why do we do this? . . . We have the strongest cause . . . for regarding that which we are doing . . . as the discharge of an absolute and imperative duty . . . We think, I may say, we know, that the power and reputation and the influence of England have for a long period of time, within these last twelve months, in the regulation of an enormous question, been employed for purposes which are in fact directly at variance with the convictions of the country.[181]

It was a grave moment and a somber mood, combining the exaltation of high purpose with the warmth of shared sentiment and the stimulus of danger. On Christmas Day, still buoyed up by the collective emotion but anxious about what might lie ahead, Gladstone recorded in his *Diary:* "The most solemn I have known for long: see that Eastward sky of storm, and of underlight!"[182]

8 ◆ A Shift in Focus

Events between September and December 1876 were critical to the success of the Bulgarian agitation. During these months, the kinds of leadership most in demand changed. For example, during the summer months, the journalist W. T. Stead played a crucial part as a "promoter." But as the movement evolved, though Stead recognized the need for innovative patterns of mobilization, his suggestions were less practicable and astute than those of seasoned political organizers like Wilson, Leader, and Mundella. It was men of their stripe who emerged during the autumn as the "bureaucrats" of the agitation.[1]

In the area of leadership, no development was more important than the increasing involvement of Gladstone. Earlier social movements had entertained uneasy and distant relations with major British statesmen. The Bulgarian agitation marked the first occasion on which a man so politically important explicitly put himself at the head of a movement "out-of-doors." It was a portentous step, and Gladstone did not take it lightly. Indeed, he avoided it as long as possible. Although many people believed (or hoped) that he had assumed leadership when he wrote the pamphlet on the "Bulgarian Horrors" and followed it up with the speech at Blackheath, evidently Gladstone did not see it that way. Rather, he thought that he was acting as a gadfly, a kind of free-floating Liberal conscience who could speak out on controversial issues about which it was desirable for someone of stature in the party to express indignation, but which were probably too tangled and complex for those actually charged with party leadership to discuss initially. It was a role, in short, uniquely suited to Gladstone's semi-retirement—a contribution he could make precisely because he was no longer at the center of day-to-day party operations.

But having made his statement, Gladstone at first did not want to recognize any further special requirements. Writing was normal enough; so were conversations with colleagues. More speeches, on the other hand, smacked of pontification, and so he did his best to avoid public appearances. In asking his counsel about the national meeting, Mundella and his associates unknowingly found the route to deeper involvement; giving backstage advice and guidance apparently seemed to Gladstone both worthwhile and responsible. It came under the heading of "conversation with colleagues" and did not, he thought, commit him to a public stand. His public stand came only in December, when he finally understood the dimensions of the movement, the chasm between the government and the people, and the unmistakable evidence of his paternity. Then and only then did the explicit assumption of leadership become "an absolute and imperative duty."[2]

The strength of the agitation derived from two sources, both important: the quantity of people who had been mobilized out-of-doors, and the quality of support within governing circles. Even influential individuals within Disraeli's own party and cabinet were shocked by stories of events in Bulgaria and were deeply uneasy about the appearance of facile British support for the Ottomans. Yet the Conservatives enjoyed significant hard-core support. In their company were large sections of the nobility and the landed gentry: the high-living, hard-drinking county society, which tended to suspect Gladstone at the best of times and was outraged by this new example of his sentimental and ill-judged missionizing and minding other people's business. Many members of the Church of England were with them, not only because of the ingrained conservative tendencies natural to an established church, but also because of an institutionally nurtured mistrust of enthusiasm. The army and navy, and all those families who were proud to count an officer among their forebears or offspring or both, characteristically took an unswervingly patriotic view of England's duty and refused to be swayed by the fact that it might now, as not infrequently in the past, be an unpleasant duty. Men who moved in high financial circles, rich bankers and commercial magnates, although far from universally favorable to the Conservative policy in this question, generally believed that England's prestige was a valuable asset, not to be squandered lightly. Although war offered certain economic risks, there would be losses if the Ottoman Empire succumbed. It might yet be possible to make the Porte pay its debts; it would be much chancier to try to transfer those obligations to successor states born in revolution and war. Finally, the Jewish community, though divided on this issue as on most others, was dismayed at the spectacle of Greek Orthodox Christian bigotry. Most Jews felt that the Ottomans' sins of omission were nowhere near as dangerous as Greek Orthodox sins of commission in emerging Balkan states such as Serbia and Romania.

These supporters were reinforced by other, less eminent partisans. Some were similar in socioeconomic background to the artisans who supported Gladstone, but whether for intellectual or for material reasons, marched to a different tune. There were workers in the arsenals, munitions factories, government dockyards, and other strategic industries. Other working men might have a Conservative employer to whom they listened, perhaps for reasons of deference, perhaps for more materialistic motives. Although some working-class government supporters were clearly self-interested (as Liberals were only too happy to point out), not all, and probably not even most, were cynical; the Conservative party had already started to win significant loyalty in the industrial towns, particularly among semiskilled and unskilled labor. Finally, there was a large contingent of casual laborers and unemployed, people who could be easily persuaded, for a few bob, a few beers, or just for the fun of it, to go out and beat up on the "rich." It was this element that dominated in the "Cockney mob"[3] which, in 1878, broke up meetings and intimidated the agitators. It appears to bear some resemblance to the "King and Country" mobs of an earlier day and a very direct relationship to the Jingo crowds who broke up peace meetings during the Boer War.[4]

In 1876, the agitators typically met with scorn, not violence; most people, especially on the Conservative side, did not think the issues important enough to call for action. Disraeli shared this dismissive attitude. During the summer he had erred in taking the situation too lightly; during the autumn and winter, he continued to underestimate the breadth and sobriety of feeling opposing him. Disraeli's highly personal reaction to Gladstone's pamphlet and speech was pure fury. He wisecracked about the pamphlet, "of all the Bulgarian horrors, perhaps, the greatest,"[5] and remarked to Corry, "what a man is Gladstone! What a scoundrel!"[6] And all the bitterness of Disraeli's own struggle to win social acceptance breathed through the comment: "Posterity will do justice to that unprincipled maniac, Gladstone, extraordinary mixture of envy, vindictiveness, hypocrisy, and superstition: and with one commanding characteristic: whether Prime Minister or

Leader of Opposition, whether preaching, praying, speechifying or scribbling—never a gentleman!"[7]

In these extreme reactions Disraeli was encouraged by his circle of close friends and associates. Corry, on vacation in Ireland, lamented "the most malignant calumnies ever forged," and reassured Disraeli, "you rightly call it a moment of national madness!"[8] Lord John Manners, writing to the "dearest of chiefs," concluded that "the country, under skilful management, has gone stark staring mad."[9] Cross clucked: "I am disturbed about this agitation: very wicked, and unprincipled though for the time telling: I can conceive nothing more reckless than Mr. Gladstone's conduct."[10] In an aside to his mentor, Lord Derby, Cross added: "I cannot imagine how any public man can have so wholly lost the sense of responsibility as Gladstone."[11]

Though outraged by Gladstone's antics, Disraeli's intimates did not expect the damage to be serious. Lord John Manners, lamenting "the tide of foolish talk," concluded "I don't think however that it will last much longer."[12] Cross, writing to Derby about Gladstone, consoled, "I feel sure that the blow will fall on his own head."[13] And Corry advised frankly against yielding to the protesters' demands. He worried that an autumn session of Parliament might be "fatal" to the cabinet. Surely the Liberals would try to force such a decision, but that did not mean that Disraeli should agree. "I do not yet see the people pulling down the railings of Hyde Park, for an idea in Turkey."[14] Others were more cautious. Disraeli's friend, Lionel de Rothschild, the great City banker, wrote anxiously about "several letters from the continent calling our attention to the mischief these meetings were causing and to the encouragement they gave to certain parties, we spoke to several friends about it, but at present it is no use to argue the position." The best solution, according to Rothschild, would be to work for an agreement among the "contending parties"; this would effectively undermine the protesters' case.[15]

This advice was easier to give than to act upon. In attempting to resolve the crisis, the cabinet was taking aim at a moving target. During the summer of 1876, in addition to the troubles in Bulgaria, the Turks were fighting Serbia and Montenegro. These two principalities attacked initially to support the revolts of Bosnia and Herzegovina, disturbances which had broken out the previous summer. There were therefore two related problems to negotiate: first, an armistice between the Ottoman Empire and Serbia and Montenegro; second, a plan to improve the lot of the Christian subjects of the Porte and assurances that the Porte would act upon it. During the autumn and winter, armistice negotiations did go forward. Partly through British urgings but mostly as result of a Russian ultimatum, the Porte reluctantly accepted an agreement on October 31.[16]

Meanwhile, Derby pressed for an international conference to reconcile the Porte with its Christian subjects. As early as August 29, he urged Elliot, the ambassador at Constantinople, to work for peace through a conference. This idea failed, but Derby did not let go. On September 21, sickened by the Baring report and mindful of the "just indignation" of the British people, he outlined a plan for Bulgaria which included reparations, punishment for the guilty, and limited autonomy.[17] Once the armistice was in place, Prince Gorchakov, the Russian Foreign Minister and Chancellor, took up the subject and urged Derby to adapt his September proposals as the basis for discussion by an ambassadorial conference in Constantinople. Derby expanded the idea to include one emissary from each power in addition to the regular representative at Constantinople, thus checking both Elliot and the wily Russian ambassador, Ignatiev. The Constantinople Conference became official.[18]

Disraeli selected Salisbury to represent Britain. It was apparently a personal choice; Salisbury's name was not the only one considered.[19] Salisbury was a candidate certain to be popular with both Conservatives and agitators. As the Conservative press immediately noted, his position in the government as secretary of state for India insured that he would be sensitive to Britain's strategic needs.[20] On the other hand, Salisbury was a Tractarian who had sided with Gladstone against the Public Worship Regulation Act,[21] and the two men were lifelong friends. He came from the same upper-class, High Church background as many protesters,[22] and certainly understood the movement as well as anyone in the cabinet. He differed from the agitators not so much on substance as on procedure; he believed that diplomacy must be the affair of experts, not ordinary individuals.[23] As a result, Salisbury enjoyed considerable credibility among the protesters. Gladstone declared, "Though Salisbury is not a very safe man, yet his appointment is in spirit the best thing the Government have done yet."[24]

Despite such hopes, the conference proved abortive. Not for the first time, Europeans had calculated without the Ottomans. Under severe pressure from the Young Ottomans and others in Constantinople who resented European interference, Sultan Abdul Hamid promulgated a constitution on the day the conference formally met and appointed its author, Midhat Pasha, as grand vizier. Although the decision ushered in a brief but significant constitutional period, its immediate international effect was to break up the conference. Neither the European delegates nor the countries they represented were prepared to accept a solution which originated in Ottoman initiative, not their own. In Britain this disposition was marked among both parties. *Punch* showing a man puffing a water pipe, expressed the rather general view: "One Bubble More!!" and later asked, "Did a Sick Man ever develop a new Constitution?"[25]

The failure of the conference left diplomacy at a standstill. In London, Disraeli and Derby had agreed beforehand that if the Ottomans proved unwilling to accept the terms, Britain would not coerce them.[26] That created a dilemma: if the Russians went to war to enforce the conference proposals, and if, as virtually everyone in Europe expected, they were quickly successful in the field, what could be Britain's response? Should Britain aid the Turks, or the Russians, or neither one? And if neutrality were the wiser course, should it be absolute or conditional? And what did conditional mean anyhow?

Since the beginning of the Eastern crisis, war had never seemed so near. The agitators in the autumn had hoped that extreme developments could be avoided by skillful diplomacy, but now a rough road lay ahead. It would test the machinery of protest organized during 1876, exposing strengths and weaknesses. And it would demand that the protesters function in new ways. In 1876 they had assumed a relatively straightforward task. Parliament was not in session at the time the enthusiastic phase developed; indeed, the absence of a Parliamentary check on policy was often urged by the protesters as the justification for their activities. Their role was to make sufficient noise, by whatever means they could, to impress the cabinet and persuade the ministers to modify policy. Now, however, as events moved toward war in the East, Parliament was sitting and major opposition leaders like Gladstone could and did avail themselves of that forum to make the protest's points. The problems, then, for the agitators turned on timing and coordination: how could pressure from without be combined with pressure from within? Although there had been earlier examples of the two proceeding side by side and tacitly complementing each other (for example, during the passage of the two Reform Acts), this occasion was unique because Gladstone was the acknowledged leader both within and without.

Looking at the protest with the benefit of hindsight, it might seem reasonable to expect that the Eastern Question Association would have stimulated and coordinated local meetings all over England to create maximum support for whatever issues Gladstone might choose to raise in Parliament. This did not happen. The Association was never able to assume such a central directing role, for reasons which go back to the debate over its founding. The leaders in Sheffield had originally conceived the Association primarily as a pressure group. At the end of November, Mundella, in a long letter to Gladstone outlining his plans, suggested that the St. James's Hall meeting would "be followed up by literature lectures and public meetings throughout the country."[27] He continued to think along these lines as he basked in the conference's success. Writing to Wilson on December 10, he expanded: "We will now set some pens at work to enlighten the *educated classes* and to strengthen the masses in their wholesome convictions. We will have *wives* to every man and organization represented at the Conference, and at the first sign of danger call for simultaneous meetings all over the country."[28] Evidently Leader, a splendid local organizer, was equally certain that priority must be assigned to grassroots mobilization. It was Gladstone who placed the emphasis instead on propaganda and forced a change in plan. Mundella had to tell Leader: "Gladstone is *not* of your opinion that there should be no publishing and lecturing machinery;" after all, "the Turks flood the country with misleading literature and it is necessary that this should be counteracted and the truth made known."[29] In Gladstone's view, the Association should not become a pressure group, but rather a propaganda organ; Mundella deferred to his vision.

The debate accordingly shifted to ways and means of propaganda. Gladstone had already showered Herbert and Mundella with ideas for an information campaign. In long letters to Herbert in November he had even provided lists of topics for pamphlets.[30] Herbert, although by that time not so closely involved, passed Gladstone's letters on to Mundella and assured Gladstone that they would be acted upon; in fact, he stated, "we had already agreed to bring out a pamphlet or two."[31]

To Mundella, Gladstone broached a related project. He wanted "to establish some journal or paper *ad hoc*," and even proposed a title, "The Star in the East."[32] The scheme was not new. Already in mid-October, he had contacted Frank Hill to suggest meeting to discuss "some special and temporary means" for spreading the message about the Eastern Question. An ordinary newspaper, committed as it was to coverage of a range of subjects, could not, he felt, say enough on the issue; he was evidently thinking of a specialized sheet, such as had been developed during the Anti–Corn Law campaign.[33] Frank Hill responded tactfully, but his lack of enthusiasm was clear. As he explained, "I doubt whether a special organ of Eastern information and politics would gain the ear of the public. However fairly conducted, it would be considered as pledged beforehand to particular news, and so dependent upon possibly biassed sources of information; and that suspicion, however erroneous, would be fatal."[34] But despite Hill's negative reaction, Gladstone continued to press for a journal as well as pamphlets,[35] and when the Association decided in favor of the latter, he was far from pleased. "I should have thought periodical issue the best," he worried in a letter to Mundella, "I hope the direction taken has been right."[36] Probably the decision was made on practical grounds. As Gladstone admitted, a newspaper "would require a very well chosen man to look after it."[37] Likely candidates were hard to find and harder still to attract.

Indeed, the launching of the Eastern Question Association was not easy at all, despite the promising start when it was formally founded at the December St. James's Hall meeting. According to the resolution setting it up, "a committee [was to] be formed . . . consisting of the Duke of Westminster, K.G., the Earl of Shaftesbury, K.G., and the members of the present National Conference Committee, with power to add to their number."[38] A general invitation to membership was issued through Association publications; those interested were asked "to forward their contributions to" the treasurer, William Morris.[39] A list of contributors published in February 1877 gave four hundred eleven names. Most memberships were individual; the major exception was Henry Richard's Peace Society. One or two Liberal Associations also gave. The group seems to have been overwhelmingly middle and upper class, with a particularly heavy representation of clergymen. Next most prominent were M.P.'s, followed by professional men, such as professors and a few doctors; there was also a sprinkling of women. The geographical distribution was sparse. Although many of the new members were listed as living outside London, and appeals for action were made to the country at large, in fact the effective scope of the organization seems to have been pretty much limited to the metropolis.[40] With a total capitalization in excess of £1,350, the new association's resources contrasted favorably with the situation during the autumn, when individual demonstrations were funded by their organizers, and was richer than Chamberlain's National Federation of Liberal Associations at the beginning.[41] But neither had the power of some of the long-established pressure groups for domestic questions; for example, in 1865–66, the Liberation Society raised £7,556 and in 1874 embarked on a crusade for disestablishment which it was hoped would run to £100,000.[42]

The most important resource in spreading the Association's message was its publication program—both a series of pamphlets and a collection of leaflets. The leaflets consisted entirely of short extracts from speeches already published, and sometimes were none too timely. The first leaflet, by John Bright, came from a talk originally delivered at Birmingham on December 4, 1876. After some more or less current offerings, the fifth reached back again to Bright's speech, while the sixth was taken from an early edition of Edward A. Freeman's *History of the Saracens*, which had first appeared in 1856. Leaflets for the most part were limited to a page in length, although some of the later ones swelled to four or even eight pages; they seem to have been produced primarily to be handed out at meetings and apparently began to appear only in the summer of 1877.[43]

The pamphlets, though billed as "written at the request of the Eastern Question Association," were not always new either. The first, "The Evidences of Turkish Misrule" by Henry Richard, had appeared in 1855 and was partially reissued in 1877.[44] Gladstone himself quickly contributed a couple of fresh manuscripts. "The Sclavonic Provinces of the Ottoman Empire" was a reprint of an address given at Hawarden on January 16, 1877, which was based on the travel account by A. P. Irby and Miss Mackenzie.[45] A more ambitious effort was his "Lessons in Massacre," drawn from papers presented to Parliament, which appeared in March 1877.[46] A later pamphlet reproduced his resolutions and the speech introducing them delivered to the House of Commons on May 7, 1877.[47]

The fervor expressed in these pamphlets cannot be doubted; more apposite questions are how they were distributed and how widely they were read. By comparison with newspapers, none was cheap. Gladstone's original pamphlet on the "Bulgarian Horrors" had appeared at the high price of one shilling sixpence, when *The Times* cost threepence and some newspapers could be obtained for halfpence.[48] A sixpenny edition was also issued, however,[49] and this was a more typical price. "Lessons in Massacre" sold for only fourpence, but even at that figure, it did not go well: while the "Bulgarian Horrors" had run up a sale of 200,000 in the first month, "Lessons in Massacre" sold only about 6500 in the first three weeks.[50]

Pamphlets were "to be had of all booksellers," and special arrangements could be made for quantity orders at a discount.[51] Naturally, a certain number of complimentary copies were sent out, sometimes to astonished recipients;[52] Gladstone, like all authors, was not above profiting by a captive audience. When "Lessons in Massacre" reached the last stages, he was staying with Sir John Lubbock; he wrote Catherine, "I had the proof sheets of my pamphlet which I gave to some of the guests here as they were not likely to have better Sunday reading."[53] And there were ways to get rid of extra copies. In January 1877, Gladstone had Murray send Catherine "a packet with a lot of the 'Bulgarian Horrors' which are to be distributed with the next Parish Magazine" at Hawarden.[54] Probably more propaganda value was derived from the "gratuitous distribution" arranged through the *Northern Echo*. Since the newspaper's daily readership counted at least 12,500, the potential for reaching large numbers was impressive. Free provision on this scale would have been expensive, however, and perhaps that is why, despite initial plans to distribute it to everyone, only 1700 were finally offered.[55]

Propaganda was clearly what the Eastern Question Association did best. The Association brought out a significant body of material which argued the case for autonomy of the Christian provinces. But, in spite of good authors and inventive distribution, the publications seem to have reached relatively few people. The "Bulgarian Horrors," a tremendous success among pamphlets, reached numbers comparable to newspaper circulation in a period when the *Daily News* went to 150,000 each day and the *Daily Telegraph* nearly 250,000.[56] Those authors less popular than Gladstone probably did not even match the 6500 attained by "Lessons in Massacre." There were inherent difficulties blocking the distribution of pamphlets, as Chamberlain noted later with his usual realism. He admitted to Stead: "I am afraid I have little confidence in the advantage of tract literature. If it be gratuitousl[y] distributed it is not valued, and at present the people are not in the habit of purchasing. To induce a sale an immense system of advertising would be necessary, which would be more costly than any existing organisation could undertake."[57]

Nonetheless, if the situation challenging the Eastern Question Association had continued to resemble conditions prevailing in the autumn of 1876, the organization might have answered very well. Facing a long-drawn-out crisis in which Britain's part was the indirect role of the interested third party, dissemination of information might logically have taken precedence over action. But during the spring of 1877, the situation in the East deteriorated sharply and suddenly. Worries had been widespread that with the coming of spring and a new campaigning season Russia would declare war, but the British hoped to avert this outcome through international pressure. On January 31, Gorchakov sent around a circular asking the powers what action might be taken in common, given the failure of the Constantinople Conference. Derby expressed his preference to Odo Russell: "We shall wait, say little, and pledge ourselves to nothing."[58] Then, in a series of imperial councils at the end of February, the Russians in a fatalistic mood debated a memorandum from D. A. Milyutin, the minister of war, urging that the European powers, or failing joint action, Russia alone, insist that the Ottoman Empire reform along the lines discussed at the Conference; if these overtures were not accepted, Russia would have to send an ultimatum and, if necessary, go to war.[59]

A last hope for peace was offered by the protocol signed by the six great powers at London on March 31. Largely the work of Shuvalov, the Russian ambassador, it softened the proposals under debate in St. Petersburg. It called for reform, but did not spell out exactly what would be required, and also did not specify what would happen if the Porte refused.[60] The British cabinet, deeply suspicious even of this modest effort to pressure the Porte, decided to sign only after word from Loftus in Russia suggested that the protocol was the one hope remaining for averting war.[61] But the protocol was stillborn. The Turks immediately rejected it, despite the advice of the powers, and the consequences were inescapable. On April 24, 1877, the Russians declared war and sent their army across the Pruth.[62]

During April, Gladstone had become increasingly alarmed.[63] But the stakes were high. Only as war was about to break out between Russia and the Porte did he seriously consider drafts for resolutions against support for the Ottomans.[64] On April 27 he recorded in his diary: "Diarrhoea in the night: kept my bed. . . . This day I took my decision: a severe one, in face of my not having a single approver in the *Upper* official circle. But had I in the first days of September asked the same body whether I ought to write my pamphlet I believe the unanimous answer would have been no."[65] On April 30, rejecting the more straightforward course of calling for a vote of no confidence in the government, he gave the House notice of five resolutions which summed up his carefully crafted policy of neutrality. The first stated that the Porte had not responded appropriately to Derby's despatch of September 21, 1876, which called for a grant of limited autonomy to Bulgaria. The second insisted that the Porte must change course, and must provide "guarantees" of future good behavior more solid than the mere verbal "promises" given in the past. The third resolution noted the war in progress between Russia and the Ottoman Empire and bound Britain to work for "local liberty and practical self-government" for the Bulgarians and an "end to the oppression which they now suffer" without the "imposition upon them of any other Foreign Dominion." The fourth resolution, revisiting one of Gladstone's favorite ideas, looked to the Concert of Europe to ensure that the Porte implemented the reforms, while the fifth proposed that an address summarizing these points should go from the House to the Queen.[66]

The resolutions were sure to face opposition in Parliament. Indeed, Gladstone had been warned, by men not unfriendly to the protest, that they might well fail ignominiously, and so actually strengthen Disraeli's hand.[67] Strong support by the movement out-of-doors was essential. In fact, the Eastern Question Association was organizing for action. On April 24, the date of the Russian declaration of war, the Central Committee in London issued a circular which summarized its activities to date and apprised its supporters of the present danger, although unfortunately it failed to make clear recommendations. The document was sent to "the numerous subscribers and supporters of the Association throughout the country," meaning probably the membership list of February with additions made since that time. It was printed a few days later in the *Daily News*, which greatly expanded the audience. The Association claimed to have received support from "the large towns," but probably did not have a well-developed network. Indeed, the Association used this crisis as an opportunity to ask for "the formation of Local Committees in those places where such action has not already been taken," suggesting that this process was not well advanced. Another sign of weakness was the vagueness of the proposals. Rather than calling for protest meetings, the Central Committee asked supporters for "their vigilance and their persistent influence" and called on them "to labour for the restoration of the concert of the Powers," without making any suggestions as to what those labors might usefully comprise.[68]

The Association faced a difficult organizational problem. Without a tightly constructed web of branches around the country, they needed to allow much time to get results. Yet until it was clear what leaders like Gladstone proposed to do in Parliament, it was hard to know what results to work for. And even when Gladstone's resolutions had been announced, they did not as they stood offer an ideal focus for collective behavior. Despite the careful wording, what Gladstone wanted was to commit Britain in advance to neutrality. It was the stuff of party politics, perhaps, but not of protest movements. The latter are notoriously reactive rather than proactive, good at fanning anger over an outrage which has happened, not so good at formulating policy for the political turns and twists of an as yet undefined future. Yet that future seemed to be developing so swiftly that Gladstone's resolutions would have lost much of their relevance had he delayed debate. Different pacing as well as different requirements for action indoors and outdoors hampered coordination.

The Labour Representation League, more independent, better organized, and therefore less constrained, was already moving into this breach. At a meeting of its Council on April 20, Broadhurst, the secretary, proposed a successful resolution that stigmatized government policy on more down-to-earth issues: "Should an attempt be made [to] involve this country in the conflict in support of Turkish interest, either direct or indirect, it will be the duty of the people of this country to take such steps as will prevent English Blood and the people's taxes being employed in such a [*sic*] unworthy and hopeless cause."[69]

The announcement of Gladstone's resolutions gave new urgency and direction to the League's efforts. Recognizing "the utmost importance" of "immediate action," Broadhurst "consulted with the officer and members nearest to hand and decided to call a conference of the Political and Trade Associations of the Metropolis" at the Cannon Street Hotel on May 2.[70] The meeting, announced hastily by a poorly reproduced handwritten letter,[71] was intended to attract any and all concerned individuals and it did. "There is a small meeting tonight at the Cannon St Hotel," wrote William Morris, treasurer of the Eastern Question Association, to his wife Janey. "I am going there to swell the crowd." Like Broadhurst and the artisans who made up the bulk of the Labour Representation League, Morris's personal worries went beyond the moral questions urged in the resolutions to frankly economic ones. "There is a great stew in political matters, and our side will be done for and war certain if we don't raise the very devil over it. Picture to yourself a 3 years war, and the Shop in Oxford Street, and poor Smith standing at the door with his hands in his pockets!"[72]

In fact, a group of about 150 representatives of working-class associations gathered, along with "a large number of Middle Class." A letter from Gladstone was read, and resolutions were passed, with only four dissenting votes, condemning the "moral and material support hitherto rendered" the Ottoman Empire and calling for "absolute neutrality" as stipulated by Gladstone's parliamentary resolutions. Plans were made for a "great mass meeting" to be held in St. James's Hall on May 7, the day debate was scheduled to begin in the Commons. It was to be sponsored by the Eastern Question Association as well as the League. Finally, a letter to the "people of the Country was adopted and ordered to be issued by the authority of the Conference."[73]

This letter expanded on the themes of economic distress. Describing the crisis created by Russia's declaration of war and the likelihood that Britain would become involved on behalf of Ottoman oppression, it laid the responsibility directly on the people to speak and urged them not to support "a policy which will paralyse our already crippled industry, cover foreign fields with the blood of English soldiers, fill our workhouses and possibly jails, with the orphans of our fellow-workers . . . English millionaires, who preferred to invest capital resulting from your labours in Turkish Bonds, rather than employ it in home speculation, should be taught that your Lives and your Taxes shall not be used for recovering their personal debts."[74] Some eight thousand copies of the letter were circulated throughout the country, a number which only hints at the real audience, since most if not all presumably went to clubs and organizations. The response, according to Broadhurst, was highly favorable, with many requests for additional copies.[75]

Yet despite this optimism, it is hard to evaluate the extent to which the Labour Representation League stimulated a response outside London. The centerpiece of their efforts was clearly the May 7 meeting, called amid hopes that it would rival the St. James's Hall meeting of the previous December.[76] But because of the very short notice, it was a much more frankly partisan affair, although an "immense crowd" was said to have turned out. The Duke of Westminster, one of the heads of the Eastern Question Association, was supposed to preside, but became ill; his place was filled by Thomas Hughes. Resolutions called for British neutrality and met with some opposition. Though a progovernment amendment offered by Maltman Barry of the Manhood Suffrage League had to be withdrawn, there was so much confusion that by the end it seemed as though two meetings were going on simultaneously.[77] Indeed, the Manhood Suffrage League went on to hold its own meeting in Hyde Park on May 13 at which Russia's illiberal record was roundly criticized and the war was blamed on the Bulgarian agitators and the impression they provoked of a possible failure of British will.[78]

Meanwhile, meetings in support of the resolutions had been organized around the country. Gladstone, keeping count in his diary, recorded an impressive response. On May 5, there were "near 140 letters . . . which took some hours to examine," while on May 7, there were "about 100 [resolutions from] meetings, and say 200 letters or 250."[79] The total number of communications was at least four hundred, with another eighty-one going directly to the House of Commons.[80]

In contrast to the earlier, largely spontaneous meetings, this round was dominated by two extremes, individuals and existing organizations. In addition to the Labour Representation League and the Eastern Question Association, the Workmen's Peace Association seized a central role.[81] Organized religion played a part, although High Churchmen and indeed Anglicans altogether were less evident than other groups. (After all, Gladstone was publicly challenging the leadership of the country and of his own party during an international crisis). The Nonconformists were active, although not so active as one might have expected. On May 1, Gladstone was presented with resolutions from the triennial conference of the Liberation Society, passed under Chamberlain's influence.[82] And on May 3, Joseph Parker, supported by Newman Hall, turned the noon service at his City Temple into a public meeting in support of Gladstone.[83] However, whereas in 1876 17 percent of the antigovernment communications about Bulgaria came from Nonconformists, in 1877 the figure was down to 11 percent.[84] In addition, the representation of sects had changed. In 1876 the proportion contributed by each denomination reflected the size of its membership; Wesleyan Methodists produced as many documents as Congregationalists and Baptists combined, and the number contributed by Primitive Methodists was negligible.[85] In 1877, on the other hand, Primitive Methodists were highly active, although Methodist participation in general declined sharply; the Baptists now took pride of place (a development that would continue in 1878). The emergence of the Primitive Methodists can plausibly be related to the apparently greater involvement in 1877 of the working classes. Godley stated that "the letters from individuals . . . probably something between one-third and one-half of the whole" were "from every class" including "labourers."[86] Although petitions to Parliament did not show a dramatic increase in working-class participation, newspaper accounts suggest that as many as 17 percent may have originated with working-class groups.[87]

In 1877, Liberal associations and other Liberal organizations (rather than spontaneous public meetings) dominated. J. A. Godley, in analyzing the communications to Gladstone, stated that "the greater number" issued from meetings "summoned" by local Liberal bodies, though he noted that "a large proportion were clearly open meetings in the strictest sense of the words, and some were presided over by the mayor or provost of the town."[88] The press undoubtedly exaggerated, but its proportion of 52 percent was more than twice as high as that described on any other occasion.[89] Those who opposed the protest were similarly divided among individuals and Conservative associations.[90] Thus, by 1877, the protest had become a political, even a partisan matter; many protesters were stirred into action by the imminence of Parliamentary debate. In spite of the change in methods, standardization had only gained a little ground. According to Godley, there was "little or no repetition in the wording" of appeals. By contrast, forms were distributed and widely used in 1878.[91]

The geographic distribution continued to favor the North, as shown in Figure 2. Wales showed remarkably little interest, perhaps because of the influence of Henry Richard, a political power in Wales and secretary of the Peace Society, who preferred to "hold back" his support.[92]

Finally although the protesters created a flurry of activity in 1877, their numbers were still very small. The signed petitions to Parliament, the only category which gave numbers, displayed only 2944 signatures between May 4 and 14. Adding the two hundred or so people who communicated directly with Gladstone,[93] and the people who attended Liberal Association meetings but were not individually listed, it still seems unlikely that the group exceeded ten thousand, no more than might have attended a single large meeting in 1876 or 1878.

In short, the response from the country was gratifying, but it was far from decisive. It certainly did not offset Gladstone's highly tenuous position in the House, where not only Conservatives but many Liberals as well opposed him. Gladstone was thoroughly worried: it was, he admitted to Granville, "a dreadful mess."[94] In the interests of avert-ing an irrevocable split in the Liberal party, he welcomed an olive branch which Granville, always the peacemaker, extended.[95] The shape of the backstage compromise unfolded quickly when the debate opened on May 7. Gladstone was asked to withdraw his third and fourth resolutions, which dealt with the unacceptable plight of the Bulgarian Christians and the desirability of reform through the Concert of Europe. The first resolution, noting that the Porte had failed to comply with Derby's despatch of September 21, would remain. The second, demanding solid "guarantees" for future good conduct, would be amended into vacuity. The fifth resolution, a technical one arranging for transmission to the Queen, would also stand. Gladstone apparently accepted the change reluctantly.[96] "Such a sense of solitary struggle," he wrote later, "I never remember." To make matters worse, he had "forgotten" his "eyeglass" and when the time came to speak, could scarcely read his notes. He was "nearly in despair . . . but resolved at least not to fail through want of effort." In the judgment of his hearers, he delivered "one of his most effective" speeches, but the

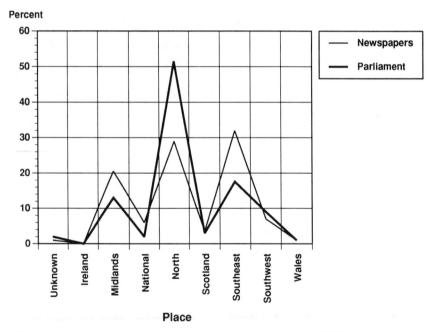

Figure 2. Geographical sources of petitions and meetings, 1877.

ordeal left him drained. "Never," he noted, "did I feel weaker and more wormlike."[97]

Brilliant as the speech apparently was, it left matters in doubt. Although Gladstone had withdrawn two of his resolutions, he spoke as though he were defending the original five; and some of his supporters, starting with Chamberlain, went on record as favoring them all.[98] The ensuing debate was exceptionally long, extending over five late nights until the cabinet threatened to cut short the Whitsun holiday.[99] By the debate's conclusion, at 2:15 A.M. on May 14, everyone was worn out. Even before the debate began, Mundella wrote disgustedly to Leader, *"after* this debate you must expect to hear less of me in the House. The very late hours are again making work with me and I have two boils this morning, and feel dreadfully queer."[100]

Gladstone's strategic retreat opened him to new criticism. First he had appeared reckless because he had put principle above party unity; now, when party unity had been exposed as a sham, he seemed to abandon principle. Backbenchers in his own party were caught unprepared and were furious.[101] Even more serious, the strategy imperilled coordination between Gladstone and his partisans out-of-doors. It was hard enough to mobilize support for the resolutions in the country given the very short notice involved. But now, just as meetings were being mounted, Gladstone gave up the central point, the commitment to neutrality. Individuals who had demonstrated in favor of the resolutions could hardly fail to feel betrayed. Indeed John Holms, Liberal M.P. for Hackney, suggested that it would be well to delay the debate so that the country might have an opportunity to respond to the change in substance.[102] Yet it is hard to see what else Gladstone could have done; had he persisted with all five resolutions, the leadership of his party was quite prepared to desert him, and his ultimate defeat would have been even more resounding than it actually was.

Once again, the relationship between Parliamentary leadership and leadership outside proved a difficult one. Gladstone's retreat, quite as much as his original proposal, was the very stuff of legislative politics; but neither maneuver worked well in the new context of a popular movement. One point obviously at issue was how to relate popular opinion to Parliamentary action; another was what kind of evidence was needed to judge the sincerity of the popular opinions expressed. Many comments made during the debate touched on precisely this question. Gladstone, always ambivalent about politics out-of-doors, came close to apologizing for the agitation. "There is not one of you opposite," he declared, "who can more deeply deplore than I do the use of the rude irregular methods to which we have been driven in order to exercise an influence upon the foreign policy of the country. I look upon these methods as, at the best, unsatisfactory and imperfect; I look upon them, in every case, except the case of necessity, as vicious and bad. It has been that necessity alone which has driven us to the point at which we stand to-night."[103] Only the belief that he was following a higher moral imperative could justify this exceptional departure from the norms of political conduct. But having unleashed popular enthusiasm, Gladstone was prepared to take it seriously; and he expected others to do the same. Somewhat acrimoniously, he pointed out that Christchurch had held a meeting in favor of the resolutions; yet their M.P., Henry Drummond Wolff, attempted to sabotage the resolutions by offering a Conservative amendment. Wolff quickly interrupted to insist that the meeting in question had been packed with outsiders "imported in waggons,"[104] a point which he developed at greater length when he was finally given the floor.[105]

In fact, a number of speakers questioned the genuineness of the sentiments expressed at the meetings. There were many objections to taking the results at face value. Cross, in his important statement for the cabinet on the first night, charged that the meetings had been got up.[106] Others, like Cross in the Conservative camp, agreed. Voicing a distrust of party organization, C. T. Ritchie declared, "Meetings that were called by telegram sent from the Liberal Association in London did not express the opinion of the people of this country."[107] "Half-a-crown-a-head," sneered the self-styled Independent Edward Kenealy, as usual belligerent, would bring out a sufficient number of Liberal agitators.[108] And Percy Wyndham, Conservative M.P. for Cumberland West, delivered a more telling, because more sober, judgment: "he did not think public meetings, though largely attended, any great index of the feeling of the people in this country. There was a type of people who attended public meetings—a type found in all classes of society, and a great number of them in the Upper House. But the main body of the people did not care for public meetings. They disliked listening to speeches—and there was only one thing they disliked more, and that was making speeches themselves."[109] An accusation often whispered was voiced by another Conservative, William Grantham: "the sufferings of the poor Christians had been more a cry for the purpose of catching votes for the poor Liberal Party of England."[110] Not all the speakers expressed skepticism about public meetings, however. Chamberlain, speaking from his own very considerable experience, declared "that money could do something, and that organization could do more; but he knew that neither money nor organization could move a popular agitation, unless there was a deep-felt popular sentiment on which to work."[111]

The common ground in these conflicting analyses is noteworthy. The debates questioned whether popular opinion had been accurately read—but no one suggested that public sentiment, if fairly expressed, was unimportant. Indeed, the Liberals challenged the Conservatives to demonstrate that opinion was on the Conservative side. As Frederick Leveson-Gower put it, "they had been told that the meetings had been got up by telegraph; if so, why had not hon. Members opposite also got up meetings in the same way to support their own particular views?"[112] Gladstone, in closing, charged that "the Government does not commonly despise popular manifestations. On the contrary, in this and that Conservative association, and in the large gatherings and combinations of these associations, there is an incessant activity wherever it can be brought to bear." Why, then, did not the Conservatives attend the protest meetings? Why did they not hold their own meetings?[113]

Yet for most people, whether Liberal or Conservative, action through party meetings was not the answer. There was a deep cynicism about political parties as they were then conceived, an assumption that parties always worked for their own advantage as vested interests. Genuine conviction would not be expressed through parties, but outside of party; seemingly spontaneous public meetings, such as had mushroomed in 1876, were generally considered more compelling than the more organized efforts of 1877.

Of course for members of Parliament, mere numbers on one side or the other out-of-doors were not conclusive. The heart of the debate turned on the substantive issue. Should Britain be neutral or should it become involved in the war? What were the stakes in either course of action? The debates reveal a focus of interest distinctly different from that of many popular meetings. Oddly enough only Edward Hermon, a Conservative cotton manufacturer from Preston, reminded the House that the "people" did not want war because it would hurt trade and might further depress industry at a moment when it had seemed to be reviving.[114] And Jacob Bright, another textile manufacturer, pointed out that waging war cost money and hence was bad for the economy.[115] Otherwise, the speakers talked in terms of British interests, of political and military strategy, of glory and prestige.[116]

The greatest concern, especially for Conservatives, was protecting the route to India, but what this might involve was less obvious. Viscount Sandon, speaking for the government at the beginning of the second evening, set the terms of debate.[117] The possession of India carried certain implications for British policy. Thanks to India, Vere Benett-Stanford insisted in the Commons, Queen Victoria ruled over ten million more Muslims than Christians.[118] Anxiety about India had been a key point in the Conservative case for action in support of the Ottomans since the beginning of the crisis, and although its more extreme formulations could be laughed off, it was not to be dismissed. Though the likelihood of a Russian army marching across the passes to challenge the British on their home ground was not great, the possibility of intrigue and sabotage was real.[119]

Speakers might doubt the extent of danger to India. But everyone on either side of the House agreed that continued access was vital. What was not self-evident, either in the cabinet or in Parliament, was what that necessitated. A series of Cabinet meetings at the end of April had resulted in a stalemate between Disraeli, who, in light of the Russian declaration of war, advocated the immediate occupation of Gallipoli, and Sir Stafford Northcote, the Chancellor of the Exchequer, who felt that Suez was the key.[120] In the end, Derby's despatch to the Russians on May 6 listed British interests in order: Suez, Egypt, Constantinople, the Straits, and the Persian Gulf.[121] Significantly, Derby put Suez and Egypt ahead of Constantinople and the Straits. It was an explicit recognition of a shift of priorities which went back to the purchase of the Canal shares in 1875, and it was expressed in Parliament as well. G. J. Goschen, toward the end of the fourth evening of debate, reflected on areas of agreement that had emerged between his own Liberal party and the Conservatives and observed that no one had called for the "maintenance of the integrity and independence of the Ottoman Empire," that shibboleth of British policy. Presumably the British were prepared to accept some modifications of Ottoman rule, and specifically were no longer willing to fight (as in the Crimean War) to keep the Balkans in Ottoman hands. This result Goschen laid to the effects of the agitation, which had worked a "change in the position of Turkey in the heart and mind of this country." It seems obvious that it also resulted from the entire course of the crisis and specifically from the war. As the long-predicted demise of the Ottoman Empire seemed to be approaching, British interests were articulated in much more precise terms than before.[122]

But despite some areas of consensus, the result of the bitter debate had never really been in doubt. As W. E. Forster put it, one didn't ask about the fate of the resolutions, one asked the size of the defeat.[123] In addition to defections among both Whigs and Radicals,[124] Gladstone had lost many moderates who agreed with the resolutions in principle but shrank from embarrassing the government in a time of tension.[125] To make matters worse, he was bitterly attacked by several Irish members. Mitchell Henry of Galway, though a Liberal, remembered the atrocities carried out by the British in Ireland, India, and Jamaica, and announced that Irishmen could not believe in any English party.[126] Why, after all, said Edward Kenealy, who, though member for Stoke, never forgot his Irish origins, should the Irish help the Liberals to win autonomy for Bulgaria when the Liberals would not concede autonomy to Ireland?[127] Little disposed to sympathize with the Bulgarians, who unlike most Lebanese Christian victims were Orthodox not Catholic, Irish members and their sympathizers freely developed the anti-British implications which had been dormant in their views of the Near East since 1860–61—the British like the Ottomans were imperial masters, and there was not much to choose between them.

These divisions were too deep for any appeal by Gladstone to overcome. Late on the fifth evening, after he had spoken for one hour and twenty minutes in closing,[128] the division was taken on the first resolution. It lost by a majority of one hundred and thirty-one. Discouraged by these dramatic numbers, Gladstone withdrew the second resolution.[129]

Possibly Gladstone would have been wiser not to have introduced the resolutions at all. Perhaps he allowed his concern for the issues to betray him into a false step, a doomed attempt to win an impracticable commitment to inaction relative to developments which had not yet occurred. And his abrupt decision to modify this stand simply made matters worse. In the absence of precedents for complementary action inside and outside Parliament, timing and coordination of activities presented major problems for the protest movement. Gladstone, an M.P. to the bone, was accustomed to the quick thrust and parry of Parliamentary infighting. At the head of a national social movement, he trailed a long following behind him. He had at his command a heavier but blunter weapon. The people were slower to rouse and slower to reconcile once they were roused. Yet there was no institutionalized way, prior to the next elections, by which Gladstone could use this anger among the masses once Parliament had declared against him. And his embarrassing retreat, logical in terms of traditional Parliamentary debate, made it difficult for his supporters outside of the House to organize an extraordinary rescue campaign on his behalf.

Yet, Gladstone persuaded himself, "much good has been done, thank God."[130] Though the resolutions lost, the vote had demonstrated a hard core of support for neutrality. The country, Gladstone believed, had declared itself strongly in one sense; Parliament had refused to follow. Some observers might blame the constitutional system. Gladstone did not. He recognized the problem; "but the case," he judged, "is a rare one."[131] The experience had renewed his faith in the people, and particularly in working men. Writing to Henry Broadhurst, he declared himself "much gratified with the Resolutions passed by the Labour Representation League" and added that he would "recollect with lively pleasure how vivid and genial an energy the people of this country have exhibited . . . and how they have shown their constancy in the sound views of the Eastern Question which they had previously adopted." Gladstone expressed the hope that the workers would remain steadfast in these opinions and would vote accordingly when elections were held.[132]

If Broadhurst and the Labour Representation League had gained credibility, the Eastern Question Association had lost. Even the meeting that was held under its sponsorship had only been mounted in cooperation with the Labour Representation League, and it had been far from unanimous. Auberon Herbert apparently believed that the problem was lack of grassroots organization, a failure to live up to the program originally sketched by Mundella and Leader. It was necessary, he declared, that the "work of the committees . . . be pushed." "Our chance now is to build up in the large towns a solid anti–Tory-war party, before a time of excitement comes." The best plan would be "to send a very efficient paid agent, who could wholly devote himself to this." If no one else were available, Herbert himself was ready to try, but he recognized that he was not the ideal person: "it wants some one much more clothed in respectability than I am."[133] Evidently nothing came of this overture. The Eastern Question Association continued to devote itself to propaganda and probably deserved the harsh judgment passed by one disgruntled supporter some months later: "I must confess disappointment at that assn [sic] which exists almost only in name."[134]

Chamberlain had a different analysis of the setback, one closely related to his own ambitions and agenda. He was convinced that thorough-going institutional reform was necessary in order that opinion in the country might be more continuously and more systematically transmitted to M.P.s and party leaders. He had watched the debacle in Parliament with mixed feelings. He was convinced, he said, that unless a compromise emerged, "a complete split in the party must result. I am not certain that this will be altogether a bad thing, since we might hope that it would be re-formed upon some more solid basis."[135] First and foremost, "the future programme of Liberalism must come from below."[136] Only that way, he implied, could the demands of the Radicals be heard. Second, he was not satisfied with the leadership; people he distrusted were too powerful and seemed likely to become more so. Chamberlain had made his calculations early in the preceding autumn: "Gladstone is the best answer . . . and if he were to come back for a few years (he can't continue in public life for very much longer) he would probably do much for us, and pave the way for more . . . If G. could be induced formally to resume the reins, it would be almost equivalent to a victory and would stir what Bright calls 'the masses of my countrymen' to the depths."[137]

What was needed was an occasion and it was Chamberlain's genius to see that the Eastern Question might provide it.[138] Even before the debate, he had invited Gladstone to come to Birmingham to speak on May 31. Chamberlain planned the gathering as the inauguration of a Federation of Liberal Associations organized along the lines he had long advocated. But he needed a star, and Gladstone, fulminating on the foreign policy topic of the spring, could be perfect. Meanwhile Gladstone had become deeply discouraged about the feasibility of effective action through Parliament. This frustration seems to explain his uncharacteristic acceptance.[139] It was in fact an opportunity to appeal to the masses over the heads of the M.P.s at a time when his own retreat in Parliament had made organization of a meeting exclusively devoted to the Eastern Question unlikely unless he took the highly unattractive step of calling it himself.

Once Gladstone had agreed to come, he and Chamberlain haggled over the details. Their correspondence speaks volumes about their contrasting purposes and conceptions of the uses of the visit. Gladstone tried to restrict his presence to events which could be carefully monitored, while Chamberlain wanted to maximize the publicity value of the occasion. For example, Gladstone wished to arrive late in the afternoon, but Chamberlain objected, because, as he finally admitted, plans were in the making for a "general half holyday" which would permit "tens of thousands" to turn out to meet Gladstone and to give him "an almost Royal welcome."[140] Reportedly, Chamberlain had assured a large audience by laying on "special trains" to bring people to Birmingham.[141] He had also scheduled some additional special events—dinner with the mayor,[142] and on the day following the meeting, a tour of the gun factory at Enfield and a visit to "one of our new Board Schools."[143] Both events were carefully calculated to win converts to Gladstone and the agitation; the Board schools had been centers of Nonconformist opposition to Gladstone, while workers in the defense industries generally supported the prospect of war in hope of increased orders.[144] All the arrangements reflected the efficient organization which Chamberlain and his associates had learned through the National Education League and the Birmingham Liberal Association. Chamberlain was not simply boasting when he wrote Stead, "the Birmingham people understand this kind of demonstration and you may rely upon it that it will be a wonderful success."[145]

Indeed all seemed to go exactly as Chamberlain had planned. The morning session considered a constitution for the proposed Federation. Chamberlain, speaking first, outlined the project. Unlike Gladstone, Chamberlain believed that the Liberal party's present difficulties were the symptom of a systemic breakdown. He pointed out that thanks to the franchise reforms, the working classes now formed the majority in many constituencies. It was therefore necessary to involve them in ways which would reflect their numerical strength. In the new Liberal associations, every Liberal voter was a member; no longer would the affairs of the party be decided locally by small cliques. Only associations of the new type were represented at Birmingham—almost one hundred of them—and only such organizations would be eligible to join the Federation. In closing, Chamberlain confidently recognized Gladstone's presence as a "happy augury" and pointed to the loneliness of his stand for "a bold, a decided, and an intelligible policy" against "the timid counsels" of the party leadership as a paradigm of the party's servitude to entrenched elites and a guide to liberation.[146]

Chamberlain and his associates were obviously trying to use Gladstone, in part for their own advancement, in part to shape the Liberal party as they thought best. "The people" had spoken in one sense and the House of Commons in another. The debate showed that many members of the House distrusted the opinions expressed by the people through their political organizations, in this case Liberal associations. One logical answer, surely, would be to make the Liberal associations more representative; to ensure that their pronouncements fairly expressed the views of Liberal voters. Such a grassroots reform could be helpful in the Eastern Question, but that, to Chamberlain and his associates, was just one among many issues on which Radicals were frustrated.

But many in the audience had little interest in these organizational questions. For most, the centerpiece was the evening meeting and Gladstone's speech at Bingley Hall. According to one worker, nothing had caused this much excitement in Birmingham in "nearly 30 years." Tickets were sold for the huge sum of five shillings each and went so fast that the hall could have been filled four times over.[147] Gladstone had been nervous when he learned that he might be expected to address a crowd of ten thousand. In fact, the audience swelled to something like thirty thousand, "said to be the largest audience ever gathered to hear one man speak" indoors.[148]

Gladstone commenced by supporting the new model for more democracy in the Liberal party, but his endorsement was brief; so brief as to suggest, to those who knew him, that he was anything but enthusiastic. Indeed he had discussed the pitfalls of the visit in advance with Granville and, alerted by Granville to Chamberlain's manipulative plans, had assured his friend that he did not intend to become embroiled in such questions.[149] The point of his speech was summed up in the resolution placed before the evening meeting, a resolution similar to the proposals which had just failed in the House of Commons. By its record of misdeeds, the Ottoman Empire had "lost all claim either to the moral or material support" of Britain. Instead of coming to the Porte's aid, Britain must work with the other European great powers to establish "local liberty and self-government in the disturbed provinces of Turkey."[150] Taking his text from recent events, he declared: "We have a great responsibility in working upon a matter of foreign policy . . . against the Executive Government, and against the sense of the House of Commons. It is a thing that is rarely done, and it is a thing which I hope will rarely have occasion to be done again."[151] For Gladstone, unlike the young Radicals of Birmingham, the altercation over Bulgaria was unique, but the need to appeal to the people, to the masses' sense of rightness, was inescapable.

Francis Herrick and others have argued that the Eastern Question and the founding of the National Liberal Federation were "related . . . only in time," not causally,[152] and in a sense this is true. The institutional models for the Federation derived from earlier experience with organizations like the National Education League, and ultimately the Anti–Corn Law League.[153] Frustration with the single-issue protest and the pressure group organized around it as the means of reforming English society had been building for some time. Chamberlain and his friends, in short, were not in agreement with Herbert that the fault in the Bulgarian agitation lay with the Eastern Question Association. Even had the Association functioned perfectly as a national pressure group, that would not have been enough in their eyes. The Eastern Question was merely one example of a kind of problem which could only be solved by a thorough-going reorganization of the party system. What the Eastern Question seemed to offer was the opportunity. Certain leaders may "lie in wait for disturbances and then move in to assume leadership," trying to shape the movement as they do so in accordance with their own political priorities.[154] This was what Chamberlain and his associates hoped to accomplish. And in a limited way, they probably did profit by the Bulgarian agitation. Between May 1877 and January 1879, membership rose from 46 associations to 101; and some of the gain may be attributable to concern over the Eastern Question.[155] But it was many years before the Federation became fundamental to party councils; when it did gain importance, it was Gladstone, not Chamberlain, who benefited.[156]

Gladstone's evaluation of the situation proved more important than Chamberlain's. Gladstone learned (or relearned) certain specific lessons which influenced his leadership when the next crisis came, at the end of 1877. First, it was a mistake to anticipate events by taking a public position too soon; one had to react to facts, not hypothetical situations. Second, organization detracted from credibility, and political organization was worst of all.[157] The more spontaneous and the more apolitical popular opinion appeared to be, the more weight it would carry. Finally, the working men, the masses, were sound and dependable in a way that the classes were not. These conclusions continued to guide him in 1878.

9 ✦ War and Counterprotest

The protesters' experience during the spring of 1877 had been frustrating. Russia's declaration of war on the Ottoman Empire raised questions about Britain's response which seemed to demand preemptive action. At least, Gladstone thought they did, and it is easy to make a case for his opinion. Movements which claim to be based on superior moral integrity lose ground if they appear indifferent or indecisive in the face of a challenge to their values, such as British entry into the war in support of the Ottomans would have offered. And the considerable aid from "the country" suggests that others agreed with Gladstone that such a challenge might be imminent. Particularly noteworthy was the strong independent backing of the Labour Representation League and the working men who formed it.

Yet there is another side to the question. There was reason to view the outbreak of war between Russia and the Porte with foreboding, even alarm, and reason as well to assume that Russia would overwhelm the Ottomans in short order. But it did not necessarily follow that Britain would renounce neutrality. In fact, the cabinet was divided. As early as the autumn of 1876, Disraeli had been revolving ambitious plans for a British military role. On October 4 he had suggested to the cabinet that if Russia invaded Bulgaria, it might be necessary for Britain to respond with a "friendly occupation of Constantinople."[1] Several British officers were sent to Constantinople to plan the possible defense of the city and the Straits area. Attention was given to a potential base of operations—if not Constantinople, perhaps Rhodes, or even Crete or Egypt.[2] Disraeli, always attracted by the possibility of picking up some likely piece of Near Eastern real estate, was very much interested and believed that if the trouble in the East led to a general redrawing of the map, Britain should seize "some

Black Sea equivalent of Malta or Gibraltar—Varna, Batoum, or Sinope." He was struck by an estimate from the War Office that forty-six thousand men could hold Constantinople, and had prepared himself for swift dispatch of aid to Turkey without a formal declaration of war or elaborate preparation of public opinion.[3] Such fantasies appealed enormously to Disraeli's restless, imaginative side. They were the stuff of which good novels could be made. But, in his guise as an exceptionally astute and realistic politician, it is not clear that he ever saw them as more than the extreme point on a spectrum of contingency plans. And, as the hot debates in the cabinet testified, if Disraeli had seriously proposed carrying out such a bold stroke, cooler heads would probably have restrained him.

Given the enormous contrast between Gladstone's and Disraeli's points of view, many people saw Gladstone's resolutions as part of the endless political jockeying between Liberals and Conservatives, not as a nonpartisan response to a moral outrage. Added to this was the very short interval during which protest could be effective, a span of time circumscribed by the Russian declaration of war (April 24), or more properly by the announcement of the resolutions (April 30), and the end of the debate on May 14. Not surprisingly, although the outburst in 1877 was concentrated and intense, it does not seem to have involved as many individuals as the agitation in 1876, or the protest in 1878 which was both long drawn out and, at moments, explosive.

Those who had participated in 1877 went away with the taste of failure in their mouths. Their protest had not overawed the House of Commons, nor were the members ready to pass Gladstone's resolutions on their merits. The protesters explained the debacle in different ways and offered different remedies. Auberon Herbert, struck by the ineffectiveness of the Eastern Question Association, wanted it to be remodeled from a propaganda organ to a pressure group. Chamberlain, in the face of the great activity of Liberal associations and the doubts about their disinterestedness, adapted the situation to suit plans of his own. He proposed frankly accepting the political side of the agitation but reorganizing Liberal associations according to the Birmingham model. Then they would be more representative and, one might hope, more convincing. Gladstone, on the other hand, apparently found confirmation for his distrust of organized, "mechanical" protest. He was grateful, however, to his supporters, particularly the working men, whose soundness seemed to have been vindicated again. Finally, although he saw benefit in his stand, he could hardly ignore the setback. He seems to have been determined in the future not to misjudge the time for action.

This sort of disunity is a perpetual problem for social movements. Quite likely, the Bulgarian agitation would have fizzled away, probably leaving the Eastern Question Association behind it,[4] had it not been reenergized by outside events. During most of 1877, the British were not faced with a need for action. It is true that almost as soon as the Russian army crossed the Danube, the British sent their fleet to Besika Bay, and upon Disraeli's initiative, the cabinet discussed plans to declare war if the Russians occupied Constantinople. Contrary to expectation, however, the decades-long Ottoman effort to build up their military forces enabled them to hold the Russians at bay. The Ottoman army in the Balkans was almost as large as the Russian; furthermore, in the aftermath of the Crimean War, the Ottomans still controlled the Black Sea. Ottoman weaponry was inferior, but their training was better. Finally, the Russian medical and supply services were atrocious. During the autumn, three Russian defeats before Pleven (Plevna) shocked observers and demonstrated that the invaders would have to work hard to win. Totleben, the great Russian siege engineer who had crafted the defenses of Sevastopol during the Crimean War, was brought to the front and recommended a blockade, rather than more attempts at assault. As the war stretched out, things looked so bad within Russia that many feared revolution.

Everything changed when the city surrendered on December 10. The Ottomans withdrew. The Russians streamed through the Shipka Pass and began their advance toward Constantinople itself.[5] Although the moral dilemma continued to trouble many Britons, Russian victories now added other, practical dimensions. The overriding concern was whether the Disraeli government would, or should, seize a material guarantee, threaten, or even declare war on Russia. And the political choice between peace and war was generally assumed to have important economic implications. The memory of the Crimean War, when Gladstone had tried, not wholly successfully, to finance Britain's military contribution without loans, was painfully fresh; it had been a time of higher taxes, business stagnation, and hardship for many members of the middle classes as well as many artisans. This precedent was not encouraging twenty-five years later, when the economy was already in the grip of a severe downturn. Yet fear of war was hardly unanimous either in business or in working-class circles. Those workers who held jobs in defense industries, such as the armor-plate factories near Sheffield or the Woolwich Arsenal in London, might gain by war and tended to be the more easily convinced of its necessity. And unskilled urban youths, who saw the army as the employer of last resort, might agree.[6]

Notwithstanding the new immediacy of the issues, the protest meetings held in 1878 resemble the agitation in 1876 and 1877 in many important respects. There was substantial overlap in leadership. Gladstone continued to be the symbol, hero, and reluctant deity of the agitators. Much of the organization behind the scenes was again handled by Mundella and Chamberlain. Stead communicated regularly with Gladstone and Chamberlain and continued to write polemics. To some extent, though, he was sidelined by the shift from propaganda to organization, a development with which he was profoundly out of sympathy,[7] and which required talents he lacked. Some leaders (for example, Henry Broadhurst, Thomas Mottershead, and J. J. Merriman) picked up where they had left off. But especially among London working men, more extreme leaders now took a larger part. Auberon Herbert and Charles Bradlaugh, two among many in 1876, played critical roles in 1878. As in 1877, Nonconformist stalwarts like Samuel Morley and Newman Hall were extraordinarily influential. But now that the issue was political as well as moral, High Churchmen and Methodists were somewhat less ready to speak out in public meetings.[8]

During the autumn of 1877, the debate about how to organize the protest intensified. Mundella apparently itched for another meeting along the lines of his triumph at St. James's Hall the preceding December, but he did not get much encouragement. Gladstone was frankly puzzled. "Last year," he wrote Mundella, "we knew exactly what we were about." Now the situation was different. "I do not altogether see my way," he admitted. Now it was difficult to isolate an issue or an accusation which might provide a suitable rallying cry for a major meeting. Gladstone did not rule out such a gathering, or even his appearance at one, but only, he said, if "I can be useful."[9] As Mundella persisted, Gladstone became firmer, warning that a meeting in 1877 would not be as successful as the one in 1876, and suggesting that instead Mundella keep in touch with "the leaders of the Nonconformists and the Birmingham men with a view to united action when the time comes."[10]

As Gladstone realized, events, not the protesters' plans, would set the schedule. Russian successes provoked a series of heated cabinet meetings, during which Britain's options were anxiously debated. The final decision, a summons to Parliament to meet early, on January 17, was announced on December 19; but the public was not informed just what the ministers' purpose might be.[11] Gladstone, "isolated" at Hawarden, was prepared to believe the worst, and, as he now wrote Mundella, "I am by no means certain that we ought to wait." The first instrument that came to mind was the Eastern Question Association. "I should think [he wrote] that the first thing for you to do at the Association will be to communicate with the Centres, or what may be called such—Such as the heads of the Nonconformists—the managers at Birmingham—and possibly the association lately formed in Scotland to look after elections; asking of them not an offhand opinion but a report on the feeling with which this intelligence has been received, and on the feeling as to war."[12]

Such a call merely for information was perhaps not very daring; but Gladstone had been burned before by premature activity. A few days later, he wrote Mundella again, backing away from the idea of a "deputation from *us*" and suggesting instead that a "deputation from Chambers of Commerce or other non-political bodies might be useful."[13]

Gladstone's instinct not to protest through normal political channels had been confirmed by the accusations of manipulation levied in 1877. It also derived from the fear that if the question became a party matter, the Conservatives would oppose as a block.[14] He had already written a long letter to Schnadhorst, Chamberlain's factotum, in which he emphasized the importance of a relatively nonpartisan approach, which would permit "the more rational Conservatives" to make common cause with the protesters.[15] It was not a foolish hope. Derby, tormented by doubt to the point of resignation, later admitted to Disraeli that "the question now dividing the whole political world is one which cuts across the existing divisions of parties, so that men who have always voted cordially together find themselves separated. It was the same in the Crimean time, as we both recollect."[16]

Chamberlain saw matters differently. He believed that there was a stiff price to be paid for such high-minded attempts at consensus, and he was bewildered that anyone should think of paying it. "Quite ready . . . for agitation," he was galvanized by a letter from Mundella on December 22.[17] But he could not fathom the attitude of Gladstone and Bright. "They agree in attaching great importance to demonstration by bodies not strictly political, and seem *almost* to deprecate a purely political agitation. I think this is a mistake. We cannot agitate except politically and the majority of the Tories will be against us no matter what we do." Although Chamberlain duly alerted a variety of groups including the local Chamber of Commerce, the expedient he preferred was an appeal to the Liberal associations belonging to his Federation.[18] It was a straightforward reaction, typically realistic, but from a certain point of view insensitive. Gladstone was not the only one to find it repugnant. Stead too objected: "the machinery should be felt not seen."[19]

What was at issue was the "direction" which the agitation, as a social movement, ought to take, what "particular strategies and tactics" should be adopted, and which leaders, as result, would have a critical role to play. Chamberlain, convinced by his experiences with the National Education League of the limitations of single-issue politics, wanted to take advantage of the excitement generated by the Eastern crisis to develop his National Federation of Liberal Associations to the point where it could "influence existing parties" on a broad range of issues.[20] Incidentally, Chamberlain expected that the Federation would advance his own career, just as Mundella tied his fortunes to the Association, and Stead took heart from his position as "editor of the best little paper in Europe."[21] The summons to Parliament simply intensified the inevitable disagreements over method.

Mundella believed that the summons might be just the call to activity that Gladstone had advised him to await. He too thought immediately of activating the Eastern Question Association. As William Morris warned his wife Janey in high excitement: "I am likely to be very busy for the next 3 weeks: public matters pressing . . . things seem most like the Jew wretch and *that* old Vic forcing us into the war . . . So we are all alive at the E.Q.A. I am so bothered by it all that I can do little else."[22]

Mundella, politically more experienced, was more cautious.[23] His hesitation was not misplaced. As Morris soon lamented, "many people are sluggish and hard to move," although "serious business men & the like do shudder back from war, even those who are Turkophile [sic]." For the moment, the committee limited itself to "issuing a manifesto and asking people to stir." The decision disappointed Morris, who evidently wanted the Association to organize its own demonstrations. Still, as Morris revealed, there was hope that "we shall arrange to have a big meeting before Parliament."[24]

Meanwhile in London, particularly in working-class neighborhoods, lines were already being drawn. A patriotic meeting organized by Maltman Barry for December 23 on Clerkenwell Green "to talk war turned all the other way by good management;"[25] but a larger meeting, planned for Trafalgar Square on December 29, soured. Free fights broke out, the police intervened, and several people were arrested, evidently all protesters.[26] In the end, the government supporters had the best of it; they celebrated victory with a procession to the Turkish Embassy and sent a series of resolutions to Disraeli, in which they denounced "the desperate and carefully planned attempt of Russian agents to break up the meeting."[27]

Meanwhile, Mundella tried again to interest Gladstone in a national demonstration. "Suppose we convene a great Northern gathering of Liberal Associations and M.P.s at Sheffield," he proposed, "would you come and make us a speech before the meeting of Parliament?" Anticipating the probable objections, he emphasized that they would not simply try to replicate the St. James's Hall meeting; in fact, (addressing another of Gladstone's previous anxieties) this "Provincial demonstration would vastly exceed it in numbers and enthusiasm."[28]

Mundella was deeply in earnest with this overture, but Gladstone did not agree. Although he recognized that the time might be ripe for "others" to act, he judged that he should not move "till there is warlike indication from [the] Government."[29] He had allowed his moral indignation to betray him into hasty action in 1877; he would not make that mistake again. But as Mundella admitted, Gladstone had become central; he pleaded, "the country is moving, its instincts are sound, but it has been so accustomed to take its tone from you on this question that your signal is needed to make the response all it ought to be."[30]

Gladstone continued to refuse; the most explicit support his friends could tease out of him was the hint which Chamberlain, as authorized, published: "I hope that . . . our friends at Birmingham . . . will . . . sleep with one eye open."[31] It was maddening, but not unwise. In 1877, independent initiatives by groups such as the Labour Representation League had been forthcoming and had proved more dynamic and more effective than the original unaided efforts of the Eastern Question Association. Gladstone's suggestive reticence left ample room for such activity to develop now.

And it did. As is typical in such situations, a variety of organized groups attempted to "move in to assume leadership."[32] Chamberlain's National Liberal Federation called for meetings; so did the National

Reform Union.[33] All the major peace organizations, Henry Richard's Peace Society, the International Arbitration Association, and the Workmen's Peace Association, issued circulars.[34] The National Agricultural Labourers' Union sent out an address to its sixty thousand members calling for neutrality; this followed an earlier spirited speech to the membership by Joseph Arch in which he warned Disraeli "that if he went to war he must not count on taking the agricultural labourers to be shot at for thirteen pence a day. They were determined that until they had obtained the franchise they would take no part in the wars of England."[35] And Samuel Morley, who had worked with J. J. Merriman and the City Neutrality Committee during 1876 until he apparently decided they were becoming too radical, formed his own Nonconformist Vigilance Committee meeting at Memorial Hall, Farringdon Street, on January 4. The gathering listened to Gladstone's letter, which seemed to favor public meetings, passed a strongly worded neutrality resolution, and sent copies of their resolutions to every Nonconformist congregation in Britain, as well as to the daily press and Nonconformist journals.[36]

This flurry of organizational activity was characteristic of the later, bureaucratic or routinized phase of mobilization. Even more than in 1877, the memorials and petitions reaching the Foreign Office and the House of Commons during the spring of 1878 originated with organized groups.[37] And the number was enormous—a total of 3,418 petitions between December 1877 and early August 1878. Although the vast majority favored the protest, for the first time significant opposition was put on paper; for example, 14 percent of the petitions reaching the Foreign Office came from Conservative groups.[38]

Although the flow of petitions was pretty steady through the spring, there were three peak periods (see Figure 3). The greatest excitement surrounded the summons to Parliament and the government's almost immediate request for a vote of credit, the money to be used, if necessary, for military purposes. This period extended for seven weeks, from December 31, 1877, to February 17, 1878, and yielded 2,368 petitions. A second peak, of 668 petitions, occurred between April 1 and 21 and was stimulated by events surrounding the call-up of the reserves. And an echo (189 petitions) was heard between May 5 and May 26 in response to the dispatch of Indian troops to Malta.

The geographical distribution resembled earlier patterns (see Figure 4). However, the proportion of petitions from the Midlands, which had previously trailed the percentage from the North, now caught up according to most measures. As before, virtually none came from

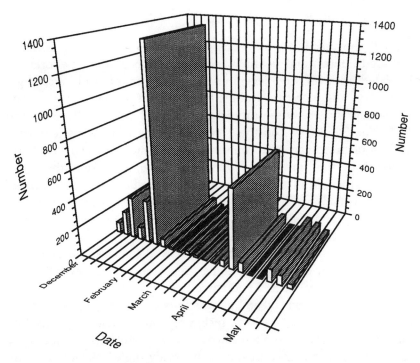

Figure 3. Petitions by the week, Parliament and Foreign Office, December 31, 1877, to May 19, 1878. Weeks are calculated from Mondays.

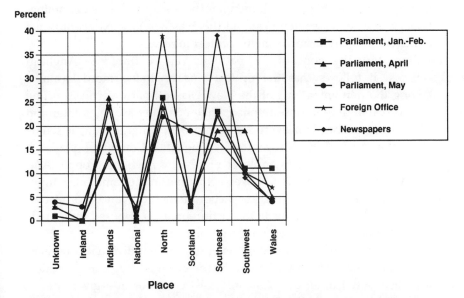

Figure 4. Geographical sources of petitions and meetings, 1878. Newspapers for 1877–1878 cover the period December 15, 1877 to March 15, 1878.

Catholic Ireland; but Wales, possibly because of the Peace Society's renewed interest and possibly because of Nonconformist efforts, re-bounded from 1877 to a level initially greater, in terms of percentage, than 1876. Although this strong interest did not seem to be maintained in the later stages, Welsh protesters remained more involved than in 1877. The Southwest, on the other hand, one of the most energetic centers of protest in 1876, only assumed a major position in April, although by that time Nonconformist outrage, apparently the motor of protest there in 1876, was beginning to dwindle. The biggest change came in Scotland, which previously had shown relatively little interest but in May suddenly accounted for 19 percent of the documents, scarcely less than the Midlands.

While the geography of the protest showed some essential continu-ity, the types of groups sponsoring the action shifted dramatically.[39] In 1876, the typical appeal had come from a public meeting. In 1877, communications from Liberal associations outstripped general meet-ings. In 1878, public meetings, including some initially organized by Liberal associations, were too rowdy for many protesters' tastes. They still took place, but many people apparently preferred more discreet methods.

Overwhelming numbers of petitions (68 percent of the petitions to Parliament in January and February 1878, for example) came from reli-gious groups (see Figure 5). Sometimes these might be local denomina-tional associations; sometimes (and this was new) the Nonconformist ministers in a city or town might protest jointly.

Since virtually none of the petitions can be traced to Anglican sources, it follows that the protest was becoming more localized among the denominations of the New Dissent: narrower in its scope but correspondingly more intense. Given Samuel Morley's intention of communicating with every Nonconformist congregation, it seems likely that he and his Nonconformist Vigilance Committee played a key part in setting the example of protest by religious groups. And the evidence of cooperation between churches in the same community is another significant feature. Local coordination of Nonconformist ef-forts could be the prerequisite for institutional, as opposed to individ-ual, grassroots influence on national politics.

Most often, however, the petitions came from individual congrega-tions. In some instances (Plymouth, for example) the same petition was distributed to all the Nonconformist churches in a given area.[40] (Although only a few such petitions list occupations of the signers, where they do appear they seem to indicate working-class origins.[41] This may, however, be a flawed sample.) The various denominations all participated, to differing extents. Primitive Methodists were not extraordinarily active. Indeed, the Methodists' role, which had declined sharply in 1877 when compared with Baptists and Congregationalists, remained low relative to their population share. Participation by Baptists, strong throughout the earlier stages, declined sharply in May (see Figure 6).

The declining role of public meetings is remarkable. In 1876, 70 percent of the Foreign Office petitions came from public meetings. In January and February 1878, that figure fell dramatically. As a result of the public's reaction to the rowdyism infecting that series of meetings, by April 1878 public meetings produced only 1 percent of the petitions. A slight recovery in May did not bring the meetings to anything like

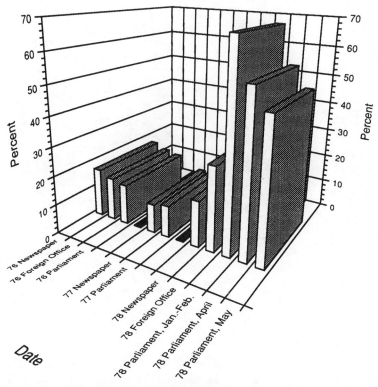

Figure 5. Petitions from religious bodies, 1876–May 1878.

their 1876 predominance; they still issued only 13 percent of the petitions (see Figure 7). The role of Liberal associations was also minimal, in spite of Chamberlain's appeal, and especially compared with their central role in 1877 (see Figure 8).[42]

Yet though public meetings were not held as widely, the numbers involved in each meeting were evidently much larger. Of course records of attendance were only guesswork, yet there seems no question that huge numbers turned out, far surpassing the crowds in 1876 and 1877. In 1876, few meetings other than the gathering to hear Gladstone at Blackheath claimed to have reached the low thousands. In 1878, many were said to have done so—2,000 at Leeds, 3,000 at Sheffield, and 3–4,000 at Bradford, to cite a few.[43] Meetings in London, even local ones, were large as well; during these weeks, 2,000 often gathered on Clerkenwell Green on a Sunday,[44] while Rev. G. M. Murphy, who

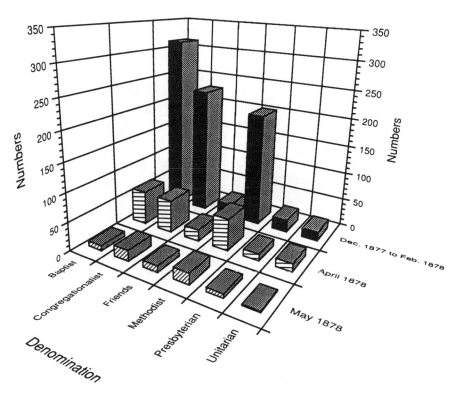

Figure 6. Petitions to Parliament by religious denomination, December 1877–May 1878.

held regular "Saturday night newspaper readings" in Lambeth, also attracted a couple of thousand at the height of the crisis.[45] And large numbers signed petitions; 124,657 people eventually signed one or another of the petitions against the vote of credit.[46]

The larger meetings were swelled by opposition. While 10,000–12,000 were meeting at Manchester for neutrality, 20,000–28,000 were meeting in another part of town to support the government.[47] The biggest meetings of all were the riotous confrontations in London; the crowd in Hyde Park on February 24 was estimated at anywhere from 60,000–70,000 up to 500,000.[48] Such figures defy credibility; even the smaller numbers are not likely to approximate the truth unless one assumes that bystanders were counted as participants. But even guesses tell us something. In giving such estimates, the journalists were saying that the Bulgarian protesters, once an annoying but rela-

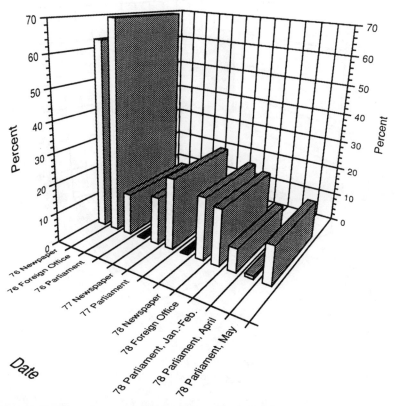

Figure 7. Petitions from public meetings, 1876–May 1878.

tively isolated group on the fringe, had now burst into the mainstream, as the international system grew more tense and the issue changed from a point of morality to fear of war.

Although it is risky to guess about the composition of crowds, it seems impossible that these numbers could have been attained without significant working-class involvement. Indeed in London the biggest meetings were the outcome of careful planning and participation by working-class neighborhoods. The Foreign Office petitions, the only petitions which were preserved in toto and so permit judgments based on handwriting and grammar, substantiate this impression of working-class activity.[49] A similar pattern of big meetings, presumably also with heavy working-class participation, can be traced in other large urban centers such as Manchester.

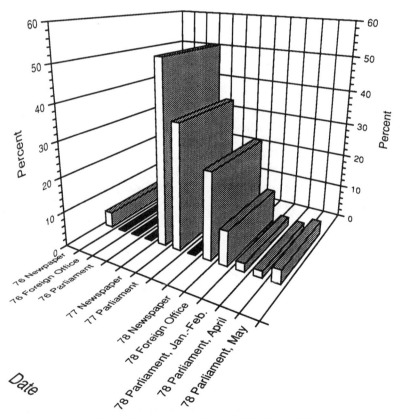

Figure 8. Petitions from Liberal associations, 1876–May 1878.

Also noteworthy is the role of agricultural laborers. To some extent, this was the result of skillful manipulation by Joseph Arch, the president of the National Agricultural Labourers' Union. Although Arch had organized meetings in 1876, beginning as early as July, and the union as a whole had petitioned,[50] it was only in 1878 that petitions from local groups of agricultural laborers began to appear in significant numbers. In West Kent, where the local branch of Arch's union boasted a printing press and a compositor,[51] petitions were printed up and distributed with an accompanying note giving instructions to sign the protest and "to take it round from house to house" throughout the village. In one instance, nineteen laborers, three bricklayers, one gardener, one wheeler, one blacksmith, one painter, and one postman signed.[52] In several instances, laborers' wives signed. Once the signatures were obtained, the organizers were requested to post the documents to a central address in Bromley, Kent, for transmission to Gladstone before the opening of Parliament.[53]

The Kent petitions represent one extreme of organization. Other working-class petitions were much simpler. Some, though less technically sophisticated than the ones from West Kent, do use common words, suggesting the activity of a single organizer.[54] Others were almost illiterate, and the absence of date, or, in some cases, even of place, indicates unfamiliarity with ordinary requirements of correspondence. Twelve laborers signed the following poignant request, which, from similarities in form and expression, may be attributed to agricultural laborers: "My Lord Dearby As Working Men we earnestly entreat your Lordships to use your utmost influence in favour of Neutrality and against any increased Expenditure on our armaments in the Horabl Ware betwen Russia & Turke."[55]

The diversity of the mature movement, reflected in the variety of petitions, was also mirrored by the variety of meetings. In 1876, a standardized pattern of mobilization, drawing heavily on radical tradition, developed quickly and was repeated time after time. In 1878, there was greater variety because so many different types of organization were involved. In some instances, such as a meeting of the Bristol Chamber of Commerce at the end of 1877, the "protest" was sandwiched in with other business and one may doubt whether more than one or two of the "protesters" knew in advance what was planned.[56] Or the discussion might form a more or less arresting part of an M.P.'s routine meeting with his constituents, in which case representations presumably were made on the spot and no petition was sent. When the matter came before a denominational meeting or a trade society, it was colored by the normal procedures of that body. The National Agricultural Labourers' Union drew up its petition to the Queen during its annual meeting at Wellesbourne in Warwickshire "under the celebrated chestnut tree, which was hung with lanterns for the occasion." The scene, as was usual with the Agricultural Labourers' meetings, purposely replicated the night when the Union had been formed.[57] In London, much of the business was transacted at the normal weekly meetings of working men's clubs. These were often lively debates, shaped by Positivist, secularist traditions, and informed by the voracious curiosity and hard-bitten skepticism of largely self-educated artisans. Other London meetings were sponsored by religious authorities or groups. Rev. G. M. Murphy's newspaper readings in Lambeth were paralleled by Rev. Newman Hall's Monday night culture meetings in Southwark; both provided a forum for discussion of the crisis.[58] A contrasting religious ambiance was offered by the Mission Preaching Tent at Mile End in Tower Hamlets, a local landmark which held about two thousand people and had been completed just a few years before, mainly with money donated by Samuel Morley.[59] Lectures were sometimes laid on, with varying degrees of success. Thomas Hughes made the circuit on behalf of the Eastern Question Association, but he was reportedly not a good speaker; when Newman Hall brought him to one of his Monday nights, the audience consisted mostly of women who had stayed around after a New Year's prayer meeting,[60] perhaps delaying the inevitable return home. Other talks were more stirring, like Annie Besant's Sunday morning address at the Hall of Science under the auspices of the National Secular Society.[61] Besant always drew a good crowd because she was surrounded by scandal—she was a clergyman's wife and accomplished speaker, to many a charlatan, and in 1876–77, the defendant with Charles Bradlaugh in a famous trial involving the dissemination of information about contraception.[62]

Despite all this variety, most of the meetings followed patterns familiar from 1876. The principal business was to pass resolutions which in one way or another favored neutrality. Resolutions usually instructed the parliamentary members to vote no to the vote of credit. As the crisis developed, some groups took more extreme steps. They might resolve that no money should be provided until the country had had a chance to render judgment on the government's policy through a general election. Resolutions expressing no confidence in the government were common. In Peckham, the local branch of the Workmen's Peace Association resolved that if Disraeli continued on his present course, he "should immediately be impeached on the charge of high treason."[63] Outright obstructionism was the last resort. Stead reported to Gladstone that there were plans in the North to set up an Anti–War Tax League, so that "the money if voted will only be collected by force."[64] Such a tactic was similar to Arch's warning that the agricultural laborers would resist conscription.[65] These extreme threats were the exception, not the rule, but they suggest that as the protest became larger and more eclectic, it also became uglier.

In many respects the protest in January and February 1878 followed and improved upon the example of 1877. The object, as before, was to create support out-of-doors for whatever positions Gladstone and the other parliamentary leaders might choose to adopt indoors, centering around the general stand for neutrality. Mindful of the tricky nature of the issues, which had betrayed him in 1877, Gladstone himself held back. Perceptive, perhaps overanxious, about the danger that a too neatly organized protest might forfeit credibility, he allowed a multifaceted, decentralized, loosely coordinated style to develop. Gladstone and his associates were gaining an instinct for this sort of operation, although they undoubtedly would not have been able to express in coherent form exactly all that they had learned, and they would not have agreed if they had tried. Certainly though, the protest in 1878 was more skillfully mounted, more intense, and therefore more likely to make a difference. And that relative success brought problems. Factionalism and marginality had been the hazards in 1876; timing and coordination had been the challenges in 1877. Now the issue was violence.

Up until the second week in January, opposition to the protest had been negligible. But from that time forward, the agitators faced a countermovement, soon nicknamed Jingoism, which by early February threatened to overwhelm the meetings in a series of hostile outbursts. Jingoism was itself an example of collective behavior. It developed out of the structurally conducive situation furnished by the war itself, by the sense that Britain had not played a role in the crisis commensurate with her true international importance, and by the very strong suspicion that Britain had actually lost ground—possibly permanently—by this failure.[66] Reinforcing these generally conducive conditions was the instinctive British conception concerning what the country was, or ought to be about, as it was propagated in music halls and popular songs. The bluff, hearty Englishman, proud of his national identity, protective of the underdog, ready to fight without asking too many questions when pushed around by a would-be foreign bully—this was the stock character which most Britons believed they resembled, or ought at least to approximate.[67] This offhand, easy masculinity, careless of hurt to itself, caring about harm to others, seemed to be subverted by the anxious, overzealous, overconciliatory, emotional makeup of the protesters. A sense of strain emerged when the cabinet called Parliament to meet early and then asked for a vote of credit. In effect, the leaders were telling the country that not enough had been done; and rather than accepting the implied reprimand and making amends, Gladstone and other protesters had the effrontery to argue, to question, and to continue to meet. Yet nothing was, or could be done about it. The agitators were free to propagate the lie that their dangerous views were the convictions of the British people.

The beliefs of the counteragitation crystallized rather quickly in midJanuary. Since 1876, several tenets of opposition to the protest had emerged, but had met with little popular acceptance. Early responses focused in one way or another on the Russian danger. The radical Manhood Suffrage League and Maltman Barry had suggested that British policy must at all costs avoid strengthening the authoritarian Russian regime by allowing it to increase its power in the Balkans. Only when the revolution had occurred in Russia would it be feasible to deal with lesser villains like the Ottomans.[68] Another attack emphasized humanitarian grounds. Turkish atrocities against Bulgarians were replaced by Russian atrocities against Turks. The form of the accusations, replicating the categories already established by the Bulgarian agitators, lent plausibility to specific charges.[69] Strategic grounds, though, afforded the most telling argument against Russia. To alarmists, it seemed all too probable that the Russians might use their recently enhanced position in Central Asia to intrigue among disaffected Indians, perhaps in collaboration with the Afghans.[70] This was the aspect of the crisis that most worried M.P.s, but it did not prove to be the stuff of which hostile outbursts are made.[71] In such episodes, "the participants . . . must be bent on attacking someone considered responsible for a disturbing state of affairs."[72] The obvious villain was Gladstone.

On January 10, Algernon Borthwick of the *Morning Post* addressed a meeting in St. James's Hall on the familiar theme of the danger to

India.[73] At the end, the Duke of Sutherland, who had presided, called for a vote of thanks. His words, probably unrehearsed, were certainly inflammatory.

[He] said he had met Russian agents in this country, in India, in Egypt, and in all parts of the world, and, if he might make a vulgar comparison, their mode of procedure was like that of a snake, which licked its victim all over before he swallowed it. The agents chosen in this country were Mr. Gladstone and General Ignatieff; and when he mentioned Mr. Gladstone of course he included a couple of dukes, a marquis, an officer of the army, and a number of clergymen who travelled about apparently with their eyes in their pockets.[74]

Some people laughed at Sutherland's venom, but as highly placed individuals seemed to create a climate in which scapegoating was condoned,[75] others let fly their rage and resentment. A cigar merchant in London wrote to Gladstone: "I consider you, an infernal traitor to your country, & shall be pleased to attend your funeral . . . P.S. These sentiments are endorsed by all my customers, & they tell me, they believe you are in Russian pay."[76]

Gladstone had received hate mail from time to time, but now there was an outpouring. "A Conservative who. will. fight. for. his. country" wrote from Manchester:

Now. you. liberal. devil

I. just. send. you. this. for. a. warning.
If. ever. you. come. to. Manchester or. Sheffield. you. will. never go. anywhere. again. For I. and three.more. have. £25– each for your life. or. as. much. as. we. can. take. of. it.
The. sicnature. below. is. the. gentlemans. that. wants. your. bones. andthe one. who. will. get. them. you. devil.

JMS

The. bordering. round. is. far. your.deth. Excuse.me. but. your days. are. short.[77]

In blaming Gladstone, the Jingoes had found a simple, dramatic belief that spoke directly to the confusion, fear, and inarticulate resentment of their recruits. Russophobia, in one guise or another, might provide intellectual justification for opposing the agitation; but it was a visceral hatred of Gladstone's pious pacifism and supposed lack of manhood that fueled the hostile outbursts. It was Gladstone, "not the Czar, who was burned in effigy."[78]

Mobilization of the Jingoes was quick and required little coordination, once events abroad and specific protest meetings at home provided precipitating factors. The movement both attracted existing fringe organizations and spawned new ones.[79] As Gladstone had feared, many Conservatives reacted against the agitation along strictly party lines. This was particularly marked after Gladstone's "violent attack" on Disraeli on January 30, but it had been foreshadowed at a meeting of Conservative agents on January 28 when the decision was taken not to restrain zealots.[80] A second group was composed of individuals who had something at stake in the Eastern Question: "armament workers, unemployed army officers, and bondholders," many prominent City financiers, and their clerks.[81] Just as the original protest attracted hangers-on of all sorts, so Jingoism pulled in a variety of marginal enterprises and stimulated the formation of ephemeral patriotic leagues and societies. The Manhood Suffrage League ceased to participate after the death of its president, John Rogers, in May 1877; but its secretary, Maltman Barry, continued to be active through the most important new group, the National Society for the Resistance of Russian Aggression and the Protection of British Interests in the East, formed in August 1877. Lord Strathenden and Campbell, who had been an avid follower of David Urquhart, was the chairman. Existing organizations which moved in included the various societies devoted to the cause of the Tichborne claimant, "the Wapping butcher who claimed to be the heir to the Tichborne estates." The connection to the counteragitation is not very clear; perhaps it was simply that these groups, rather like the earlier Urquhartite foreign affairs committees, were infused with a "backward-looking . . . nationalism of the free-born Englishman." Equally cranky were the Fair Traders and their leader, Lieutenant R. H. Armit, who argued that free trade was undermining the British economy; in this and in other questions "a more nationalist and British policy" would help the working classes.[82] In contrast to the Manhood Suffrage League, which moved in briefly from the extreme left, the Fair Traders occupied a niche on the extreme right. In the 1880s, they competed with the Socialists for working-class loyalties and were involved on February 6, 1886, in the Pall Mall Affair, a riot in which they opposed the Socialists much as they had earlier opposed the agitators.[83] Last but not least, there was a casual element spoiling for a fight. Possibly these motives stirred the medical students.[84] They were joined by others, less educated, who could be alarmed, or stirred up, or bought, or who simply joined in for the fun of it.

Particularly at the end of January and during the first part of February, the Jingoes broke up protest meetings and mounted their own. Newspaper reports give some sense of the patterns.[85] To be sure, the vast majority of meetings apparently unrolled with no opposition whatsoever, or with very minor opposition. This included not only protest meetings, but also the progovernment Conservative gatherings, which were often organized around a Conservative Association meeting or a meeting with a Conservative member of Parliament. In about 5 percent of the cases, however, there was a major disturbance, taking the form either of an organized effort to break up a meeting, or of a rival assemblage which might or might not pass over to the attack. Clearly, the most vulnerable were large urban meetings out-of-doors, but public meetings held indoors could be disrupted as well, if a few determined people gained admittance. All the halls available had limited seating. It was not too difficult to find out when a meeting would be held and then get the partisans out. If these opponents came in advance, they could grab enough seats to overwhelm the proceedings. They might even be instructed to come at an hour earlier than the time set for the meeting,[86] so as to be sure to get seats. The obvious remedy was to admit by ticket only, a practice rather generally followed. It did not solve all problems. Tickets might be forged or might fall into the "wrong" hands.[87] It was difficult to turn people away if the room was not full.[88] Ultimately, for big meetings where trouble was expected, it might be a matter of stationing key individuals at the entrance and letting them use their best judgment. At one large meeting in London, "Henry Broadhurst was in charge of a party of stewards at the doors, 'all acquainted with the features of the leaders of the Jingo mob,' and [he] personally threw one suspect on the floor."[89]

Once the meeting started, the dissidents might simply offer amendments or they might take the low road of disruption and intimidation. Many individuals on either side showed up with "props": banners or flags, especially the British and the Turkish, and signs or placards, with messages such as "Vote for Gladstone," "Vote for Bright," "Down with the traitor Gladstone."[90] As the meeting wore on, these items became prime targets for attack, especially at outdoor meetings, where fist fights generally ensued. At a slightly more intellectual level, both sides usually prepared handbills which could be given out at the meeting or tossed to the crowd from the platform and which could comunicate the salient points if the speaker were hooted down.[91] Even inside, scuffles and fights were accompanied by hisses, groans, and catcalls, and could become brutal. Sometimes the interruptions were orchestrated and either side might be "guilty". At the Cremorne Gardens meeting, arranged by the Conservatives, some members of the Eleusis Club, a local Radical working men's organization, apparently managed to get up on the platform and signaled their followers in the crowd below when to drown out the speaker.[92] But much of the noise, including the ubiquitous singing,[93] was spontaneous.

Such scenes, repeated to a greater or lesser degree in many London working-class districts and around the country,[94] show the gratuitous brutality that was still very much a part of British political life. What shocked was that this violence was associated with an agitation; had it been part of an election campaign, no one would have been astonished.[95] Disruption came in two forms. A meeting called by one side might actually be broken up by the other, or meetings called simultaneously might compete.[96] Naturally, whatever form violence took, things were worst at meetings held largely or wholly outdoors. In Manchester on January 30, the Liberal Association sponsored an anti-war meeting indoors at the Free Trade Hall. At the same time, a Jingo group met outdoors in Albert Square, and after passing resolutions in support of government policy, set out in quest of their anti-war opponents. "Prevented by an extra detachment of police from breaking into the hall, they smashed the boards containing the placards announcing the meeting, and hooted and hustled the audience as it dispersed." They ended the evening by roaming around the city, groaning outside the Reform Club, cheering outside the Conservative and the Junior Conservative Clubs, singing rousing choruses as they went.[97] A similar pair of meetings in Exeter led to considerably more trouble because the police were not so quick. The protesters, meeting at the Reform Club to pass resolutions against the vote of credit, were "blocked in" by the Jingoes "till the police came to their rescue."[98]

Later meetings in Manchester continued this pattern of confrontation, but were competitive rather than violent. On Saturday afternoon, February 2, a Jingo group met in Pomona Gardens, where they burned Gladstone in effigy as "England's traitor." Meanwhile, the protesters gathered in Stevenson Square. It was feared that the two groups might fight it out, but they did not, although for most of the evening, gangs wandered through the streets singing.[99] Apparently the point, here and at the parallel meetings a week later on February 9,[100] was to see which side could get out the most people. In a sense, these gatherings became, in Cunningham's words, "almost ritual trials of strength in localities where politics was a prolonged duel, and a striking victory something to be treasured over the years." It is noteworthy that whereas episodes of disruption usually appear to have been organized by a few determined individuals, who may then have been joined by a greater or lesser number of bystanders, outside London such competitive incidents seem always to have depended ultimately on party organizations. Quite possibly, as Cunningham believes, these confrontations took on a life of their own, in which the contest was more about turf than it was about policy.[101]

A final observation to be made about Jingo activity is that it was extremely concentrated in time.[102] A modest spurt of activity during the two calendar weeks before Parliament's new session (January 5–18) was followed by a peak during the three weeks spanning the announcement of the vote of credit and its passage (January 26–February 15). But though limited in the scope of their operations, the Jingoes were wonderfully effective. During the most critical days, between January 31 and February 15, not a single public meeting was reported to have been held under quiet conditions. The protest could not continue without violence.

Violence was precisely what the agitators did not want. The notion that protest meetings were attended by rowdyism had plagued every movement out-of-doors since anti-slavery; and much of the elaborate organizational tradition was designed to prevent or at least minimize violence, while assuring maximum participation. For many Parliamentary leaders, abhorrence of disorder, thought to give free play to the baser passions, justified their distrust of consulting the masses. Jingo violence, then, struck to the roots of the protest; and finding solutions became, in 1878, a major concern of what was by now an effectively if loosely organized and directed movement.

The problems of violence facing big urban protest meetings were nowhere more significantly illustrated than in London. There crowds were the largest, brawls the most uproarious, and the need to confront tactical issues the most implacable. As before, mobilization in London was the work of different groups who still cooperated somewhat uneasily, with the Eastern Question Association functioning as coordinator rather than prime mover. The Association, at the end of December, had been discussing the advisability of a large gathering before Parliament convened. Then on December 31 a meeting of working men "representing the various clubs" and chaired by Thomas Mottershead began to make plans for a big meeting in Exeter Hall immediately before the opening of Parliament. "A permanent workmen's committee" was set up to arrange demonstrations in London for neutrality. "For this purpose the cooperation of all other organized bodies . . . [was] cordially invited."[103]

A second meeting of "delegates from the various workmen's clubs and other organizations of London," on January 2 at the Labour Representation League with F. W. Campion presiding and Henry Broadhurst acting as secretary, resolved to seek the help of the Eastern Question Association in organizing the projected Exeter Hall meeting.[104] As organizational meetings continued, Mottershead's neutrality committee circularized working men's clubs.[105] District meetings to organize participation were held in working-class areas throughout London such as Lambeth, Southwark, Hackney, Chelsea, Tower Hamlets, and Finsbury.[106] Economic concerns were prominent; the war policy "meant nothing short of desolate hearths and homes for the working classes."[107]

The result was a big neutrality meeting at Exeter Hall on the eve of the assembly of Parliament.[108] William Morris crowed, "the . . . meeting was magnificent: orderly and enthusiastic; though mind you, it took some very heavy work to keep the enemies roughs out; and the noise of them outside was like the sea roaring against a lighthouse."[109]

Parallel meetings of protesters and Jingoes were held outside by torchlight in Trafalgar Square and a brawl broke out when a group of Clerkenwell costermongers, headed by Mottershead, rushed the Jingo platform. Undaunted, the Jingoes marched off to see Musurus, the Ottoman ambassador, and then Disraeli. They were in luck; "the Premier, who was giving his full dress parliamentary dinner at the Foreign Office, was induced to appear, and thank the deputation."[110] It was a ceremonial passage; hardly any event could have been more effective in bonding the crowd to the prime minister as fellow actors in great events.[111]

Meanwhile, influential businessmen in the City had been working independently along similar lines. As in September 1876, working- and middle-class committees were organizing separate but virtually simultaneous protests. On January 1, a group of about sixty met under the leadership of J. J. Merriman. Merriman "deprecated agitation in the streets," but, noting the unusual situation, suggested that the group constitute itself a committee to organize a protest meeting in the Guildhall.[112]

Only a day or two later, the Earl of Carnarvon, the colonial secretary, arranged to speak on the Eastern crisis during a meeting about colonial policy.[113] When Carnarvon's widely reported remarks seemed to promise conciliation, the committee, more optimistic about cabinet intentions, thought better of a big demonstration. Instead they set up an executive committee to watch developments.[114] There were now three vigilance committees in permanent session: one for the working men of the clubs, one for the City, and a third organized by Samuel Morley for Nonconformist ministers, which, keeping its distance from the large London protest meetings, had been contacting Nonconformist congregations all over the country. Perhaps because of this show of feeling, the cabinet displayed moderation when Parliament met on January 17.[115] A conciliatory speech from the throne lulled apprehension. "The Agitation is over for the present I suppose," William Morris wrote Janey, and he gave much of the credit to "the last fortnight's agitation."[116] When the executive committee of the City group met on January 18, Merriman suggested that "no further action . . . [was] necessary." A disagreement developed with representatives of the Eastern Question Association who were present; the incident shows the different objectives of the two groups. William Morris called for continued "watchfulness" and pointed out that while the City Committee seemed to be concerned solely about neutrality, the Eastern Question Association had a broader agenda, that is, freedom for the eastern Mediterranean peoples. In a controversial compromise, it was decided to keep the City executive committee alive.[117]

It was no mistake, for the situation in the East worsened. The Russian armies pressed forward to Edirne (Adrianople), but the Porte continued to balk at accepting preliminary peace terms demanding a big, autonomous Bulgaria. Meanwhile, telegrams from St. Petersburg reinforced the Russian commander-in-chief's inclination to march on and enter the capital. Alarming news from Henry Layard, who had replaced Elliot as British ambassador in April 1877, sparked fears in the cabinet that the Russians were about to occupy Gallipoli and settle the status of the Straits unilaterally with the Turks. Afraid of being left behind by events, the cabinet, at a tumultuous meeting on January 23, decided to send the fleet to Constantinople and to proceed with the vote of credit. The measures were intended as warnings, rather than as first steps into war; but they were too much for Derby and Carnarvon, both of whom immediately resigned.[118] Rumors flew. Next day (January 24), the City executive committee agreed to "meet day by day" until further notice. They still hesitated to stage a demonstration, however.[119]

On January 25 Disraeli, since August Earl of Beaconsfield, outlined in the Lords the confusing events of the last few days. No sooner had the cabinet ordered the fleet to Constantinople to cope with what appeared to be a complete breakdown of "security for life and property," than word was received from Layard indicating that acceptable conditions of peace had been approved by the Sultan. The order to the fleet had accordingly been countermanded.[120] Nonetheless, as Northcote officially announced in the Commons, the Cabinet proposed to request a vote of credit to total £6,000,000. Questioned, Northcote admitted that this sum was intended for the current fiscal year, that is, for the next two months only.[121]

This peculiar position was not greatly clarified when Northcote introduced the question in the Commons on January 28. He outlined the frustrating series of communications from the East and admitted that during the last few weeks the English had had no firm idea of how far the Russians intended to go, or what kind of peace they sought. That sounded alarming. Then he explained that things seemed better at the moment; the vote of credit, though still necessary, was precautionary. Probably the money would never be spent. Its importance was political, not military; this was not a "Vote of Credit, but a Vote of Confidence."[122]

This speech, rife with contradiction, offered an easy target for the Liberals. If the government did not intend military measures, asked Bright, why request the money at all?[123] On the other hand, as Gladstone said, if under the guise of a supplementary appropriation the government were really seeking approval of their entire Eastern policy, the question became portentous; more time should be allowed to consider all the implications.[124] Whether Gladstone had thought of it or not, more time would allow for more expression of public opinion. William Beckett-Denison, member for East Retford, objected:

> A habit had grown up lately which, in his opinion, did not conduce to the dignity of the House . . . he alluded to the system of telegraphic wire pulling on questions on which the Members did not happen to be of one mind. . . . he now protested, and always should protest, against degrading the Members of the House into the position of delegates, and against a system of what he might call wired-up agitation on a subject of the most extreme gravity, for the purpose of bringing pressure to bear upon them . . . he objected to be ruled by the mobocracy.[125]

In fact, meetings were being held all over the country. The petitions and memorials which had showered upon Parliament and the Foreign Office earlier in January had let up momentarily but now resumed and would soon reach flood proportions—1,376 documents during the week of February 4.[126]

On January 29, after "grave and anxious consideration," the executive of the City Neutrality Committee decided to support the Liberals in Parliament by a public meeting at the Cannon Street Hotel on January 31.[127] Hopes that the City Liberal Club under Samuel Morley might participate were dashed when Morley preferred to continue his independent work with the Nonconformist Vigilance Committee.[128]

The Cannon Street Hotel meeting was unusually boisterous. An "immense crowd" of Jingoes gathered and moved into the hotel, packing stairways and halls, singing, making speeches, and holding up messages on big pieces of paper. Eventually, after they had broken some plate glass doors and engaged in free fights, the police were called and a strong force cleared the hotel.[129] William Morris, "very low & muddled about it all," was convinced the opposition had been carefully orchestrated: "They behaved very disgracefully . . . they had 400 roughs down in waggons from Woolich [sic] Dockyard, & generally played the gooseberry: people on our side had to hide away in cellars & places & get out anyhow: all of this is very enraging, & I am beginning to say, well if they will have war let them fill their bellies with it then!"[130]

The meeting continued outside and a crowd proceeded to the Guildhall, "guided by a gentleman who took his seat on the roof of a hansom cab, with his legs hanging over in front, who alternately waved his hat and a large placard" announcing where the group was going. In the new location, they were addressed, amid much tumult, by leading Conservatives such as the Lord Mayor and Edward Howley Palmer, a Governor of the Bank of England and a leading Turkish bondholder and speculator.[131] The resolutions eventually passed were delivered to the House of Commons and accepted by Lord John Manners, the Postmaster-General and one of Disraeli's closest associates. He thanked the group profusely and said that he "hoped and believed . . . the manifestation would be generally followed throughout the country."[132] Disraeli personally wrote the Lord Mayor next day to express his thanks. A copy of the letter was posted in public view on the side of the Mansion House until it was ripped off by a man who was then beaten up by onlookers and taken into custody by the police.[133]

Meanwhile, the debate on the vote of credit continued. An armistice between Russia and the Ottoman Porte had been announced by Musurus Pasha on February 1; but there were no details as to the terms and no explanation of why the Russian army continued to advance.[134] The uncertainty and the sense of impending danger put the Liberals on the defensive. Finally, Gladstone suggested that the vote of credit be adjourned; in return, Parliament would offer an address of support for the cabinet, which would receive bipartisan backing.[135] It was a clever move, far more astute than the compromise he had accepted in May 1877. On that occasion, his attempt to buy unity in Parliament inadvertently cut him adrift from the wave of meetings around the country. This time he tried to appear as a peacemaker in the House but did not abandon opposition to the vote of credit, a key demand of the agitators out-of-doors. However, his overture was not taken up, and the international situation disintegrated further.[136] On the afternoon of February 7, as William Morris entered the Strand, he found that the newspapers were announcing (mistakenly) that the Russians had reached Constantinople and Gallipoli.

Morris was thunderstruck; as he instantly recognized, "here was a spoke in our wheel!" The stock market crashed, and excited crowds roamed the streets. It was a classic panic. After a long buildup of tension, a "dramatic event" seemed to "confirm" the fears, an event which was at once "immediate," "uncontrollable," and "ambiguous" in its implications.[137] A band of about three thousand met in Trafalgar Square, heard speeches in favor of war, then, after missing Disraeli at Downing Street, went on, cheering and singing, to Parliament, where the police closed the gates of Palace Yard. Rumors flew about what was happening inside. Morris wrote his daughter, Jenny, "I heard that the confusion in the H. of Commons was beyond Everything; that was like a French revolutionary assembly . . . many people thought that war would be declared in a few hours." Although the situation was enormously exaggerated, anxiety helped the Conservatives win a procedural vote which served as a test of sentiment on the vote of credit.[138]

Next day things scarcely looked better. It was unclear where the Russian army actually was, but fears were rife that even if they were not yet in Constantinople, they might march in at any time. The cabinet determined to send up some ships from the fleet.[139] On February 9, a carefully organized Jingo meeting was held in Chelsea, in the "once popular," now rather dilapidated and lugubrious, amusement park, the Cremorne Gardens.[140] But even before this meeting, the House of Commons, on the evening of February 8, knowing the orders to the fleet, passed the vote of credit by a majority of 204.[141]

For the agitators, it was a major disappointment. Independent meetings of different protest groups, although large and well-timed, had
not impressed Parliament. As in 1876, the solution seemed to be to
organize a more inclusive demonstration uniting working men and
Liberals in the City, with Gladstone as speaker. Already, on February
2, the Workmen's Neutrality Committee had determined "to hold a
monster demonstration of all the trades and political clubs in the metropolis in favor of continued peace"[142] and to ask Gladstone to speak.
Unlike 1877, when he had distanced himself from the popular protest
by his compromise on the resolutions, Gladstone had held fast to the
principal demand of the protesters, and so was well placed to appeal
directly from the House to the country.

Morris was delegated to present the invitation to speak on behalf
of the Workmen's Neutrality Committee and the Eastern Question
Association. He recounted excitedly, "I went to Gladstone with some
of the workmen & Chesson, to talk about getting him to a meeting at
the Agricultural Hall: he agreed & was quite hot about it, and as brisk
as a bee: I went off strait [sic] to the Hall, & took it for tomorrow:
[February 21] to work we fell, & everything got rite [sic] into train."[143]

Obviously order would be problematic at such a meeting; but Gladstone and the working men were not deterred. Gladstone suggested
to Broadhurst that it might "disarm hostility" if the resolutions to be
proposed were published in advance. To this end, he sent Broadhurst
both a rough draft and later an emended series of resolutions, calling
for British neutrality "in the absence of any substantial and just cause
of war" and for efforts "to promote the interest of freedom" in the
Balkans in the "Xian Provs in & near" [sic] the Ottoman Empire.[144]

Specific measures to restrain troublemakers also engaged Gladstone's attention. He insisted that everyone must be *"seated"*; there
must be no general "admission"; and there must be an adequate number of "stewards" present to handle any disturbances. The working
men agreed.[145] Henry Broadhurst later revealed that arrangements had
been made to appoint special constables to keep order. Probably with
some exaggeration he claimed that the force would number fifteen
hundred from "three trade societies" and about the same number from
"the fourteen or fifteen political clubs," five hundred from the Greenwich Association and eight hundred from Southwark, with the rest,
up to five thousand, "made up by similar organized bodies of workmen." With such precautions, Broadhurst had no fears for the harmony of the occasion.[146]

Then, as these plans were still being made, the meeting was suddenly abandoned. Gladstone learned the decision at the House.[147] Though apparently surprised, he was probably secretly relieved; he had admitted to Granville that though he could not now get out of the meeting "by an act of shabbiness," he would be glad to be released from it in a way that would save face.[148] William Morris, astounded, was thoroughly disgusted; after hours spent in committee work, there would be no result. What had happened, he disclosed to Janey, was that "our parliamentarians began to quake."[149] Westminster and Shaftesbury, the titular heads of the Eastern Question Association, instructed Mundella on February 17 to insist that the Association drop the meeting in view of the rumors of violence.[150] The fact that the Eastern crisis seemed to be moderating on February 18 and 19 gave them a pretext.[151] But canceling was easier said than done: the meeting of the Eastern Question Association, according to Morris, was "stormy" and "full of wretched personalities" and the working men were "in a great rage about it,"[152] as Broadhurst made clear in a circular sent out next day.[153]

In the minutes of the Labour Representation League, of which he was secretary, Broadhurst never mentioned these complex maneuvers. Perhaps he regarded them as a shameful episode, a false start not worth recording alongside other, more successful, initiatives. Nonetheless, the working men's disgruntlement does not seem to have affected their relations with Gladstone. Whatever their real feelings, Broadhurst and his friends were on their best behavior when they called him from dinner to discuss "in much dismay but without any murmuring or ill temper the business of the withdrawal."[154] Gladstone was impressed. And probably the working men felt that it really had not been his fault. According to Morris, he "was quite ready to come up to the scratch & has behaved well throughout."[155]

The abandonment of the Agricultural Hall meeting was a major setback for the protest. The working men's efforts to preclude violence by careful advance planning had not reassured key upper-class leaders, and the protesters had yielded to intimidation. As in other protest movements, "in this atmosphere of disorganization following the successive failure of several lines of agitation, extreme militancy began to grow."[156] A working men's committee led by Auberon Herbert and Charles Bradlaugh had been busy for some time organizing an outdoor demonstration in Hyde Park. This Hyde Park Demonstration Committee, working out of the Southwark Radical Club and Auberon Herbert's home, met regularly to coordinate efforts by receiving "offers of personal assistance and subscriptions."[157] Once again, security measures were a major concern. On the evenings of February 21 and 22, rosettes and wands of office for two thousand marshals and deputy marshals were distributed by the committee to representatives of the working men's clubs. Instructions for the special constables were drawn up: "Gentlemen: Should our party be attacked you are requested not to interfere in any way unless a white flag is waved on the platform which will be a signal that your help is required. We shall be much obliged however if you will endeavour to repress as gently as possible any attempts to create a breach of the peace by throwing eggs or stones."[158] Efforts to get everything in order kept the committee busy "until a late hour."[159]

The meeting itself, the largest held during the Bulgarian agitation, numbered by some estimates sixty to seventy thousand. The Jingoes mounted a parallel meeting.[160] Both sides emphasized economic questions. One anti-war protester cried: "To the rich it would mean fewer bottles of champagne, to the poor it would mean short Saturday nights and meagre Sunday dinners."[161] Fair Traders among the counteragitators argued that the Russians had hurt British trade wherever possible and thus were responsible for economic distress in their own right; indeed, on this and many counts, the protesters were "the baffled agents of Russia." A melee ensued. Ultimately one group went on to Downing Street to be assured by Lord Barrington that Disraeli was "much gratified with the enthusiastic reception you have given him."[162] Another group went on to Gladstone's home where they broke windows, attacked the police, and indulged in petty theft. During the evening, Gladstone's street had to be cordoned off by the police.[163]

The Hyde Park meeting confirmed the fears of those Liberal leaders who believed that any mass meeting at this stage, however well organized in advance, would become a pitched battle. The two leaders associated with it, Auberon Herbert and Charles Bradlaugh, were widely viewed as extremists. Herbert, a daredevil and an adventurer who was never happier than when he was doing something outrageous in a good cause, tried to draw the moral that violence was inevitable but must be faced down in the interests of free speech.[164] But others, such as Henry Broadhurst, judged the Hyde Park meeting to have turned out badly.[165]

Undaunted, the extremists continued plans for another Hyde Park extravaganza.[166] Held on March 10, it was even rougher.[167] Warned by the experience of February 24, the police were also more in evidence. Major concern centered around Gladstone's home at Harley Street, where several men were posted. Despite this precaution, reinforcements had to be sent. They blocked off the area and settled things by "riding through the street gently pushing the crowds before them."[168] Gladstone and his wife, about to go out, were sufficiently jostled by the crowd that they decided to stop at a neighbor's house and eventually left in a hansom cab.[169]

In the aftermath of this March 10 meeting there could be no doubt that the strategy of open-air protest meetings was untenable unless the protesters were willing to accept a high level of disorder. Auberon Herbert and some of his friends were ready to go on; but when they attempted to organize a meeting for April 6, Herbert was allegedly warned by Scotland Yard that he would be held responsible for the consequences.[170] No meeting took place, but both the counteragitators and the police were prepared.[171] By now, Herbert's extremism had long since cost him the support of "the better class of trade unionists and working men."[172]

Middle-class leaders had turned away even from large meetings indoors in mid-February, when the Agricultural Hall meeting was canceled. By March, all but a few extremists agreed that meetings held under such conditions would not give credible results.

Rowdiness was the most serious problem facing the agitators in 1878. As early as the end of January, the worrisome question of how to respond occupied protest leaders. Insight into the rationale for a shift in methods can be gained from the debate after a rough meeting in Sheffield on January 29. Thirty thousand were said to have come out to an exceptionally noisy meeting at which the protesters were outnumbered and a progovernment amendment passed "nearly two to one."[173] The feeling among some, at least, of the Jingoes was vindictive and gleeful: "What do you think of that my hearty," one individual wrote Gladstone anonymously, enclosing the description in the *Standard*, copiously underlined.[174] Given Mundella's prominence in the agitation, this was a shocking reversal; indeed Chamberlain, no friend to Mundella, called it "the worst news I have had for a long time."[175]

In fact, the Liberals' hold on the Sheffield constituency was not as solid as it appeared. Some of the trouble could be laid to Conservative intrigue aimed at gaining a seat at the next election.[176] But whatever reasons can be adduced retrospectively, the Liberal collapse came as an almost total surprise. Some were inclined to pass it off as an aberration.[177] Mundella was too realistic to suppose that that was all. He confided to Leader: "H. J. W. writes me a letter which shows that organization and drink had much to do with our disaster, but I cannot think they were the sole causes of it. A meeting so large as that appears to have been must have had a good deal of the popular as well as the rowdy element in it."[178]

The question now was what to do. Auberon Herbert, breakfasting with Mundella in London the morning after, counseled that the most important thing was not to be intimidated. Holding another meeting as soon as possible would put the rowdies on notice "that nothing alters our fighting temper . . . that to lose one fight is only to enter on another."[179] Mundella was not so sure. He forwarded a letter to Leader from Herbert pleading the case directly, but he himself was prey to an unwonted indecision. "I say it would be a very good thing if it could be done," he admitted to Leader, "but I don't want to make things worse." Mustering only a thin attempt at pluck ("we must *keep heart*, and show a bold front"), he refused to take the responsibility, telling Leader, "As to the best steps to be taken I must leave this with you and other friends to devise."[180]

Perhaps Mundella, and other protest leaders as well, were not sufficiently bold. Undoubtedly Herbert felt so. The confrontations still did not involve more than a miniscule proportion of the population, nor were they violent, by modern standards. But there were sound reasons for considering other methods. Most protesters felt a deeply rooted distaste for brawling. This was emphatically true of Gladstone, and he shared the sentiment with most members of Parliament. It was also accepted by many working men, particularly the artisans to whom Gladstone especially appealed. It was self-control, they thought, which had made possible the achievements, moral and material, that differentiated them from ordinary laborers; and it was the same discipline which, they rightly believed, would give them a hearing with their betters.

There were also valid strategic arguments against big public meetings. Chamberlain astutely summed up the case some weeks later.

I do not see what possible action can be taken which would not be more likely to do harm than good. I do not think the Government desire war, though it is quite possible they may blunder into it; but any attempt on the part of a minority to protest against war would only call forth another outburst of rowdy patriotism by which the Government might be forced farther than their own intentions. I do not think it would be useful even if it were possible to hold public meetings.[181]

In addition to distrust of extremism, there were other reasons why the protest meetings seemed to taper off early in March. After a very tense period during mid-February, the Eastern crisis seemed momentarily to be receding, and the likelihood of British military involvement, never large in actuality, lessened for a time. The Russians and Ottomans signed a peace treaty at San Stefano on March 3; during the next two weeks, arrangements were made for ratification. Although the concessions exacted by the Russians were considered shockingly extensive, there was hope that they could be at least partially revised.[182] To this end, on March 7 Austria called for an international conference. But the members of the British cabinet continued to be deeply divided and in a long session on the same date argued bitterly, with no resolution, about Britain's course.[183] There had been much general discussion earlier of the need for a naval station which would position the British to safeguard their interests at the Straits and Suez and protect the routes to India.[184] Now such options were examined in the cabinet, and Disraeli, overlooking Derby's horrified opposition, believed that he had won assent. As a minimum, the British insisted that the entire treaty of San Stefano be laid before the conference for revision. This the Russians were not willing to concede, and as they stalled for time, briefly war again seemed imminent. The Tsar, furious with the British and under great pressure from the Panslavs, felt certain that hostilities were unavoidable and continued to bombard headquarters with instructions to go forward and seize the Bosporus. Believing (rightly) that the Russian army, if not the Tsar, was too exhausted to fight further, Disraeli decided to call the bluff. The cabinet meeting of March 27 accepted his "dangerous gamble" of "calling out the Reserves," to the number of "two *corps d'armée*," and ordering troops from India to the area. It was too much for Derby. After the meeting, he gave his resignation; this time there was no going back.[185]

Once again, the country was awash with rumors that war might be just hours away. But the strategy of big public meetings had been called into doubt, and many leaders, like William Morris, had had their fill of protest.[186] They needed a different approach, one which could preclude violence. In fact, most of the activities of the protesters

had gone unchallenged. Where meetings could be limited to an identifiable group whose members were known to each other, when a deputation could be arranged, or when a petition could be circulated within
a congregation or from house to house in a village or neighborhood,
problems did not arise. Just public meetings, widely announced and
only imperfectly limited by devices such as admission by ticket, had
proved vulnerable. The lesson must have seemed inescapable. As the
Peace Society counseled its members, "It may not be possible in some
places to hold public meetings, because they may be broken up by
violence and tumult. But some of you are members of religious corpo-
rations, or connected with religious congregations whom you may
induce to join in a protest against war." Or it might be possible to
appeal through local newspapers, or directly to members of Parliament.[187] Following such observations, protest in April was dominated
by meetings and deputations of specific, self-selected groups, and by
circulated petitions. The pattern continued, somewhat less markedly,
in May.

As tension mounted again early in April, several groups called for
meetings and memorials. In addition to suggesting that its branches
"provide resolutions," the National Reform Union joined the National
Liberal Federation in asking Liberal associations all over the country
to send representatives to a deputation to Hartington and Granville.
Gathering in London on April 3, the group was led by John Bright.
Other members of Parliament—Chamberlain, Jacob Bright, Mundella,
Henry Richard, and Samuel Morley—were much in evidence; they
were the most illustrious of 450 representatives from 120 constituencies. Not surprisingly, the vast majority were either from the Midlands
and the North, the areas of Chamberlain's greatest strength, or from
southeastern England, convenient to the event. The talk with Hartington was disappointing,[188] but the opportunity to meet first as a group
and to discuss resolutions against war helped community feeling. Far
more than the earlier scattered local meetings, this sizeable deputation
testified to Chamberlain's skill in using the Eastern Question for his
own purposes. It also demonstrated his uneasy relationship with Gladstone, who was loudly cheered despite his conspicuous absence.[189]

Gladstone did speak at a meeting early in April of the Workmen's
Peace Association. The mood was militant; one of the agricultural labor
leaders declared that "if the Government declared war without a just
cause, not only would armies be sent abroad, but an army would have
to be kept at home."

But the highest drama came when "Gladstone unexpectedly entered the room."[190] He had agreed to speak with a mere two hours' warning;[191] and his somewhat rambling remarks were uncharacteristically brief (only half an hour).[192] Musing on the tremendous volume of mail he was receiving, both adoring and vindictive, he lamented the failure of leadership at the top and absolved the working classes.[193]

Another group Gladstone addressed during these tense weeks was Samuel Morley's Nonconformist Vigilance Committee. An anti-war resolution which had been drawn up and made available for signature at Farringdon Street was presented to Gladstone[194] in a ceremony which evidently moved him deeply in a time of some distress. He recorded in his diary: "Even on this solemn day [Maundy Thursday] I could not manage evening Church. Indeed the circumstances of this Lent have been singularly adverse to that recollection which is the very first condition of a due & profitable observance. . . . To the Memorial Hall for the remarkable meeting of Nonconforming Ministers, when I spoke for an hour. The preparation was very small: perhaps all the better. Never did I address a better audience."[195] To the ministers, Gladstone could speak from the heart.

Meetings brought people together and knit ties between them. But as long as the meetings were restricted to groups with a defined membership, there were limits on how large and how impressive they could be. Furthermore, the groups were preexisting organizations with their own agendas; the whole was less than the sum of the parts. Had the Eastern Question Association formed itself from the beginning as a pressure group with a national network of branches, these problems could readily have been overcome. As it was, the meetings held in early April did not impress the government, nor have they received much notice from historians. Fortunately for the protesters, another approach was possible. Both in 1877 and earlier in 1878, Parliament had been showered with petitions. Most noteworthy, in January and February 1878, were the petitions from religious sources, often individual congregations—68 percent of the total communications in that period. There was much similarity in wording and even in format in many localities,[196] a clue that the campaign was highly organized. Indeed, it is tempting to see the impetus as coming from Samuel Morley's Nonconformist Vigilance Committee, which had planned to circularize every Nonconformist congregation early in January. In April, petitions mushroomed on secular ground; they were carried around from house to house in a neighborhood, or circulated through a factory or other organization. By no means new, they dramatically outstripped religious petitions as a source for signatures and quickly developed into an important weapon (see Figure 9).

The next step was finding efficient ways to gather enormous numbers of signatures quickly around a single text. In mid-March, the Labour Representation League sent out an address and a suggested model for a petition against increased armaments, emphasizing harmful economic effects. They were circulated widely, even beyond the network of labor clubs: for example, the Birmingham Liberal Association printed up 25,000 copies of the address for distribution. In "less than a week," the petition was signed by 15,314 individuals, said to be "leading men of the various trade unions," and was presented by John Bright to Parliament.[197] And this was part of a more general effort. In the first sixteen days of April, 71,960 individuals signed nonreligious petitions to Parliament opposed to the cabinet's policy. To an extent quite new in the campaign, these petitions used similar wording. Earlier in 1878, the same form had sometimes been used in a given area, indicating that one leader, or a group of local leaders, had

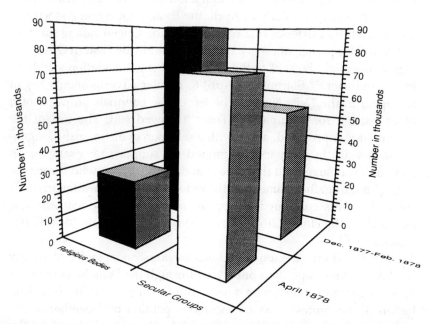

Figure 9. Signatures on petitions by religious bodies and secular groups, December 1877–April 1878.

organized protest in that restricted region. Now the same texts began to appear nationwide from widely separated localities, demonstrating efforts coordinated on a far more ambitious scale. Petitions from religious groups continued, but now fell far behind in number of signatures. However, it soon became artificial to separate religious from secular sources; a group of local chapels might join with neighborhoods, groups of women, and others.[198] Religious, now primarily Nonconformist, participation had evolved steadily in the course of the protest. Starting with action by denominations, or by prominent individuals or their chapels, it had come to involve coordinated stands by different Nonconformist congregations in a particular town. Now these crossdenominational, geographical groupings were working closely with likeminded nonreligous groups.

The problem was still inclusiveness. Local groups might coordinate their efforts, but only a national leadership could orchestrate a single chorus. And to be most effective, this national group could not be identified with a particular, parochial interest like the Labour Representation League. The need for an organization like the Eastern Question Association was obvious; the difficulty was how it could function as a national pressure group without a national structure. The answer was the newspapers. Early in April, the Eastern Question Association announced the existence of a memorial to the Queen calling for neutrality and for participation in a congress to settle the Eastern Question. Signatures might be sent to the secretary at the Association's address in Westminster.[199] Starting on April 8, regular advertisements began to appear in the *Daily News* to the left of the editorials on page four; other papers, for example *The Times,* followed suit. The text of the statement was provided, along with a selection of distinguished signatures. Articles in the paper drummed up support; for example, on April 8, it was suggested that "those in our large towns who favour the object" might gather names locally and send them to headquarters.[200] Advertisements continued to appear, and when the document was delivered to the Home Office early in May there were said to be 17,000 signatures.[201]

The method thus demonstrated was obviously adaptable. Also early in May a women's petition publicized through the *Daily News* received 11,955 signatures in just nine days.[202] But the biggest effort, the culmination of the protest, was an enormous petition put together in the course of about a month, between mid-April and mid-May. Like the other two, this final upsurge of protest was pushed forward by the dispatch of Indian troops to the Mediterranean. This decision, taken earlier, was not announced until April 17, when Parliament was on the point of recessing for Easter; it stimulated a proliferation of activity.[203] The last petition, described as a declaration against war, apparently started in reaction to the Eastern Question Association memorial. Many of the signers of the declaration were more radical than those of previous petitions, and the anti-war message was less equivocal: "We believe that there has not existed during the last 12 months, and that there does not exist now, any justification whatsoever for a war between Russia and Great Britain, and we should hold our Government guilty of the greatest crime towards this nation should they lead us or allow us to drift into war."[204]

Whatever the origins of the declaration, the Eastern Question Association quickly took it over. On April 13, William Morris's name appeared as one of the sponsors,[205] and from then on, the project ballooned, quickly flying ahead of the more modest memorial. The advertisement on April 16 gave a list of prominent individuals who would be willing to collect the names and addresses of signers, as well as accepting monetary contributions.[206] As correspondence mounted, forms for collecting signatures were offered. At first the individual to contact was Jacob Bright, but evidently the task grew too heavy; Mrs. Bright took over and her address was helpfully provided. By this time 20,000 signatures were said to be coming in every day.[207] When the petition was finally ready for presentation on May 18, it supposedly contained more than 220,000 signatures from a broad cross section of the protesters, including many Church of England clergy as well as Nonconformists; Radicals like Chamberlain, Bright, and Morris; intellectuals; professional do-gooders like Shaftesbury; and even the occasional aristocratic Whig like Leveson-Gower.[208] Despite this impressive pedigree, Salisbury, Derby's successor as foreign secretary, refused even to see the deputation which asked to present the declaration to him, arguing that anything which needed to be said could better be said in Parliament.[209]

The period from January to May 1878 marked the crest of the protest, now a very different movement from that which had started so modestly in the summer of 1876. By 1878 the issues had changed dramatically and so had the strategies appropriate for dealing with them. While the Nonconformists launched a nationwide campaign of petitions, many secular protesters initially tried to organize public meetings. The effort was similar to that in 1876, but existing organizations played a larger part. Instead of small groups gathered more or less spontaneously for speeches and discussion, there were now well-orchestrated mass meetings.

And there was opposition. In 1876 and 1877, few people took the agitation seriously enough to think it worth countering. In 1878 counteragitators protested because they perceived that the war was going badly, the cabinet was worried (witness the vote of credit), and despite this evidence of danger to British interests, Gladstone and his friends continued to mount protest meetings. Jingoism, a social movement in its own right, developed an extremely effective grassroots opposition. Whether by instinct or design, the Jingoes quickly found where the protesters were most vulnerable. Abhorrence of policy making through violent confrontation had made many opponents of government policy wonder from the start whether they wanted to run the risk of association with the protest. By February 1878, the Jingoes effectively broke up public protest meetings wherever they were held; it began to seem as though additional gatherings might only encourage warmongering.

The solution was a major shift in strategy. The protesters largely gave up public meetings, so difficult to control; instead, they emphasized circulated petitions and deputations. It is an interesting reversal of usual procedure; in many instances, petitions have been the prelude to violent demonstrations, not the sequel.[210] It shows once again how determined the leaders were to maintain order, and how effective they were in holding their followers. They were helped too by the fact that the Eastern crisis, rather than reaching new heights, gradually dissipated in April and May.

Inevitably, this fundamental shift in strategy affected individual leaders and their prominence. Men who had been associated with the organization of big meetings tended to lose influence. Mundella was never as important as he had been in 1876 at the time of the launching of the Eastern Question Association. That group's assumption of a backstage, facilitating, organizational role rebounded unfavorably on his position. Herbert suffered from perceptions that he was an extremist; William Morris, thoroughly disillusioned by what he construed as the cowardice of middle-class leaders, turned eventually to socialism.

But other men rode the current. Samuel Morley, who had disassociated himself from the City protest to work through Nonconformist groups, was proven wise. Chamberlain was able to adapt the role of "his" Liberal associations to take advantage of shifting tactical demands. Broadhurst, though he chafed at the change, fell in with it and did good service; he was rewarded.

Most important was Gladstone's contribution. Methods might change, but Gladstone's stature did not. Involvement in failed attempts like the Agricultural Hall meeting did not diminish him in the eyes of his admirers. Unlike the promoters and bureaucrats, who rose or fell with the fortunes of a particular gambit, Gladstone's involvement in organizational matters remained subordinate to his grasp of the overall purposes, the beliefs, of the movement. He was its symbol and its prophet.

10 ◆ Conclusion

The Bulgarian agitation certainly generated a tremendous amount of activity. But did anyone listen? Did all the meetings and petitions and memorials make a difference? Did the agitation affect foreign policy, its ostensible target, and if so, to what extent? Finally, what is the nature of the protest's influence on domestic affairs?

The agitation was bound up with British diplomatic decisions, and it was noted abroad. In the autumn of 1876, although Disraeli's instinct was to discount it, Derby listened, and he mentioned the agitation in his September 21 dispatch as a factor in his insistence that the Porte reform. The agitation probably played some slight role in the proposal for a conference at Constantinople to concert reforms, and in the choice of Salisbury as chief British representative. Such conferences in the past had succeeded in patching up Eastern crises; that this one did not can be laid to the newly intransigent mood in Constantinople, where a younger generation saw such accommodation as truckling to the West.

Once the conference failed, war between Russia and the Ottoman Empire became likely; what attitude should Britain take? The issues had shifted significantly. In 1876, attention focused on the moral problem of British support of the Ottomans. The protesters occupied the high ground, and it was difficult to oppose them without seeming to favor rape and murder. In 1877, the discussion concerned peace or war, neutrality, conditional neutrality, or maybe in the long run, participation. Many working men were even more willing to speak up on this basis. The memories of economic hardship during the Crimean War were still fresh. Many did not wish to suffer for what they perceived to be the benefit of army officers, bondholders, and the Turks. But so many members of Parliament hesitated to tie the cabinet's hands that Gladstone's resolutions for neutrality failed resoundingly. Still, the debates indicate that many M.P.s, no longer willing to maintain the Ottoman Empire unquestioningly, were beginning to differentiate between parts of the Empire and to weigh the merits of types of involvement. Some of this thinking reflected ideas floated at the time of the purchase of the Suez Canal shares, but much was surely owed to the Bulgarian agitation as well.

During the rest of 1877, the Ottomans' unexpectedly strong showing in the field afforded Britain the luxury of postponing a decision. But at the beginning of the new year, the Russian march on Constantinople forced Disraeli's hand. Without the protest, it seems quite likely that Britain would have occupied some strategic point, perhaps Gallipoli, fairly early in the year. The Ottomans might not have liked it, but they would hardly have opposed Britain militarily, and a British presence might have deterred the Russians from advancing so far and so fast. But what would have happened then? It might be argued that the British, by their patience, made a better deal in the end. A treaty less outrageous than San Stefano might have stood, and the British might have been worse off than they were after the Congress of Berlin.

Certainly, the protest affected Disraeli, who acted inconsistently. The Russians' resultant confusion about what he intended greatly increased the danger of war by inadvertence. He did not send up the fleet in January, when there was reason to do so; instead, he waited until February, when the Russians had halted their advance. The Ottomans were not pleased; in fact, Ahmed Vefik Pasha, the grand vizier, warned Layard against the gesture. Layard himself had to admit that such action might frighten the Russians into advancing further.[1] Indeed, the consequence was to enrage the Tsar, to convince him that it was impossible to deal with the British, and to provoke the series of peremptory telegrams in which he ordered occupation of Constantinople or its environs. That the Russian commander in chief did not comply had only partly to do with the fact that the British did not follow up their move; the critical determinant was probably the utter exhaustion of the Russian troops.[2]

Because the Tsar's commands were not immediately followed, there was time for P. A. Shuvalov, the pacifically inclined ambassador to London, to moderate the crisis. He offered assurances to Derby, the foreign secretary. The fact that it was Derby who talked to him was crucial, and once again had much to do with the protest. Had Disraeli wished to push ahead with a belligerent policy in 1878, a logical beginning would have been to rid himself of Derby, who opposed any steps which seemed likely to lead to war. There were many reasons why it would have been difficult to replace Derby, until the foreign secretary himself provided the opportunity by resigning at the end of January. Significantly, Disraeli did not avail himself of this piece of luck; instead, he begged Derby to stay. Derby had a powerful network of friends, particularly in Lancashire, where he was a major landowner.[3] W. Hart Dyke reported to Disraeli that Derby's departure would have a harmful effect among "the commercial element" in Lancashire.[4] Disraeli admitted his misgivings to Queen Victoria in a letter in which he tried (successfully) to convince her to retract her acceptance of Derby's resignation. Disraeli confided, "Our friends in Lancashire, who were organising public meetings on a large scale to support your Majesty's Government, and answer the mechanical agitation of the last month, have telegraphed that, in consequence of the assumed resignation of Lord Derby, they must relinquish the attempt."[5] The end of January was the critical moment, when big displays of progovernment sentiment turned the tide against the protesters. And to judge by the many letters and the statements in the press which expressed confidence in Derby's judiciousness, much more was at stake than a few meetings in Lancashire, important though this was. A great many Englishmen of both parties distrusted Disraeli's rootless and unpredictable ambition. They believed, however, that as long as Derby, an aristocrat who had proved again and again his caution, good sense, and total unconcern with the empty aspects of prestige was a member of the cabinet, Britain was safe. And they were not wrong to trust him. Responding to a fiery letter from a member of the county set, Derby pointed out mildly but firmly that his correspondent and friends would not be the ones to pay most heavily for war; since a significant number of those who would had declared themselves against it, it behooved leaders to listen.[6]

By the time Derby resigned for good at the end of March, the situation had changed in the East. Disraeli's gamble of calling up the reserves and shifting troops from India to Malta would prove less risky than it appeared, because the Russians were finally beginning to face the implications of the sorry state of their army and the real likelihood that they might have to fight not only the Ottoman Empire and Britain but Austria-Hungary and Romania as well.[7] Salisbury, Derby's successor, had always sympathized with the views, if not the methods, of the protest. Now he used Britain's show of force not as the entering wedge for a military campaign but as a bluff to win good terms in the final settlement. Salisbury's April 1 circular outlined British objections to the San Stefano treaty. Thanks to the continued intransigence of the Austrians, who were infuriated by the Russians' apparent disregard of earlier promises to them, the way was opened for secret negotiations between Salisbury and Shuvalov, and the arrangements agreed upon at the Congress of Berlin began to take shape.

The terms of the Treaty of Berlin came as no great surprise. The big Bulgaria of San Stefano was cut down drastically and divided in two. The northern part was to receive autonomy under a foreign prince; the southern part of Bulgaria, Eastern Rumelia, would remain under direct Ottoman rule. Austria was assigned occupation of Bosnia and Herzegovina. Romania, Serbia, and Montenegro all received formal recognition of independence. Territory was traded in the area of the Danube mouth. In effect, Ottoman control of the Balkans was severely limited; after the two parts of Bulgaria were united ten years later, only Albania, Macedonia, and eastern Thrace would remain under the Porte's full jurisdiction. In Asia, Ottoman control was maintained, although the Russians were allowed to keep a substantial part of their conquests and to add Batum. But Salisbury had arranged a coup; the Cyprus Convention with the Porte, signed on June 4, allowed Britain to occupy that island and potentially oversee Asiatic Turkey. Advice to the Porte had failed to save the Balkans for the Ottoman Empire; now the British were theoretically in a position to enforce reform in Asia, keep the area out of Russia's clutches, and guard the routes to India.[8]

In the end, Disraeli and Salisbury ranged themselves with the middle ground in both parties—the people who wanted "peace with honour" and believed that Britain must maintain its prestige and protect communications with India, but who were disgusted with the Ottomans and hoped that, through wise diplomacy, British interests could be upheld without resort to war. The influence of the protest was visible in the Cyprus Convention. Salisbury believed that control of Cyprus would commit Britain to a strong military policy in the eastern Mediterranean; it would, in short, be an antidote against future protests. As he wrote Layard in connection with the negotiations:

> The point to which your attention should be most distinctly drawn is that this country, which is popularly governed, and cannot, therefore, be counted on to act in any uniform or consistent system of policy, would probably abandon the task of resisting any further Russian advance to

the Southward in Asia, if nothing but speculative arguments can be advanced in favour of action. But it will cling to any military post occupied by England as tenaciously as it has clung to Gibraltar; and if any movement were made which would threaten it, while assailing the Ottoman dominions, its action might be counted on.[9]

Salisbury was right as far as Cyprus went; but it did not follow that the British would involve themselves in Ottoman Asia. The ambitious policy conceived by Salisbury and Layard remained largely a dead letter, partly because the Sultan, Abdul Hamid, had become convinced that Britain was no longer his friend, and that it was time to look elsewhere for support. Layard blamed Gladstone for this outcome,[10] and he was partly right. But even had the Sultan wished to, he could not have undertaken the extensive military and judicial reforms envisioned without financial relief. When it came to lending more money, the British were adamant. The decree of Muharrem, which grew out of discussions at the Congress, set up the Public Debt Administration and the Porte began orderly repayment of its obligations. Other countries, notably the French, had also suffered when the Ottomans defaulted; but once things were put right, new monies were forthcoming. In Britain, however, financial caution was reinforced by moral revulsion.[11]

Although the protest was closely intertwined with foreign policy, its greatest significance was domestic. The real opportunity offered by this eccentric, originally symbolic, issue was construction of a broadly representative coalition from elements which did not generally work well together, and in some cases did not work at all. Gladstone himself realized this when he looked back on the crisis in November 1878. In an article in *The Nineteenth Century*, musing on the Liberals' electoral prospects, he noted with satisfaction the party's "healthy individuality," adding, "The composition of a Tory majority is pretty uniform. That of a Liberal party is apt to be diversified, not to say heterogeneous." Historians have concurred. As Lubenow points out, the Liberal party, partly as a function of its long record of success, was a "coalition party" built up from different, competing, often contentious groups, rather than a "consensus party" like the Conservatives or later the Irish Nationalists. Such a loose alliance would obviously be more biddable if there were an ideological focus, but such a goal was elusive. Even the Bulgarian agitation alienated many important elements. Still, Gladstone believed, since January 1876 more Liberal candidates had won by-elections and these new members had been gratifyingly loyal to the party position in major House votes. He offered these observations as evidence that an issue such as the Eastern Question, transcending mere sectional interests, could help to create a solid working majority.[12]

The Bulgarian agitation enhanced the importance of the Nonconformists and reconciled them to Gladstone. Tentative and not wholly successful efforts were made to bridge the gap between Nonconformists and radical secularist working men. The agricultural laborers, usually alienated from politics, soldiered manfully for the cause. So did many urban working men; they joined ranks with "enlightened" middle-class factory owners like Samuel Morley and A. J. Mundella, whom some of them respected, some disliked, and some didn't know at all. The initial prospect of involving High Churchmen and the occasional representative of the right wing of the party like Argyll, plus Tories like the Marquess of Bath, did not wholly materialize.[13] However, any narrowing of the movement was compensated for by the remarkable deepening of working-class and Nonconformist support as the issues shifted to peace or war, and by the increasingly powerful link between the protesters and Gladstone.

What might come of this casual coalition, above and beyond its immediate goals, was at first far from apparent. The period between 1876 and 1878 afforded opportunities to experiment with novel forms of organization appropriate to the new franchise laws, to grapple with the conceptual problem of how to bridge the gap between popular opinion and official action. The Bulgarian agitation made an immediate difference to the Liberal party in terms of group as well as individual participation. It was strikingly evident that certain persons held the key to certain communities. For example, when Henry Richard hesitated to support Gladstone's neutrality resolutions in 1877, Welsh participation in the protest dropped dramatically; in 1878, when he was once more active, it revived. The agricultural laborers were represented by Joseph Arch, who had for years resisted pressure to join in a variety of Radical causes. He become involved in the peace movement and from this went on to the Bulgarian agitation and then to protest against Disraeli's imperialistic foreign policy during the 1880 election.[14] The Liberals came back into power in 1880, and faced increasing pressure to extend the franchise in the traditionally Conservative counties. Surely they must have been reassured to note the enthusiasm for their party demonstrated by the group that would benefit most from this electoral reform, finally enacted in 1884–85.[15]

Arch's ambition to capture a parliamentary seat was frustrated until 1885, when his natural constituency had been enfranchised.[16] But in 1880 many leaders with working-class backgrounds or identifications were elected to the Commons, including both Bradlaugh and Broadhurst. Henry Fawcett, only slightly less involved in the protest, went to the post office in Gladstone's second ministry. Broadhurst became undersecretary of state for the Home Office in his third. The role of the Bulgarian campaign in their rise was not incidental, as Broadhurst later admitted. Writing in 1901 he testified: "I took part in nearly every public event connected with the Eastern Question and the Bulgarian Atrocities, and this brought me into close contact with a class of people whom I otherwise should never have met."[17] Furthermore, when he met those people, he had something to talk about: he was saved from the isolation so often meted out to those who are perceived to have just one issue on their minds—their own position and entitlement to advancement. When Broadhurst campaigned at Stoke-upon-Trent in 1878–1880, he recognized that "though primarily a representative of Labour interests, [he] should fight the election on general political principles," and his experience and concerns were by now wide enough to enable him to do so convincingly.[18] Finally, when Gladstone asked him to become a junior minister in 1886, the Grand Old Man revealed how he had come to adopt Broadhurst as a protégé. As Broadhurst put it, when he called on Gladstone to discuss the proposal

> he gave me a hearty welcome, and in subsequent conversation he referred to the dark days of Liberalism from 1876 to 1878, and assured me that he had never forgotten my labours and my devotion to the cause of Liberty during those exciting times, when all the worst passions of mankind seemed to pervade the metropolis. He went on to impart to me the fact that he had then determined, when a favourable moment arrived, to recognise my services to the Eastern Question Association in some adequate fashion.[19]

But Broadhurst's welcome came with limits. As his autobiography reveals, he suffered all the torments of recently assimilated individuals conscious of having been accepted not primarily because of what they are, but because of their ability to mimic a style not originally their own. Faced with the prospect of functioning as a minister, he worried about his lack of formal education. As he admitted: "Visions of humiliation arising from the duties of my new office and my meagre capacity and endowments rose before me with startling vividness."[20] And an encounter with "dear old Sir John Mowbray," member for Oxford from 1868 to 1899, demonstrated the tenuousness of his position. As Broadhurst told the story,

Our talk ran on the university, and on his remarking that I seemed to have a good deal of knowledge about the various colleges, I informed him that I had been at Christ Church. I shall never forget the look of bewildered incredulity that passed over his benevolent countenance, pain mingling with pity at the thought that I was trying to delude him into a belief that I had been a student at "The House." His relief was instantaneous and perceptible when I gently explained that my connection with Christ Church College was confined to the roof, where I had assisted in fixing a number of new chimney-pots.[21]

After all, Broadhurst knew his place.

Not everyone did. It has been suggested that working men as a body were far more radical in the 1870s than they were in the 1880s. In part, the turn away from extremism was the price of survival during worsening economic conditions.[22] But in part it may be traceable to the Bulgarian agitation. Radical extremism, expressed through huge rallies organized in the expectation that they would lead to violence, was categorically rejected by the party leaders in favor of big petitions and self-screened deputations. This decision set nonviolent terms for working-class and Nonconformist participation. Those like Broadhurst, who were willing to work their way into the system, took the road through Bulgaria. Those Radicals who were not, like William Morris, turned toward revolutionary socialism.

For the near term the Bulgarian agitation certainly broadened the Liberal party and won back doubtful elements. And it was tremendously important in creating a bond between Gladstone and the mass of Liberal supporters, in making him indeed a "reluctant icon." "Most reluctant," as he said, "for God knoweth how true it is that my heart's desire has been for that rest from conflict & from turmoil which seems almost a necessity for a soul that would be prepared in time to meet its God for eternity." Yet there was the sense of being buoyed up by the group emotion, of being empowered, "as it were upheld in an unusual manner." "Was not all this for a purpose?" Gladstone asked himself.[23] A year later, already embarked on the Midlothian campaign, he noted "special gifts of strength" as he seemed to transcend his own person and speak "for millions who themselves cannot speak." To be called to "this work," so he explained it to himself, is "a great and high election of God."[24] It was also a compelling movement; Gladstone's appeal to the people over the heads of the entrenched Whig leadership summoned a response that amazed and overwhelmed political pundits and, as Gladstone recognized more quickly than they, left them with no real alternative but to restore him to power with as much joyfulness as they could muster.[25]

But it was very much a personal triumph, unique to Gladstone and his extraordinary style. Chamberlain had tried to use the Eastern Question as a motivating force to found a new type of local party organization which would wrest control from entrenched and ingrown elites. Liberal associations on the Birmingham model would potentially give a voice to a wide spectrum of Liberal voters; the National Federation would coordinate the effort. Whatever Chamberlain's personal hopes, such changes implied restructuring the party to make it independent of personality. But these reforms were not yet widely adopted. If, in the 1880s, Gladstone seemed to be lurching from one crisis to another, always talking of retirement yet always held back by the need for his cementing presence,[26] he was simply following the logic of his return to power. The Liberals were held together by shared emotion, not institutional discipline. The approach helped to initiate a crisis management style of leadership which could be amazingly effective, but was hard to maintain on a routine basis.

Jenkins has pointed out that such "hand-to-mouth" practice evidently answered one of Gladstone's deep psychological needs. It assuaged his guilt over clinging to power when successors, no longer so young, were ready and waiting to take over. Ironically, Gladstone had suffered the same fate at the hands of Palmerston in the early 1860s. But beyond guilt and anger was seduction. In the 1880s, he sought to replicate the magical moments between 1876 and 1878 when he had seemed to be lifted on a wave of enthusiasm to accomplishments beyond the norm of politics. And the party, so often indistinguishable from the fractious cabals of ambitious politicians, seemed at such moments to realize a God-given potential as an instrument for good in a sordid world.

The difficulty was that emergency management tended to perpetuate itself beyond the point where it could be constructive. Jenkins shrewdly remarks that since the leadership was always in doubt, no one except Gladstone could engage in long-term planning. Derby, who joined the Liberal cabinet in 1882, complained of "the careless, slipshod way in which . . . business is done." One crisis led to another as "the manifestations of Gladstone's failure of leadership became the 'cause' of his need to carry on."[27] Meanwhile, colleagues at both ends of the ideological spectrum were in a state of near-constant frustration with Gladstone's new approach. Whigs suspected that the parliamentary party had been delivered over to manipulation by "popular" opinion of dubious provenance, while some Radicals, like Chamberlain, fumed at Gladstone's unwillingness either to institutionalize broadened lines of communication himself or let others do it for him.

There was a substantive problem as well. Only certain questions were susceptible to development as ingathering issues. The Bulgarian massacres were ideal; because they mattered scarcely at all to Britons in a practical sense, they assumed symbolic significance and could be colored differently by different groups. Hence they could serve in important ways as a unifier. During his second ministry, Gladstone adduced a number of emergencies as excuses for staying in power— Ireland, the Transvaal, franchise reform, Russia[28]— but none of these had the same potential for rallying diverse groups of people behind a common cause. And Ireland, as Gladstone came to understand it, was positively divisive. Home Rule for the Irish, as Shannon pointed out long ago,[29] may have followed logically for Gladstone from his support for autonomy for the Bulgarians; after a certain point, national feeling was national feeling, wherever one met it. At another level, it was impossible for Gladstone to berate the Turks for failing to shoulder the burden of empire without recognizing sooner or later that England was guilty too. Ireland was "a warning & a judgment for our heavy sins as a nation."[30] Few of Gladstone's Liberal colleagues agreed. Calling the Ottomans to account was prophetic; dismantling the British Empire was dastardly.

Notes

1. Introduction

1. For a useful examination of the composition of the Bulgarian agitation, see R. T. Shannon, *Gladstone and the Bulgarian Agitation, 1876,* 2nd ed. (Hassocks, Eng.: Harvester Press, 1975; originally published 1963), pp. 147–238.

2. R. W. Seton-Watson, *Disraeli, Gladstone, and the Eastern Question* (London: Macmillan, 1935); W. N. Medlicott, *The Congress of Berlin and After* (London: Methuen, 1938); David Harris, *A Diplomatic History of the Balkan Crisis of 1875–1878: The First Year* (Stanford, Calif.: Stanford University Press, 1936); Richard Millman, *Britain and the Eastern Question, 1875–1878* (Oxford: Clarendon Press, 1979). See also B. H. Sumner's magisterial *Russia and the Balkans, 1870–1880* (Hamden, Conn.: Archon Books, 1962; originally published 1937).

3. Shannon, *Bulgarian Agitation,* p. vi.

4. This view is sketched out by G. S. R. Kitson Clark in his illuminating introduction to Shannon's *Bulgarian Agitation* (pp. xi–xxviii), which has strongly influenced this study.

5. Neil J. Smelser, *Theory of Collective Behavior* (New York: Free Press, 1963). The potential usefulness of this approach was pointed out by Donald C. Richter in "The Role of Mob Riot in Victorian Elections, 1865–1885," *Victorian Studies,* 15 (September 1971), 27–28, and in his *Riotous Victorians* (Athens, Ohio: Ohio University Press, 1981), pp. 166–167. Turning his attention "not . . . [upon] the rioters, but the forces of riot control," Richter did not follow up this suggestion; I arrived at this methodology independently.

6. See for example Edward N. Peterson, *The Limits of Hitler's Power* (Princeton: Princeton University Press, 1969).

7. Akaby Nassibian, *Britain and the Armenian Question, 1915–1923* (Oxford: Oxford University Press, 1984), p. 109.

8. See Kitson Clark in Shannon, *Bulgarian Agitation,* p. xxviii.

9. See Patricia Hollis, ed., *Pressure from Without in Early Victorian England* (New York: St. Martin's Press, 1974).

10. The best treatment of such plans remains Dwight E. Lee, *Great Britain and the Cyprus Convention Policy of 1878* (Cambridge, Mass.: Harvard University Press, 1934).

11. A. J. P. Taylor, *The Trouble Makers* (Bloomington, Ind.: Indiana University Press, 1958), p. 74.

12. Fine treatments of nineteenth-century Ottoman internal history are provided by Roderic H. Davison, *Reform in the Ottoman Empire, 1856–1876* (Princeton: Princeton University Press, 1963); Niyazi Berkes, *The Development of Secularism in Turkey* (Montreal: McGill University Press, 1964); Bernard Lewis, *The Emergence of Modern Turkey*, 2nd ed. (London: Oxford University Press, 1968); and S. J. Shaw and E. K. Shaw, *History of the Ottoman Empire and Modern Turkey*, 2 vols. (Cambridge, Eng.: Cambridge University Press, 1976–1977), vol. 2, "Reform, Revolution, and Republic: The Rise of Modern Turkey, 1808–1975."

13. See Robert Devereux, *The First Ottoman Constitutional Period* (Baltimore, Md.: The Johns Hopkins University Press, 1963).

14. Edward Said, *Orientalism* (New York: Vintage Books, 1979).

15. William Ewart Gladstone, "The Past and Present Administration," *Quarterly Review*, 104 (October 1858), 560. For discussion of Gladstone's developing views on the Ottoman Empire, see Chapter 5.

16. William Ewart Gladstone, *The Gladstone Diaries*, ed. M. R. D. Foot and H. C. G. Matthew, 11 vols. to date (Oxford: Clarendon Press, 1968–), VII, 120.

17. Ann Pottinger Saab, "The Doctor's Dilemma: Britain and the Cretan Crisis, 1866–69," *Journal of Modern History*, 49 (December 1977), On-Demand Supplement, pp. D1402–1404, © The University of Chicago.

18. The standard life is still Stanley Lane-Poole, *The Life of the Right Honourable Stratford Canning, Viscount Stratford de Redcliffe*, 2 vols. (London: Longmans, Green, 1888). It was authorized by the Foreign Office and based on Stratford's papers and a memoir, which Lane-Poole lost; see also Allan Cunningham, "Stratford Canning and the Tanzimat," in *Beginnings of Modernization in the Middle East: The Nineteenth Century*, ed. William R. Polk and Richard L. Chambers (Chicago: University of Chicago Press, 1968), pp. 245–264. On Stratford's ethnocentrism, see Cunningham, pp. 250 and 260.

19. Article on Sir Austen Henry Layard, *Dictionary of National Biography*, XXII (supplement; London: Oxford University Press, 1917–), 954–957, hereafter *DNB*; Sir Austen Henry Layard, *Sir A. Henry Layard . . . Autobiography and Letters*, 2 vols. (New York: Charles Scribner's Sons, 1903), see especially II, 42–111. See also Gordon Waterfield, *Layard of Nineveh* (London: J. Murray, 1963).

20. Gladstone, *Diaries*, VIII, 157.

21. Ibid., p. 511.

22. See Chapter 3.

23. *The Times*, October 20, 1866, p. 8, col. e.

24. Gladstone, *Diaries*, VII, 283 and n. 8, 285–286, 290–296, 303, 306–307, 310–311, 335, 337.

25. These visits are treated at greater length below in Chapter 5 (Gladstone) and Chapter 6 (Disraeli). See also Robert Blake, *Disraeli's Grand Tour* (New York: Oxford University Press, 1982).

26. Lane-Poole, *Stratford Canning*, I, 69–81, 110–111, 177–183; II, 1–6.

27. New York: D. Appleton, 1916.

28. *Daily News*, December 20, 1877, p. 6, col. f.

29. See Richard Shannon, "David Urquhart and the Foreign Affairs Committees," in Hollis, *Pressure from Without*, pp. 239–261; article on David Urquhart in *DNB* XX, 44–45.

30. Hollis, ed., "Introduction," *Pressure from Without*, pp. 3–23.

31. Smelser, *Collective Behavior*, pp. 8–9. The strategy Smelser adopts has been subjected to searching criticism by Charles Tilly, *Big Structures, Large Processes, Huge Comparisons* (New York: Russell Sage Foundation, 1984), pp. 97–100. While Tilly's objections are cogent, the advantages of informed use of Smelser's scheme seem to outweigh the disadvantages in the present instance at least, for reasons given in the text.

32. For a brief summary of the determinants of collective behavior, see Smelser, *Collective Behavior*, pp. 13–17.

2. The Crisis in the Ottoman Empire

1. Quoted in Alexander L. George, "The 'Operational Code': A Neglected Approach to the Study of Political Leaders and Decision-Making," *International Studies Quarterly*, 13 (1969), 190–191.

2. See Edward Ingram, *The Beginning of the Great Game in Asia, 1828–1834* (New York: Oxford University Press, 1979), pp. 1–15.

3. V. J. Puryear, *International Economics and Diplomacy in the Near East* (Hamden, Conn.: Archon Books, 1969; originally published 1935), pp. 227–228; Beatrice Marinescu, "Economic Relations between the Romanian Principalities and Great Britain (1848–1859)," *Revue roumaine d'histoire*, 8 (1969), 272–273.

4. Feroz Ahmad, "The Late Ottoman Empire," in *The Great Powers and the End of the Ottoman Empire*, ed. Marian Kent (London: George Allen and Unwin, 1984), pp. 5–30; see especially p. 23.

5. Puryear, *International Economics*, p. 228.

6. Ibid., p. 125.

7. Orhan Conker, *Les Chemins de fer en Turquie et la politique ferroviaire turque* (Paris: Librairie du Recueil Sirey, 1935), p. 37.

8. Ibid., pp. 9, 15, 17, 22.

9. *Morning Post*, July 20, 1867, p. 6, col. d.

10. Şevket Pamuk, *The Ottoman Empire and European Capitalism, 1820–1913* (Cambridge, Eng.: Cambridge University Press, 1987), p. 135.

11. Conker, *Chemins de fer*, pp. 9–10.

12. *Pall Mall Gazette*, September 26, 1876, p. 6, cols. a–b.

13. Disraeli Papers, B/XVI/A/125 (Box 68), Western Manuscripts, Bodleian Library, Oxford.

14. Ahmad, "Late Ottoman Empire," p. 25.

15. Charles Issawi, "Middle Eastern Economic Development, 1815–1914: The General and the Specific," in *Studies in the Economic History of the Middle East*, ed. M. A. Cook (New York: Oxford University Press, 1970), pp. 395–411; see especially pp. 395 and 408. Hereafter cited as "General and Specific."

16. Niyazi Berkes, *The Development of Secularism in Turkey* (Montreal: McGill University Press, 1964), pp. 144–145, 152–153.

17. D. C. Blaisdell, *European Financial Control in the Ottoman Empire* (New York: Columbia University Press, 1929), p. 74.

18. S. J. Shaw and E. K. Shaw, *History of the Ottoman Empire and Modern Turkey*, 2 vols. (Cambridge, Eng.: Cambridge University Press, 1976–1977), vol. 2: "Reform, Revolution, and Republic: The Rise of Modern Turkey, 1808–1975," pp. 86–87.

19. Charles P. Issawi, *Economic History of Turkey, 1800–1914* (Chicago: University of Chicago Press, 1980), pp. 362–363.

20. Issawi, "General and Specific," pp. 399–400.

21. For a sociologist's expectations concerning the outcome of such situations, see Neil J. Smelser, *Theory of Collective Behavior* (New York: Free Press, 1963), pp. 226–227.

22. For a short summary of these events, see Shaw and Shaw, *History*, pp. 142–144 (Lebanon); pp. 151–152 (Crete); pp. 160–162 (Bulgaria). The figures for Lebanon and Damascus appear on p. 143; those for Bulgaria on p. 162. Leila Tarazi Fawaz, *Merchants and Migrants in Nineteenth-Century Beirut* (Cambridge, Mass.: Harvard University Press, 1983), p. 24, in discussing the events in Damascus, gives the much smaller, but still horrifying figure of "5,000 . . . out of a population of about 10,000 or 12,000 males."

23. Smelser, *Collective Behavior*, pp. 226–230 is relevant here. For a not altogether successful attempt to describe this sort of event in essentially economic terms, through Immanuel Wallerstein's world systems approach, see Bruce Masters, "The 1850 Events in Aleppo: An Aftershock of Syria's Incorporation into the Capitalist World System," *International Journal of Middle East Studies*, 22 (February 1990), 3–20.

24. See Shaw and Shaw, *History*, pp. 133–134, 142.

25. See Smelser, *Collective Behavior*, pp. 231–241.

26. Shaw and Shaw, *History*, p. 143.

27. Masters, "1850 Events," pp. 9–11, analyzes the earlier example of Aleppo, in which Muslim accounts exaggerated the role of outsiders in order to exonerate the Sunni Muslim urban elite. Something similar may have happened in Damascus.

28. Smelser, *Collective Behavior*, pp. 254, 263, 268, discusses such characteristic features of social protest.

29. Moshe Ma'oz, *Ottoman Reform in Syria and Palestine, 1840–1861* (Oxford: Clarendon Press, 1968), p. 227.

30. *Osmanli Tarihi* (Ankara: Türk Tarih Kurumu Basimevi, 1947–), vol. 7: Enver Ziya Karal, *Islâhat Fermani Devri, 1861–76*, p. 19.

31. Emmanuel Zambettakis, "Anekdota diplomatika eggrapha tes proepanastatikes periodou tou 1866 en Krete," *Kretika Chronika*, 13 (1959), 90–94.

32. Stanford J. Shaw, "Some Aspects of the Aims and Achievements of the Nineteenth-Century Ottoman Reformers," in *Beginnings of Modernization in the Middle East: The Nineteenth Century*, ed. William R. Polk and Richard L. Chambers (Chicago: University of Chicago Press, 1968), pp. 32–34.
33. Shaw and Shaw, *History*, p. 151; Smelser, *Collective Behavior*, pp. 246–247.
34. See Ann Pottinger Saab, "The Doctors' Dilemma: Britain and the Cretan Crisis 1866–69," *Journal of Modern History*, 49 (December 1977), On-Demand Supplement, pp. D1394–1395. For revolutionary organization and civil war, see Smelser, *Collective Behavior*, pp. 255–256.
35. Shaw and Shaw, *History*, pp. 116–118; Smelser, *Collective Behavior*, p. 247.
36. Kemal H. Karpat, *Ottoman Population, 1830–1914* (Madison, Wis.: Wisconsin University Press, 1985), p. 50.
37. According to Ottoman figures prepared for the Congress of Berlin, in the kazas of Vidin, Tirnovo (Türnovo), Niş (Niš), and Sofia, Bulgarians outnumbered Turks only by a ratio of 2:1.6; in Rusçuk (Ruse or Ruschuk), Varna, Tulca (Tulcea), Islimiyye, and Filibe (Plovdiv or Philippolis), they were actually a minority (Karpat, *Ottoman Population*, p. 51; see also the table on p. 116). Although the objectivity of such findings is suspect, it is clear that Bulgaria was and has remained very different from Serbia and Greece, the first Ottoman provinces to break away, where there were overwhelming Christian majorities.
38. Shaw and Shaw, *History*, pp. 117, 162.
39. See Smelser, *Collective Behavior*, pp. 254–263.
40. Shaw and Shaw, *History*, p. 162.

3. British-Ottoman Strain

1. Neil J. Smelser, *Theory of Collective Behavior* (New York: Free Press, 1963), p. 51.
2. Ibid., pp. 64–66.
3. *Newcastle Guardian*, December 17, 1853, annexed to Musurus Bey to Reşid Pasa, December 17, 1853 (Hariciye Iradesi 1270 #5151), Başvckôlet Arşivi, Istanbul.
4. John H. Gleason, *The Genesis of Russophobia in Great Britain* (Cambridge, Mass.: Harvard University Press, 1950).
5. This is Kingsley Martin's contention in *The Triumph of Lord Palmerston*, rev. ed. (London: Hutchinson, 1963; originally published 1924).
6. Ibid., pp. 50–52.
7. For a discussion of the revolts, see Ann Pottinger Saab, *The Origins of the Crimean Alliance* (Charlottesville, Va.: University Press of Virginia, 1977), pp. 139–149.
8. François Lenormant, *Histoire des Massacres de Syrie en 1860* (Paris: L. Hachette, 1861), pp. 7–9.
9. Ibid., pp. 128–129; C. H. S. Churchill, *The Druzes and the Maronites under Turkish Rule, from 1840 to 1860* (London: B. Quaritch, 1862), pp. 232–233.
10. Kamal S. Salibi, "The 1860 Upheaval in Damascus as Seen by al-Sayyid Muhammad Abu'l-Su'ud al-Hasibi," in *Beginnings of Modernization in the*

Middle East: The Nineteenth Century, ed. William R. Polk and Richard L. Chambers (Chicago: University of Chicago Press, 1968), pp. 185–202.

11. *Osmanli Tarihi* (Ankara: Türk Tarih Kurumu Basimevi, 1947–), vol. 6: Enver Ziya Karal, *Islâhat Fermani Devri, 1856–1861*, p. 35.
12. Serif Mardin, *The Genesis of Young Ottoman Thought* (Princeton: Princeton University Press, 1962), p. 17.
13. Smelser, *Collective Behavior*, pp. 224–225.
14. *Freeman's Journal*, August 3, 1860, p. 3, col. f; August 21, 1860, p. 3, col. c.
15. Ibid., August 14, 1860, p. 3, col. c.
16. Ibid., September 4, 1860, p. 3, cols. d-e.
17. Ibid., September 10, 1860, p. 2, col. g; p. 3, col. a.
18. Ibid., September 12, 1860, p. 3, col. g.
19. See *Hansard Parliamentary Debates*, 3rd series, vol. 160, 1860, col. 1479, cols. 158–185; vol. 161, 1861, col. 1230; vol. 162, 1861, cols. 250–252.
20. *Irish Times*, July 17, 1860, p. 2, cols. d-e.
21. Ibid., August 24, 1860, p. 4, col. c.
22. Ibid., July 30, 1860, p. 3, col. e; September 3, 1860, p. 2, col. d; *Freeman's Journal*, August 8, 1860, p. 2, col. g; August 30, 1860, p. 3, col. g; September 3, 1860, p. 4, col. b.
23. By way of comparison, the same fundraiser gathered only £1,200 in the far richer cities of Manchester and Liverpool combined, and just £800 in Birmingham (*Morning Post*, December 13, 1860, p. 3, col. d).
24. *Irish Times*, December 26, 1860, p. 3, col. e.
25. Ibid., November 10, 1860, p. 3, col. e.
26. *Punch*, August 18, 1860, vol. 39, p. 64, cols. b-c.
27. *The Times*, July 12, 1860, p. 8, col. f.
28. Ibid., July 25, 1860, p. 9, cols. c-d.
29. Ibid., September 17, 1860, p. 7, cols. e-f; Leila Tarazi Fawaz, *Merchants and Migrants in Nineteenth-Century Beirut* (Cambridge, Mass.: Harvard University Press, 1983), p. 110.
30. Ibid., October 19, 1860, p. 4, col. a; October 20, 1860, p. 7, col. a.
31. Ibid., April 4, 1861, p. 8, col. e.
32. Wood to Ponsonby, October 14, 1839, in Sir Richard Wood, *The Early Correspondence of Richard Wood: 1831–1841*, ed. A. B. Cunningham (London: Royal Historical Society, 1966), pp. 136–137.
33. "Introduction" in ibid., pp. 8–36.
34. Ibid., p. 30; *Manchester Guardian*, July 24, 1860, p. 2, col. g; July 30, 1860, p. 3, col. a.
35. *The Times*, September 21, 1860, p. 8, col. c.
36. "A Lebanon Sheik," in, *All the Year Round*, ed. Charles Dickens, May 14, 1861, p. 63, col. b; p. 64, col. a. My colleague, Professor William G. Lane, suggests that the author may well have been E. J. Jones, an Englishman who spent several years in Betela (Beit Allah?) and contributed to Dickens's *Household Words*; see *Household Words*, comp. Anne Lohrli (Toronto: University of Toronto Press, 1973), p. 329, cols. a-b. Another possibility is M. R. L. Meason, who published "The Druses of Lebanon" in *Once a*

Week on July 28, 1860 (ibid., p. 329, col. b and p. 362, col. b) and who wrote to the *Morning Post* on October 10, 1860 (p. 7, col. a) that he had another general article on Lebanon which he hoped to publish in *All the Year Round*.

37. T. E. Kebbel, *Lord Beaconsfield and Other Tory Memories* (New York: M. Kennerley, 1907), pp. 219–220. Kebbel does not tell us exactly when he did this work for the *Morning Post*, but he places it just subsequent to the demise of the *New Quarterly*, which folded after two issues in 1860, according to the *British Union Catalogue of Periodicals*. An inspection of the leading articles in the *Morning Post* during the summer and autumn of 1860 shows that they often reveal an unusually detailed knowledge of Ottoman affairs and contrast in their strongly pro-Ottoman point of view with the articles sent in by the *Post's* correspondents in Paris and in Constantinople. The connection between the *Morning Post* and Musurus went back to the Crimean War and was still operative in 1876; see Lucy Brown, *Victorian News and Newspapers* (Oxford: Clarendon Press, 1985), p. 236.

38. Brown, *Victorian News*, pp. 116–117.

39. *Morning Post*, September 1, 1860, p. 4, cols. b-c. This article was reproduced in the *Irish Times*, September 4, 1860, p. 4, cols. c-d.

40. *Morning Post*, July 21, 1860, p. 4, col. c.

41. Ibid., July 24, 1860, p. 4, col. d.

42. *Manchester Guardian*, July 21, 1860, p. 5, col. f (full length); July 24, 1860, p. 4, col. b (summary). The coincidence in dates is explained by Francis Sheppard, "London and the Nation in the Nineteenth Century," *Transactions of the Royal Historical Society*, 5th series, vol. 35 (1985), p. 66; sometimes material was worked up for "simultaneous publication" in London and the provinces.

43. *Morning Post*, September 3, 1860, p. 5, col. f; September 4, 1860, p. 4, col. f.

44. Ibid., August 11, 1860, p. 4, col. f.

45. Ibid., September 17, 1860, p. 4, col. c; a similar point was made by the *Manchester Guardian*, October 15, 1860, p. 4, col. a, borrowing this time from the *Post's* Paris correspondent.

46. Ann Pottinger Saab, "The Doctors' Dilemma: Britain and the Cretan Crisis, 1866–69," *Journal of Modern History*, 49 (December 1977), On-Demand Supplement, pp. D1390–1391, © The University of Chicago, reprinted with permission.

47. *Morning Post*, July 19, 1860, p. 4, col. c.

48. Ibid., August 9, 1860, p. 4, col. b.

49. Ibid., July 27, 1860, p. 4, col. d.

50. Hansard, vol. 185, 1867, cols. 1512–1531; vol. 191, 1868, col. 811. This speech was reprinted as a pamphlet in 1876.

51. Ibid., vol. 185, col. 1537.

52. Ibid., vol. 191, cols. 814–815.

53. *The Times*, August 26, 1868, p. 10, col. f (letter from John Vickers).

54. Stanley to Cowley, March 27, 1867, *Sessional Papers: House of Commons*

(Great Britain, 1867–1868), vol. 73, "Correspondence Respecting the Disturbances in Crete," p. 56.

55. Alan J. Lee, *The Origins of the Popular Press in England, 1855–1914* (London: Croom Helm, 1976), p. 165.

56. Kebbel, *Tory Memories*, p. 220.

57. "The Cretan Rebellion," *Pall Mall Gazette*, November 29, 1866, p. 3, col. b.

58. Francis G. Hutchins, *The Illusion of Permanence* (Princeton: Princeton University Press, 1967).

59. *Freeman's Journal*, September 10, 1860, p. 2, col. g; p. 3, col. a.

60. Hansard, vol. 186, 1867, cols. 838–842.

61. Ibid., vol. 189, 1867, col. 173; for an excellent summary of the position of the Jews in Moldavia and Walachia, see Fritz Stern, *Gold and Iron* (New York: Knopf, 1977), pp. 351–355.

62. Hansard, vol. 187, 1867, cols. 1497–1498.

63. Ibid., vol. 188, 1867, cols. 748–750.

64. Ibid., vol. 230, 1876, col. 1181. On events in Jamaica, see Bernard Semmel, *Jamaican Blood and Victorian Conscience*, 1st American ed. (Boston: Houghton Mifflin, 1963).

65. Robert Blake, *Disraeli* (Garden City, N.Y.: Doubleday, 1968), p. 579.

66. Hansard, vol. 231, 1876, cols. 140–141.

67. Ibid., vol. 231, col. 221.

4. Conflicting Visions of the State

1. For a general definition of structural conduciveness, a term which seems to fit Britain's situation, see Neil J. Smelser, *Theory of Collective Behavior* (New York: Free Press, 1963), pp. 15, 278–279, 383–384.

2. Patricia Hollis, ed., *Pressure from Without in Early Victorian England* (New York: St. Martin's Press, 1974), "Introduction," pp. 3, 20.

3. John R. Vincent, *The Formation of the British Liberal Party* (New York: Charles Scribner's Sons, 1966), pp. 59–60.

4. Stephen E. Koss, *The Rise and Fall of the Political Press in Britain: The Nineteenth Century* (Chapel Hill, N.C.: University of North Carolina Press, 1981), p. 69; Francis Sheppard, "London and the Nation in the Nineteenth Century," *Transactions of the Royal Historical Society*, 5th series, vol. 35 (1985), pp. 65–66.

5. Hollis, *Pressure from Without*, pp. 21–25.

6. Vincent, *Liberal Party*, p. 123.

7. Donald Southgate, *The Passing of the Whigs, 1832–1886* (London: Macmillan, 1962), see especially pp. xiii–xvi, 193–227, and Appendix III.

8. Michael Brock, *The Great Reform Act* (London: Hutchinson, 1973), pp. 317, 320.

9. Robert Stewart, *The Politics of Protection* (Cambridge, Eng.: Cambridge University Press, 1971), p. 218.

10. Brock, *Reform Act*, p. 331.

11. Vincent, *Liberal Party*, pp. 95–96.

12. Ibid., p. 107.

13. Ibid., pp. 89–93, 124.
14. F. B. Smith, *The Making of the Second Reform Bill* (Cambridge, Eng.: Cambridge University Press, 1966), p. 236.
15. H. J. Hanham, *Elections and Party Management*, 2nd ed. (Hamden, Conn.: Archon Books, 1978; originally published 1959), p. xxviii; this point is also implied by Vincent's treatment, which looks at the period before and after 1867 as a unit.
16. Hanham, *Elections*, pp. xiii, xxiii–xxv; John P. Mackintosh, *The British Cabinet* (Toronto: University of Toronto Press, 1962), pp. 161–162, 165, 182–184, 216.
17. On the agricultural laborers see Pamela Horn, *Joseph Arch* (Kineton, Eng: Roundwood Press, 1971) and Joseph Arch, *Joseph Arch. The Story of His Life, Told by Himself* (New York: Garland, 1984, reprint of 2nd edition, originally published 1898).
18. Henry Broadhurst, *Henry Broadhurst, M.P.; The Story of His Life from the Stonemason's Bench to the Treasury Bench* (London: Hutchinson, 1901) provides a fascinating account of the rise of this early working-class M.P. and junior minister.
19. Walter L. Arnstein, *The Bradlaugh Case* (Oxford: Clarendon Press, 1965), pp. 21, 79.
20. J. P. Parry, *Democracy and Religion: Gladstone and the Liberal Party, 1867–1875* (Cambridge, Eng.: Cambridge University Press, 1986), p. 214.
21. Hanham, *Elections*, pp. 324–327, outlines this general view of working-class leadership.
22. Royden Harrison, *Before the Socialists* (London: Routledge and Kegan Paul, 1965), p. 139.
23. See Harrison, *Before the Socialists*, for an opinion that pressure from without was critical; most recent treatments, however, like F. B. Smith, *Second Reform Bill*, and Maurice Cowling, *1867: Disraeli, Gladstone and Revolution* (London: Cambridge University Press, 1967) emphasize the importance of negotiation among individuals, factions, and parties within Parliament.
24. Harrison, *Before the Socialists*, p. 204; Geoffrey Crossick, *An Artisan Elite in Victorian Society* (London: Croom Helm, 1978), p. 139.
25. Article on George Howell, *Dictionary of National Biography, Supplement 1901–11*, (London: Oxford University Press, 1917–), 308–309.
26. Harrison, *Before the Socialists*, p. 163.
27. Brock, *Reform Act*, p. 318.
28. Harrison, *Before the Socialists*, p. 139.
29. Hanham, *Elections*, p. 93.
30. Harrison, *Before the Socialists*, pp. 141–200, provides a detailed and instructive account of the role of working-class leaders in the 1868 elections.
31. Ibid., pp. 194–199.
32. Ibid., pp. 211, 215; E. P. Thompson, *William Morris*, rev. ed. (New York: Pantheon, 1977; originally published 1955), pp. 211–213; Broadhurst, *Life*, pp. 64–68; Parry, *Democracy and Religion*, p. 400.
33. For a fascinating discussion of this problem, see Agatha Ramm, "The

parliamentary context of Cabinet government, 1868–1874," *English Historical Review*, 99 (1984), 739–769.

34. Hanham, *Elections*, p. 93.

35. Darlington, *Northern Echo*, September 5, 1876, p. 2, col. f.

36. Stephen E. Koss, *Nonconformity in Modern British Politics* (Hamden, Conn.: Archon Books, 1975), p. 15.

37. William Ewart Gladstone, *The Gladstone Diaries*, ed. M. R. D. Foot and H. C. G. Matthew, 11 vols. to date (Oxford: Clarendon Press, 1968–), VII, xxix.

38. Parry, *Democracy and Religion*, p. 39.

39. Brock, *Reform Act*, p. 333.

40. J. L. Garvin, *The Life of Joseph Chamberlain*, 4 vols. (London: Macmillan, 1932), I, 104.

41. Parry, *Democracy and Religion*, pp. 295–306.

42. Garvin, *Chamberlain*, I, 102–104; John Morley, *The Life of William Ewart Gladstone*, 3 vols. (New York: Macmillan, 1903), II, 298–301.

43. John Lawson and Harold Silver, *A Social History of Education in England* (London: Methuen, 1973), pp. 315–316.

44. Marjorie Cruickshank, *Church and State in English Education, 1870 to the Present Day* (New York: St. Martin's Press, 1963), pp. 29–30, 38–39, 41.

45. Ibid., p. 31.

46. Morley, *Life of Gladstone*, II, 303–304, 308–309; Garvin, *Chamberlain*, I, 104–105.

47. Koss, *Nonconformity*, pp. 24–26; Hanham, *Elections*, pp. 121–122. Parry *(Democracy and Religion)* believes that the education issue had been settled by 1874 as Nonconformist candidates seized control of local school boards; he emphasizes the defection of the Whigs, especially in the counties (pp. 393–398).

48. H. C. G. Matthew, *Gladstone 1809–1874* (Oxford: Clarendon Press, 1986), p. 203; Parry, *Democracy and Religion*, pp. 332, 427.

49. Crossick, *Artisan Elite*, p. 140.

50. Harrison, *Before the Socialists*, pp. 37–39, 209; Gareth Stedman Jones, *Outcast London* (New York: Pantheon, 1984; originally published 1971), p. 167.

51. *Daily News*, September 6, 1876, p. 3, col. f.

52. Ibid., January 28, 1878, p. 2, col. b.

53. Stan Shipley, *Club Life and Socialism in Mid-Victorian London* (Oxford: History Workshop, 1972), p. 24. A general description of the clubs is given on pp. 21–34.

54. Richard Price, *An Imperial War and the British Working Class* (London: Routledge and Kegan Paul, 1972), pp. 46–70, discusses the patronage of the club movement at length and, unlike Shipley, views the clubs in these early years as instruments of bourgeois control; Shipley, *Club Life*, p. 13; *Daily News*, September 13, 1876, p. 3, col. a.

55. Shipley, *Club Life*, pp. 28–33.

56. Even when he concluded that Muslims were unacceptable as rulers over Christians, Gladstone was quite prepared to believe that they could rule effectively over other Muslims; see William Ewart Gladstone, "Aggres-

sion on Egypt and Freedom in the East," *Nineteenth Century,* 2 (August 1877), 160.

57. Parry, *Democracy and Religion,* p. 175.
58. Gladstone, *Diaries,* VIII, 532.
59. For useful definitions of Ritualism, see P. T. Marsh, *The Victorian Church in Decline* (Pittsburgh: University of Pittsburgh Press, 1969), pp. 112–115, and James Bentley, *Ritualism and Politics in Victorian Britain* (Oxford: Oxford University Press, 1978), pp. 20–30.
60. Bentley, *Ritualism,* pp. 23–27, 124.
61. Parry, *Democracy and Religion,* p. 186.
62. Marsh, *Victorian Church,* pp. 111–40; see also D. A. Hamer, *The Politics of Electoral Pressure* (Hassocks, Eng.: Harvester Press, 1977), pp. 94–99.
63. Marsh, *Victorian Church,* pp. 117, 140–144, 154–157.
64. Ibid., pp. 158–172.
65. Parry, *Democracy and Religion,* pp. 98, 413.
66. *Hansard Parliamentary Debates,* 3rd series, vol. 221, 1874, col. 1086.
67. Ibid., col. 1172.
68. Bentley, *Ritualism,* pp. 64–65.
69. Parry, *Democracy and Religion,* p. 409; Agatha Ramm, *William Ewart Gladstone* (Cardiff: University of Wales Press, 1989), pp. 70–72; Gladstone, *Diaries,* IX, 4–6.
70. Morley, *Life of Gladstone,* II, 498.
71. Bentley, *Ritualism,* pp. 75–79.
72. Crossick, *Artisan Elite,* pp. 248–251.

5. Gladstone's Pursuit of Singlemindedness

1. R. T. Shannon, *Gladstone and the Bulgarian Agitation, 1876,* 2nd ed. (Hassocks, Eng.: Harvester Press, 1975; originally published 1963), p. 90: "far from being a decisive agent, Gladstone was practically carried into the agitation by others. Far from being the conscious meditator of a diabolically cunning coup of right timing against Disraeli, Gladstone was, at most, absentmindedly waiting for something to turn up; and then remained for long unconscious of the fact that something had turned up. Far from being excited into activity by the atrocities in Bulgaria, Gladstone's excitement was related almost exclusively to the popular movement in England. Far from being an impatient crusader against Disraeli, Gladstone, even after committing himself on 6 September, wasted a vital and precious month in delays and vacillations. Far from deliberately boosting forward the agitation in September, in effect Gladstone did more than anyone else to put a drag on its impetus." See also R. T. Shannon, "Midlothian 100 Years After," in *Gladstone, Politics and Religion,* ed. Peter J. Jagger (New York: St. Martin's Press, 1985), pp. 88–103.
2. William Ewart Gladstone, *The Gladstone Diaries,* ed. M. R. D. Foot and H. C. G. Matthew, 11 vols. to date (Oxford, Clarendon Press, 1968–), VII and VIII.
3. *Hansard Parliamentary Debates,* 3rd series, vol. 231, 1876, cols. 174–177.

4. John Morley, *The Life of William Ewart Gladstone*, 3 vols. (New York: Macmillan, 1903), I, 492.

5. Gladstone, *Diaries*, V, 77; Richard Millman, *Britain and the Eastern Question, 1875–1878* (Oxford: Clarendon Press, 1979), pp. 183–184.

6. Richard Shannon, *Gladstone*, vol. I (London: Hamilton, 1982), pp. 352–353.

7. Gladstone's speech is given in Hansard, vol. 150, 1858, cols. 44–66; quotation from col. 59.

8. Hansard, vol. 150, cols. 59–60.

9. [William Ewart Gladstone], "The Past and Present Administrations," *Quarterly Review*, 104 (October 1858), 554–560. Shannon contends (in Jagger, *Politics and Religion*, pp. 93–97) that Gladstone definitively wrote off the Ottoman Empire in this article and then forebore to act on his convictions for eighteen years: first, because it was not expedient to oppose Palmerston; second, after Palmerston's death, because he felt public opinion would not support him. This interpretation presupposes a level of hypocrisy on Gladstone's part which would be implausible in hardened cynics; it also neglects Gladstone's own argument that decentralization might prove the answer to the Ottoman Empire's problems. This was not a foolish suggestion: at least, neither the Russians nor, as Gladstone notes, the French thought so.

10. Michael Pratt, *Britain's Greek Empire* (London: Collings, 1978), pp. 145–146; Agatha Ramm, *William Ewart Gladstone* (Cardiff: University of Wales Press, 1989), pp. 30–33.

11. Bruce Knox, "British policy and the Ionian Islands, 1847–1864: Nationalism and imperial administration," *English Historical Review*, 99 (1984), 506.

12. For a short summary of the tribulations of British rule of the Islands, see Knox, "British Policy," and Pratt, *Greek Empire*, pp. 104–145.

13. Pratt, *Greek Empire*, pp. 145–146.

14. H. C. G. Matthew, "Introduction," in Gladstone, *Diaries*, V, lxx.

15. S. G. Checkland, *The Gladstones* (Cambridge, Eng.: Cambridge University Press, 1971), pp. 400–401.

16. Hugh Lloyd-Jones, *Blood for the Ghosts* (Baltimore, Md.: The Johns Hopkins University Press, 1983), p. 123.

17. Ibid., p. 120; Frank M. Turner, *The Greek Heritage in Victorian Britain* (New Haven: Yale University Press, 1981), pp. 164–165, 449.

18. Turner, *Heritage*, p. 448.

19. Lloyd-Jones, *Blood*, pp. 114–115.

20. Matthew, "Introduction," in Gladstone, *Diaries*, V, lx; see also on this whole subject H. C. G. Matthew, "Gladstone, Vaticanism, and the Question of the East," *Studies in Church History* 15 (1978), pp. 417–441.

21. Morley, *Life of Gladstone*, I, 597.

22. Pratt, *Greek Empire*, pp. 113, 146–148.

23. Morley, *Gladstone*, I, 611–614; Charles Lacaita, *An Italian Englishman, Sir James Lacaita* (London: G. Richards, 1933), pp. 113–114.

24. Pratt, *Greek Empire*, pp. 147–148.

25. For a description applicable to the Ionian movement, see Neil J. Smelser, *Theory of Collective Behavior* (New York: Free Press, 1963), pp. 270–273.

26. Shannon, *Gladstone*, p. 475.
27. Lacaita, *Italian Englishman*, pp. 114–115.
28. Morley, *Gladstone*, I, 605; Lacaita, *Italian Englishman*, pp. 115–116.
29. Gladstone, *Diaries*, V, 357–358.
30. John R. Vincent, *The Formation of the British Liberal Party* (New York: Charles Scribner's Sons, 1966), p. 212.
31. Gladstone, *Diaries*, V, 367. Matthew mistakenly refers to the Valide Jaffir Pasha in n. 3 as "civil governor of the province" (vali); since valide means mother, she must have been the "hostess" later described as interceding for her son, Jaffir Pasha.
32. Pratt, *Greek Empire*, p. 148. It is instructive to contrast Gladstone's discomfort during his visit to Albania with the sense of adventure with which Disraeli had welcomed his even more arduous excursion into the same general area some twenty-five years before. See Benjamin Disraeli, *Letters: 1815–1834*, ed. J. A. W. Gunn, John Matthews, Donald M. Schurman, and M. G. Wiebe (Toronto: University of Toronto Press, 1982), I, 166–171, and Chapters 1 & 6. An illuminating comparison of Disraeli and Gladstone is offered by Robert Blake, "Disraeli and Gladstone," in Jagger, *Politics and Religion*, pp. 1–20; Blake considers Gladstone "the more cosmopolitan and cultivated of the two" (p. 15). It is certainly true, as Blake states, that Gladstone traveled more, and doubtless this had a cumulative effect over a lifetime; but documentary evidence suggests that Disraeli approached the very different world of the eastern Mediterranean in a far more open and receptive frame of mind than did Gladstone, a contrast not entirely to be explained by the fact that he was a younger man at the time.
33. Shannon, *Gladstone*, I, 438–439.
34. Gladstone, *Diaries*, VI, 489.
35. Hansard, vol. 171, 1863, cols. 140–147.
36. Shannon, *Gladstone*, pp. 474–475.
37. Gladstone, *Diaries*, VI, 475.
38. Ibid., p. 489.
39. Hansard, vol. 185, 1867, cols. 441–445.
40. For a brief summary of the diplomatic crisis, see S. J. Shaw and E. K. Shaw, *History of the Ottoman Empire and Modern Turkey*, 2 vols. (Cambridge, Eng.: Cambridge University Press, 1976–1977), vol. 2, "Reform, Revolution, and Republic: The Rise of Modern Turkey, 1808–1975," pp. 151–152.
41. Gladstone to Clarendon, January 18, 1869, quoted in Gladstone, *Diaries*, VII, 13.
42. Gladstone to Clarendon, October 18, 1869, quoted in Gladstone, *Diaries*, VII, 151.
43. Gladstone to E. Hammond, October 28, 1870, quoted in Gladstone, *Diaries*, VII, 388.
44. Gladstone, *Diaries*, IX, 103 and n. 3, quoting Gladstone's speech to the House of Commons from Hansard, vol. 227, 1876, col. 106.
45. See Chapter 7 and Shannon, *Bulgarian Agitation*, pp. 24–25.
46. Gladstone, *Diaries*, IX, 121 and n. 4, 141.

47. Ibid., p. 142 and Hansard, vol. 230, 1876, cols. 1741–1748.
48. Gladstone, *Diaries*, IX, 129 and n. 2, 132 and n. 3; Shannon, *Bulgarian Agitation*, pp. 93–95.
49. Edmund Sheridan Purcell, *Life and Letters of Ambrose Phillips de Lisle*, ed. Edwin de Lisle, 2 vols. (London: Macmillan, 1899), II, 153, 163. The *Diaries*, in which Gladstone kept careful account of his reading, do not show that he read either Fleming's or de Lisle's book during 1876.
50. Shannon, *Bulgarian Agitation*, pp. 94–95.
51. Gladstone, *Diaries*, IX, 142–144; Shannon, *Bulgarian Agitation*, p. 95.
52. Hansard, vol. 231, cols. 192, 198.
53. Shannon, *Bulgarian Agitation*, p. 96.
54. Ibid., p. 98; Gladstone, *Diaries*, IX, 146 and n. 9.
55. Gladstone, *Diaries*, IX, 139 n. 1; Shannon, *Bulgarian Agitation*, p. 98.
56. Gladstone, *Diaries*, IX, 148.
57. Gladstone to Granville, August 20, 1876, #1 in Agatha Ramm, ed., *The Political Correspondence of Mr. Gladstone and Lord Granville, 1876–1886*, 2 vols. (Oxford: Clarendon Press, 1962), I, 1.
58. Shannon, *Bulgarian Agitation*, pp. 98–99.
59. MacColl to Gladstone, August 21, [1876], British Library, Additional Manuscript 44243, ff. 173–174.
60. MacColl to Gladstone, [August 26, 1876], Add. MS 44243, f. 182.
61. MacColl to Gladstone, September 1, [1876], Add. MS 44243, f. 189.
62. Shannon, *Bulgarian Agitation*, p. 102; W. T. Stead to Gladstone, August 26, 1876, Add. MS 44303, ff. 230–231.
63. W. T. Stead, ed., *The M.P. from Russia*, 2 vols. (New York: Putnam, 1909), I, 236.
64. Gladstone to Stead, September 2, 1876, Add. MS 44303, f. 232.
65. See Madame Novikov to Gladstone, July 2, 1875, and September 12, 1876, Add. MS 44268, f. 27; ff. 31–32.
66. Granville, consulted, advised against this, but his letter arrived too late. Gladstone to Granville, August 27, 1876, #3, in Ramm, *Political Correspondence*, I, 3.
67. Gladstone, *Diaries*, IX, 149 and n. 9; Shannon, *Bulgarian Agitation*, pp. 100–101.
68. Gladstone to Granville, August 29, 1876, #4, in Ramm, *Political Correspondence*, I, 3.
69. Shannon, *Bulgarian Agitation*, pp. 92, 100–101; Shannon, "Midlothian," in Jagger, *Politics and Religion*, pp. 95, 100–102.
70. Agatha Ramm, "Gladstone as Politician," in Jagger, *Politics and Religion*, pp. 104–116, quotation p. 105.

6. The First Stirrings of Protest

1. Neil J. Smelser, *Theory of Collective Behavior* (New York: Free Press, 1963), pp. 298–299.
2. Ibid., p. 297; the terms are Smelser's.

3. R. T. Shannon, *Gladstone and the Bulgarian Agitation, 1876,* 2nd ed. (Hassocks, Eng.: Harvester Press, 1975; originally published 1963), p. 90.

4. These two groups were more typically at war: see D. A. Hamer, *The Politics of Electoral Pressure* (Hassocks, Eng.: Harvester Press, 1977), p. 8.

5. Gordon L. Iseminger, "The Old Turkish Hands: The British Levantine Consuls, 1856–1876," *Middle East Journal,* 22 (1968), 299–301, 312 n. 61.

6. G. Muir Mackenzie and A. P. Irby, *Travels in the Slavonic Provinces of Turkey-in-Europe* (London: Bell and Daldy, 1867).

7. David Harris, *Britain and the Bulgarian Horrors of 1876* (Chicago: University of Chicago Press, 1939), p. 42; Sir Edwin Pears, *Forty Years in Constantinople* (New York: D. Appleton, 1916), pp. 8, 12–16, 59.

8. Shannon, *Bulgarian Agitation,* pp. 40–41.

9. Pears, *Forty Years,* pp. 17–18; Shannon, *Bulgarian Agitation,* p. 54.

10. Shannon, *Bulgarian Agitation,* pp. 45–48, 59, 61–62.

11. Darlington, *Northern Echo,* July 4, 1876, p. 3, cols. c-d; July 11, p. 3, col. b; July 22, p. 3, col. b.

12. Strangford to Corry, June 25, 1876, Disraeli Papers, B/XVI/B/113 (Box 69), Western Manuscripts, Bodleian Library, Oxford.

13. *Hansard Parliamentary Debates,* 3rd series, vol. 230, 1876, cols. 1181–1182.

14. Robert Blake, *Disraeli* (Garden City, N.Y.: Doubleday, 1968), p. 593.

15. Hansard, vol. 230, cols. 1494–1495.

16. Ibid., vol. 231, 1876, col. 203.

17. John Morley, *The Life of William Ewart Gladstone,* 3 vols. (New York: Macmillan, 1903), II, 551.

18. Blake, *Disraeli,* p. 594.

19. Cecil Roth, *Benjamin Disraeli, Earl of Beaconsfield* (New York: Philosophical Library, 1952); pp. 1–23 give a full account of Disraeli's origins.

20. Benjamin Disraeli, *Letters: 1815–1834,* ed. J. A. W. Gunn, John Matthews, Donald M. Schurman, and M. G. Wiebe (Toronto: University of Toronto Press, 1982), p. 165 (editorial note on Benjamin Disraeli to Isaac D'Israeli, October 25, 1830, Prevesa, Greece).

21. Ibid., Disraeli to E. Lytton Bulwer, Constantinople, December 27, 1830, p. 179.

22. Ibid., Benjamin Disraeli to Isaac D'Israeli, Prevesa, Greece, October 25, 1830, p. 167.

23. Ibid., Benjamin Disraeli to Benjamin Austen, November 18, 1830, p. 174.

24. This fact cannot have escaped Disraeli; it was the subject of several Parliamentary debates and must have been brought to his attention by Jewish friends. See for example William Demo to Corry, June 15, 1877, enclosing a pamphlet by Armand Levy, April 1873, entitled "The Position of the Jews in Rumania," Disraeli Papers, B/XVI/B/145–47 (Box 69).

25. See Richard W. Davis, *The English Rothschilds* (Chapel Hill: University of North Carolina Press, 1983), pp. 86–89.

26. *Jewish Chronicle,* September 8, 1876, p. 356, cols. a-b; September 22, 1876, p. 396, col. a (commentary on the Earl of Derby's view of the Bulgarian crisis).

27. Ibid., October 20, 1876, p. 458, col. a.

28. Darlington, *Northern Echo*, September 22, 1876, p. 2, col. f.

29. Agatha Ramm, *William Ewart Gladstone* (Cardiff: University of Wales Press, 1989), p. 73.

30. Stephen E. Koss, *The Rise and Fall of the Political Press in Britain: The Nineteenth Century* (Chapel Hill: University of North Carolina Press, 1981), pp. 118–136, 210.

31. Alan J. Lee, *The Origins of the Popular Press in England, 1855–1914* (London: Croom Helm, 1976), p. 118.

32. Darlington, *Northern Echo*, July 7, 1876, p. 2, col. f. More than a third (35%) of the petitions sent to Parliament during the summer of 1876 came from the North (House of Lords Record Office: *Report of the Select Committee on Parliamentary Petitions, 1876*).

33. *Northern Echo*, July 14, 1876, p. 3, cols. b-c.

34. Ibid., August 28, 1876, p. 2, col. f.

35. See for example ibid., August 17, 1876, p. 3, col. c.

36. Ibid., July 10, 1876, p. 3, col. d.

37. Stead to Gladstone, August 26, 1876, British Library, Additional Manuscript 44303, ff. 230–231.

38. Gladstone to Stead, September 2, 1876, Add. MS 44303, f. 232.

39. Shannon, *Bulgarian Agitation*, p. 75.

40. William Ewart Gladstone, *The Gladstone Diaries*, ed. M. R. D. Foot and H. C. G. Matthew, 11 vols. to date (Oxford: Clarendon Press, 1968–), IX, 150–152; Gladstone to [Frank Hill], September 1, 1876, Add. MS 44451, f.102.

41. Morley, *Life of Gladstone*, II, 552; Ramm, *Gladstone*, p. 73.

42. Stead to Gladstone, September 6, 1876, Add. MS 44303, f. 233.

43. The word "revivalist" is Shannon's (*Bulgarian Agitation*, pp. 115–116).

44. William Ewart Gladstone, *The Bulgarian Horrors and the Question of the East* (London: J. Murray, 1876), pp. 7–33.

45. It may seem strange that Nonconformists were willing to accept Gladstone's lead on an issue of official religious intolerance in light of the Education Act of 1870. Two points may, however, be urged. First, the Education Act was even more identified with W. E. Forster than with Gladstone. Second, Gladstone's anti-Catholic writings after leaving office in 1874 had helped to reestablish his credibility with Nonconformists.

46. Gladstone, *Bulgarian Horrors*, pp. 13, 22, 24–25, 33.

47. *Punch*, October 7, 1876, vol. 71, p. 149; November 25, 1876, vol. 71, p. 229.

48. Gladstone, *Bulgarian Horrors*, pp. 31–53.

49. Ibid., pp. 61–62.

50. Shannon, *Bulgarian Agitation*, p. 101.

51. Gladstone, *Diaries*, IX, 153 and n. 4, n. 13. The low estimate of numbers present at Blackheath appears in *Daily News*, September 11, 1876, p. 2, col. b.

52. See W. T. Stead, ed., *The MP for Russia* (New York: Putnam, 1909), I, 257.

53. Morley, *Life of Gladstone*, II, 554.

54. Smelser, *Collective Behavior*, p. 6, quoting J. B. Gittler, ed., *Review of Sociology: Analysis of a Decade* (New York: John Wiley, 1957), p. 130.
55. Morley, *Gladstone*, II, 550.
56. Smelser, *Collective Behavior*, p. 6.

7. *The Movement Matures*

1. Neil J. Smelser, *Theory of Collective Behavior* (New York: Free Press, 1963), pp. 296–299.
2. Darlington, *Northern Echo*, September 7, 1876, p. 2, col. f.
3. Glynne-Gladstone MSS, St. Deiniol's Library, Hawarden, Thomas McConcas to Gladstone, Upper Teddington, Middlesex, September 11, 1876 (Box 55).
4. William Ewart Gladstone, *The Gladstone Diaries*, ed. M. R. D. Foot and H. C. G. Matthew, 11 vols. to date (Oxford: Clarendon Press, 1968–), IX, 154.
5. Ibid., pp. 154–156; Gladstone's remarks for the press were published on September 16. See Gladstone, *Diaries*, IX, 155 n. 6 and R. T. Shannon, *Gladstone and the Bulgarian Agitation, 1876*, 2nd ed. (Hassocks, Eng.: Harvester Press, 1975; originally published 1963), p. 126.
6. Gladstone to Granville, October 7, 1876, #18 in Agatha Ramm, ed., *The Political Correspondence of Mr. Gladstone and Lord Granville, 1876–1886*, 2 vols. (Oxford: Clarendon Press, 1962), I, 13.
7. Gladstone, *Diaries*, IX, 161 and n. 10.
8. Gladstone to Granville, October 18, 1876, #20, Ramm, *Political Correspondence*, I, 15; Glynne-Gladstone MSS, J. Sword to Gladstone, October 21, 1876 (Box 87).
9. Gladstone to Granville, October 3, 1876, #15, Ramm, *Political Correspondence*, I, 10–11. It has never been exactly clear what Gladstone's motives were—avoidance of agitation, promotion of agitation, both at once, or simply acceptance of social obligations he could not now duck. Shannon, although he judges the trip "innocent" and emphasizes that Gladstone did not wish to become further involved in the agitation, explains that many Whigs "were nervous" about it, suspecting that Gladstone intended to stir up the country (*Bulgarian Agitation*, pp. 126–127). The Gladstones actually decided upon "extending a little the circle of . . . visits" (Ramm, *Political Correspondence*, I, 10–11) once Gladstone concluded they could be innocuous. However, a series of visits on this scale must have been arranged at least tentatively weeks or months in advance; simple politeness, a strong consideration with Gladstone, would have argued against any major change of plans at the last minute. I am indebted to Dr. Agatha Ramm for this suggestion.
10. Gladstone, *Diaries*, IX, 157.
11. Glynne-Gladstone MSS, Thomas Cruddass to Gladstone, September 22, 1876 (Box 18).
12. Ibid., September 23, 1876 (Box 18).
13. Gladstone, *Diaries*, IX, 157 and n. 11.

14. Ibid., pp. 158–160; see also Glynne-Gladstone MSS, Thomas Melrose to Gladstone, September 27, 1876 (Box 59) for Coldstream, and *Daily News*, October 20, 1876, p. 3, col. c for Alnwick.

15. Gladstone to Hill, September 28, 1876, British Library, Additional Manuscript 44451, f. 258.

16. Shannon, *Bulgarian Agitation*, pp. 148, 239, n. 1. To facilitate comparison with later stages of the protest, petitions for and against the government have been lumped together. The percentage of antigovernment petitions coming from such meetings was even higher. The newspapers examined (*Daily News, Morning Post,* and *Standard*) give a similar impression. The bulk of petitions to Parliament in 1876 were apparently circulated without meetings. They were limited to the period when Parliament was in session; the last ones are dated August 10, 1876, and so they do not fall into the period under discussion (House of Lords Record Office: *Report of the Select Committee on Parliamentary Petitions, 1876*).

17. Remarks here and throughout are based on a close reading of the *Daily News,* the *Morning Post,* and the *Standard*.

18. Shannon, *Bulgarian Agitation*, pp. 148–153. This was especially clear at the national level; of the three protests submitted by nationwide organizations, two were religious in origin (the British and Foreign Unitarian Association and the Baptist Union of Britain and Ireland). On the other hand, the initiatives taken by party associations, although sometimes a stimulus behind the scenes, were largely and designedly invisible. In Exeter, for example, since no move to requisition the mayor developed spontaneously, the Reform Association "issued placards" (*Daily News,* September 1, 1876, p. 3, col. c).

19. Article on W. R. Cremer, *Dictionary of National Biography* (supplement 1901–11), (London: Oxford University Press, 1917–), I, 441–442; article on George Howell, II, 308–309; XXII, 248–250; Walter L. Arnstein, *The Bradlaugh Case* (Oxford: Clarendon Press, 1965).

20. Thomas Mottershead, for example, had been heavily involved (and was probably remunerated for his work) in rallying the working-class vote behind Liberal party candidates in the 1868 elections; see Royden Harrison, *Before the Socialists* (London: Routledge and Kegan Paul, 1965), pp. 153–156. Mottershead nonetheless chaired the General Council of Marx's First International in 1871; see Stan Shipley, *Club Life and Socialism in Mid-Victorian London* (Oxford: History Workshop, 1972), pp. 16–17.

21. Cremer had been trained as a carpenter, Howell as a bricklayer, Henry Broadhurst as a stonemason (for the latter's career in brief see article on Broadhurst, *DNB* (supplement 1901–11), II, 228–230; also Henry Broadhurst, *Henry Broadhurst M.P.: The Story of his Life from a Stonemason's Bench to the Treasury Bench* (London: Hutchinson, 1901), especially pp. 3–30.

22. Examples are the barrister and Christian Socialist, Thomas Hughes, who had been member for Lambeth, 1865–1868 (article on Thomas Hughes, *DNB*, XXII, 879–882, best remembered for writing *Tom Brown's School Days*) and the blind Cambridge professor, Henry Fawcett, who had been elected for Hackney in 1874 (article on Henry Fawcett, *DNB*, VI, 1116–1121).

23. Bradlaugh, the founder of the National Secular Society, was militantly, even crankily, secular.

24. Shannon rather underestimates the agitation in London *(Bulgarian Agitation,* pp. 149–155); it was more than "very respectable," and should not be judged solely on the number of petitions produced (only 33 out of a total of 455 for the agitation). In the more populous boroughs of London, one petition might issue from a series of meetings and might represent the opinions and organizational efforts of a considerably larger group of people than in the more decentralized provinces.

25. Shannon discovered at least 455 petitions of protest addressed to the Foreign Office during the autumn and winter, 407 of them, or 90 percent, originating between September 1 and October 9 (Shannon, *Bulgarian Agitation,* pp. 147–149). In addition 54 petitions supported the government, all but 11 of them coming after October 10 (ibid., p. 239, n. 1).

26. Fifty percent of the first 50 protests against government policy and 40 percent of the anti-government petitions in the first two weeks of September; Shannon's important statistical analysis appears in *Bulgarian Agitation,* pp. 149–150.

27. Fifty percent of the anti-government protests between October 10 and December 27 came from the North. Shannon's geographical categories (from *Bulgarian Agitation,* p. 149, n. 4) have been retained in this study and extended to the later protest:

    Midlands: Shropshire, Staffordshire, Derby, Nottingham, Lincoln, Rutland, Leicester, Northampton, Warwick, Worcester, and Hereford
    North: Northumberland, Cumberland, Durham, Westmorland, Lancashire, Yorkshire, and Cheshire
    Southeast: Norfolk, Cambridge, Hunts and Peterborough, Bedford, Buckingham, Oxford, Berkshire, Hampshire, Sussex, Surrey, Kent, Greater London, Hertford, Essex, and Suffolk
    Southwest: Cornwall, Devon, Somerset, Gloucester, Wiltshire, and Dorset
    Wales: includes Monmouthshire

28. The precise figures were: Southwest, 1:29; Wales, 1:48; the North, 1:54. Shannon relates this to the prominence of Nonconformists in the movement *(Bulgarian Agitation,* pp. 150–151). This hypothesis, though plausible, is not supported by the lesser role played by the Southwest in the later protest in 1878, when Nonconformists were particularly active (see Figure 4, Chapter 9).

29. Gladstone noted this with some chagrin and suggested, first to Granville (Gladstone to Granville, September 14, 1876, #10, Ramm, *Political Correspondence,* I, 7) and then to Stead (Gladstone to Stead, October 18, 1876, "Private," Add. MS 44303, ff. 245–246), that something ought to be done. But, as Stead recognized, the counties, each one still very much a world unto itself largely untouched by the Reform Act of 1867, were not fertile ground for this kind of protest; see Stead to Gladstone, October 18, 1876, Add. MS 44303, f. 248. On the counties, see H. J. Hanham, *Elections and Party Management,* 2nd ed. (Hamden, Conn.: Archon Books, 1978; originally published 1959), pp. 3–4. Indeed, to the extent that the Eastern

Question was addressed in the counties, typically at agricultural shows, support was generally expressed for the government (see for example the Winchcombe Agricultural Show on September 15, *Daily News*, September 18, 1876, p. 2, cols. c-d and the Banbury Agricultural Association on September 19, *Daily News*, September 20, 1876, p. 6, col. f). The most famous speech in such a setting endorsing the Cabinet's policy was Disraeli's speech at Aylesbury.

30. Shannon, *Bulgarian Agitation*, pp. 149–150, and Figure 1.

31. *Daily News*, October 7, 1876, p. 2, col. b.

32. Glynne-Gladstone MSS, E. Davis to Gladstone, September 10, 1876 (Box 19). To capitalize on the feeling aroused by the Blackheath speech, Davis suggested setting up a *"Shilling* Relief Fund"; it would be named for William and Catherine Gladstone and would involve women as well as men as each artisan household contributed one shilling.

33. Newspaper reports, an obvious source, are doubtless exaggerated. For example, George Graham wrote to the *Standard* about the protest meeting at Penge, enthusiastically reported by the *Daily News*. Graham, who claimed to have been present, reported that no more than thirty-four voted in favor of any one of the resolutions, in a district in London which claimed eighteen to twenty thousand inhabitants *(Daily News*, September 8, 1876, p. 2, col. a; *Standard*, September 9, 1876, p. 5, col. c).

34. *Daily News*, September 5, 1876, p. 3, col. a; *Morning Post*, September 5, 1876, p. 2, col. c; September 6, 1876, p. 6, col. c.

35. Specific figures were generally not reported; meetings were ambiguously billed as "crowded" or "numerously attended." London meetings offered the largest potential crowds; at a low estimate, Gladstone was said to have drawn six to seven thousand at Blackheath *(Daily News*, September 11, 1876, p. 2, col. b), but this was far smaller than the estimated audiences on some previous occasions when he spoke to his constituents *(Standard*, September 5, 1876, p. 3, col. d).

36. *Morning Post*, September 28, 1876, p. 4, col. e.

37. The terms are Smelser's in *Collective Behavior*, p. 296.

38. For a description of a typical meeting, see Darlington, *Northern Echo*, July 14, 1876, p. 3, cols. b-c. See also ibid., September 2, 1876, p. 3, col. d.

39. Freeman stressed the advantage of "plain, practical points" rather than empty moralizing. In addition to Elliot's dismissal, he suggested calls for an extraordinary session of Parliament during the autumn; withdrawal of the British fleet from Eastern waters so as not to encourage the Turks in false hopes of British support; and "the uselessness of all terms of peace which do not set free the revolted lands from Turkish rule" *(Daily News*, September 5, 1876, p. 6, cols. d-e).

40. Regular columns were run in the newspapers; see, for example, the *Northern Echo's* feature entitled "The North Country and the Atrocities," August 29, 1876, p. 3, cols. c-d.

41. For an important discussion of the nature of the Victorian press, see Lucy Brown, *Victorian News and Newspapers* (Oxford: Clarendon Press, 1985), especially pp. 57, 63, 66–67, and 277.

42. Denbigh to Corry, September 28, [1876], "Private," Disraeli Papers, B/ XVI/C/357 (Box 71), Western Manuscripts, Bodleian Library, Oxford.

43. H. Drummond Wolff to Disraeli, September 8, 1876, Disraeli Papers, B/ XVI/B/115 (Box 69).

44. William Crawshay had made a fortune by supplying iron to the railroads as they were constructed, taking his payment in the form of shares in the railroad companies (article on William Crawshay, *DNB*, V, 63).

45. See Richard Shannon, "David Urquhart and the Foreign Affairs Committees," in *Pressure from Without in Early Victorian England*, ed. Patricia Hollis (New York: St. Martin's Press, 1974), pp. 255–257. Pears relates that when the Porte announced a contract for a hundred iron buoys to mark the channel in the harbor at Constantinople, Crawshay wanted it, and made a bid which scarcely covered his expenses. Unfortunately, a continental country which offered a substantially higher bid won the contract through bribery. When the buoys arrived, they did not have the proper airholes and would not float. Crawshay was furious, but he rationalized his disappointment by saying that the transaction must have been handled by some Levantine Christian; see Sir Edwin Pears, *Forty Years in Constantinople* (New York: D. Appleton, 1916), pp. 6–7.

46. Other causes of the Crawshays' financial problems were the general changeover to steel from iron. The branch of the family in Wales also had to contend with unrest in their collieries near Merthyr Tydvil (article on Robert Thompson Crawshay, *DNB*, V, 62).

47. At the time of the default, the Crawshays engineered a resolution of support by the local Foreign Affairs Committee favoring efforts to win better compensation from the Porte through a plan put forward by Hamond (*Sessional Papers: House of Commons* [Great Britain: 1876], vol. 84, pp. 844–845).

48. Nonetheless, a motion more or less favorable to Bulgaria was passed at Gateshead. (*The Times*, September 7, 1876, p. 8, col. f). An early meeting, supportive of the government, had been held at Newcastle in July ("Resolutions passed by a public meeting at Newcastle upon Tyne," July 18, 1876, Public Record Office, FO 78/2532). Neither the Crawshays nor Hamond were present at the September meeting, but two individuals, David and George Rule, again attempted to attenuate the protest resolutions. David Rule, who served as consul for the Ottomans, had been a leader in the local Foreign Affairs Committee, and, through common support of Urquhart's movement, was linked with the Crawshays. The effort to create opposition was not very successful; the Rules' version received only half a dozen votes (*Daily News*, September 7, 1876, p. 2, col. c; for David Rule, see Shannon, *Bulgarian Agitation*, p. 237, n. 7).

49. Article on Robert Thompson Crawshay, *DNB*, V, 62 and *Daily News*, September 14, 1876, p. 3, col. d.

50. Hanham, *Elections*, p. 68.

51. In addition to the examples already mentioned, two specifically progovernment special meetings were organized, one of "honest hard-working Conservative working men" at St. James's Hall on September 16, drawing

between 100 and 150 participants (*Daily News*, September 18, 1876, p. 2, col. d) and one outdoor meeting called by the radical Manhood Suffrage League in Hyde Park on October 8 (*Standard*, October 9, 1876, p. 3, col. f). Of course, support for the government was routinely expressed at meetings with Conservative M.P.s and at agricultural meetings in the counties.

52. *Daily News*, August 18, 1876, p. 3, col. b.
53. *Standard*, August 22, 1876, p. 5, col. a.
54. *Daily News*, August 30, 1876, p. 3, col. c.
55. Levy Lawson to Derby, September 6, 1876, "Confidential," Derby Papers (15th Earl), 920 DER(15) 16/2/17, Liverpool Record Office. Levy Lawson was strategically well placed to act as a go-between; the *Daily Telegraph* was a Liberal paper whose traditions went back to Palmerston, but Levy Lawson, perhaps because of his Jewish background or perhaps because of the paper's reputed connections with the Turkish bondholders, rejected the Liberal position on the Eastern crisis and followed the government (Shannon, *Bulgarian Agitation*, p. 25). Throughout the tense months of 1876 to 1878, he was in frequent and fruitful contact with Derby.
56. The Workmen's Peace Association had been organized by W. R. Cremer in 1871, when it seemed likely that Britain might intervene against the French Republic, which was championed by many working men because of its republican ideals; see A. C. F. Beales, *The History of Peace* (New York: Dial Press, 1931), pp. 136–137.
57. See *Daily News*, September 12, 1876, p. 2, cols. d-f. Cremer gave assurances that his group was quite willing to join the others.
58. *Sessional Papers: House of Commons* (Great Britain: 1876), vol. 84, p. 872; D. C. Blaisdell, *European Financial Control in the Ottoman Empire* (New York: Columbia University Press, 1929), p. 39.
59. One of Disraeli's regular correspondents was Weguelin, said to have the largest interest in Russia of any man in the City; Corry to Disraeli, November 5, 1876, Disraeli Papers, B/XVI/B/11 (Box 69).
60. Harrison, *Before the Socialists*, p. 176.
61. *Daily News*, September 9, 1876, p. 2, col. e; *Standard*, September 9, 1876, p. 2, col. d.
62. Glynne-Gladstone MSS, Merriman to Gladstone, September 8, 1876, telegram (Box 59). It is not clear whether the telegram was sent by Josiah J. Merriman or by his confrere Arthur P. Merriman.
63. Glynne-Gladstone MSS, Arthur P. Merriman to Gladstone, September 11, 1876, telegram (Box 59).
64. *Standard*, September 16, 1876, p. 3, col. b.
65. Glynne-Gladstone MSS, [J. J.] Merriman to Gladstone, September 13, 1876, telegram (Box 59).
66. *Daily News*, September 16, 1876, p. 2, col. c.
67. Gladstone, *Diaries*, IX, 155.
68. *Daily News*, September 14, 1876, p. 3, col. c.
69. Ibid., September 19, 1876, p. 2, cols. b-e; *Morning Post*, September 19, 1876, p. 2, cols. a-f; September 22, 1876, p. 6, col. a. Quote is from the

Morning Post, September 19. Later Merriman charged that efforts had been made to stop the Guildhall meeting: "The day before the meeting a circular was sent out calling upon the Conservative party to 'come and show their accustomed discipline' . . . The worst electioneering devices were resorted to, but he was happy to say, with total and significant failure." (*Daily News,* September 28, 1876, p. 2, col. a.)

70. *Daily News,* August 29, 1876, p. 2, col. c.
71. Ibid., September 9, 1876, p. 2, col. c.
72. *Standard,* September 11, 1876, p. 3, col. e.
73. *Daily News,* September 12, 1876, p. 3, col. d.
74. See Harrison, *Before the Socialists,* pp. 239–241.
75. *Daily News,* September 16, 1876, p. 2, col. e.
76. Ibid., September 18, 1876, p. 2, col. e; Whaley, one of the members of Parliament, studied a copy of proposed resolutions at the Clerkenwell Patriotic Club. *Standard,* September 18, 1876, p. 3, col. f.
77. *Daily News,* September 19, 1876, p. 2, col. e to p. 3, col. b.
78. Shannon, *Bulgarian Agitation,* p. 129 and notes 4 and 5.
79. Derby to Elliot, September 21, 1876, in *Sessional Papers: House of Commons* (Great Britain, 1877), vol. 90, "Correspondence Respecting the Affairs of Turkey," #316, pp. 237–238. For publication, see Shannon, *Bulgarian Agitation,* pp. 130–131.
80. *Morning Post,* September 21, 1876, p. 5, cols. d-f.
81. Stead to Gladstone, September 22(?), 1876, Add. MS 44303, f. 237.
82. *Daily News,* September 22, 1876, p. 2, col. a; September 28, 1876, p. 2, col. a for the reaction of the Mottershead committee; Shannon, *Bulgarian Agitation,* pp. 130–131 for general reactions.
83. *Standard,* September 28, 1876, p. 2, col. a; *Daily News,* September 28, 1876, p. 2, cols. a-d. Samuel Morley warned that the general mood was revolutionary.
84. *Daily News,* September 28, 1876, p. 2, cols. a-d; ibid., September 19, 1876, p. 2, col. e.
85. Ibid., September 22, 1876, p. 2, col. a.
86. Glynne-Gladstone MSS, J. Alfred Giles to Gladstone, September 21, 1876 (Box 32).
87. Glynne-Gladstone MSS, J. Alfred Giles to Gladstone, October 3, 1876 (Box 32).
88. Gladstone, *Diaries,* IX, 161 and n. 6. Gladstone explained himself at some length to Granville: "I have for the moment more than your responsibilities to the country in this sense that I feel myself compelled to advise from time to time upon the course of that national movement which I have tried hard to evoke and assisted in evoking. I have tried and shall try to avoid speaking: but if I do not speak I must write, only taking care not to do it except under a clear sense of necessity and within the limits established by it." (Gladstone to Granville, October 7, 1876, #18, Ramm, *Political Correspondence,* I, 13.)
89. Gladstone to Giles, October 7, 1876, Add. MS 44452, ff. 37–42. According to William Saunders, proprietor of the Central News, such letters

were hot property; he claimed that Giles had attempted to sell his editor a copy of the letter before the meeting, and cited other examples of such profit making; Glynne-Gladstone MSS, Saunders to Gladstone, October 10, 1876 (Box 79).

90. *Daily News*, September 23, 1876, p. 2, col. c; on Langley see *Morning Post*, September 7, 1876, p. 4, col. e; *Daily News*, October 10, 1876, p. 3, col. d.

91. *Daily News*, September 29, 1876, p. 2, col. a.

92. Ibid., September 30, 1876, p. 2, col. d.

93. Ibid., October 9, 1876, p. 3, col. f.

94. Derby had by now published the dispatch in which he disparaged Ottoman hopes of British support, and there were rumors in the press that an armistice would be concluded in the Balkans. Although Langley insisted that such "paper promises" were no good, they did take some of the urgency out of the protest. *Daily News*, October 10, 1876, p. 3, cols. d-e; *Standard*, October 10, 1876, p. 3, col. b; quotes are from the *Daily News*. For the resolutions, see Glynne-Gladstone MSS, J. Baxter Langley to Gladstone, October 5 and 11, 1876 (Box 50).

95. Stead to Gladstone, October 16, 1876, Add. MS 44303, f. 244.

96. W. H. G. Armytage, *A. J. Mundella, 1825–1897* (London: Benn, 1951), p. 169.

97. Glynne-Gladstone MSS, Robert Leader to Gladstone, October 2, 1876 (Box 51); Shannon, *Bulgarian Agitation*, pp. 142–143.

98. *Daily News*, October 5, 1876, p. 6, col. c; October 6, 1876, p. 2, col. e; October 10, 1876, p. 3, cols. a-d; *Morning Post*, October 10, 1876, p. 2, cols. c-d; *Standard*, October 10, 1876, p. 3, col. b. Morley did not participate in the Hyde Park demonstration, which was the fruit of Merriman's attempts at cooperation; when Merriman revived the City agitation in 1878, Morley worked through his own, explicitly Nonconformist group at Memorial Hall, Farringdon Street.

99. Wilson Papers, Sheffield University Library, Leader to Wilson, October 2, 1876 (37P/8/75/i).

100. Glynne-Gladstone MSS, Leader to Gladstone, October 2, 1876 (Box 51).

101. Mundella Papers (6P/66), Sheffield University Library, Mundella to Leader, October 4, 1876 (AJM/RL/9/57/i-ii).

102. Shannon, *Bulgarian Agitation*, p. 144.

103. Ibid., pp. 245–246.

104. For further statements of approval, see Mundella Papers, Mundella to Leader, October 6, 1876 (AJM/RL/9/58/ii) and October 7, 1876 (AJM/RL/9/59/i-ii).

105. Article on A. J. Mundella, *DNB*, XXII (supplement), 1081–1084; Harrison, *Before the Socialists*, p. 171; more generally, see Armytage, *Mundella*.

106. Mundella Papers, Mundella to Leader, October 10, 1876 (AJM/RL/60/i).

107. Mundella Papers, Mundella to Leader, October 11, 1876 (AJM/RL/9/61/i).

108. Shannon, *Bulgarian Agitation*, p. 144.

109. Mundella Papers, Mundella to Leader, October 20, 1876 (AJM/RL/9/64/iii).

110. Shannon, *Bulgarian Agitation*, pp. 245–246.

111. Mundella Papers, Mundella to Leader, October 11, 1876 (AJM/RL/9/63/i).
112. Shannon, *Bulgarian Agitation*, pp. 245–246.
113. Mundella Papers, Mundella to Leader, October 14, 1876 (AJM/RL/9/60/i).
114. Gladstone, *Diaries*, IX, 164.
115. Glynne-Gladstone MSS, Leader to Gladstone, October 19, 1876 (Box 51).
116. Mundella Papers, Mundella to Leader, October 20, [1876] (AJM/RL/9/64/ii-iii).
117. Shannon, *Bulgarian Agitation*, pp. 251–252.
118. Mundella Papers (6P/66), Herbert to Mundella, October 20, 1876, telegram (AJM/RL/9/64 Annex).
119. Mundella Papers, Mundella to Leader, August 12, 1876 (AJM/RL/9/49/ii), describes Mundella's plans to vacation with Herbert at the end of the parliamentary session; Mundella Papers, Mundella to Leader, October 20, [1876] (AJM/RL/9/64/ii).
120. Chesson Papers, Rhodes House Library, Oxford, MSS British Empire 518, Auberon Herbert to Chesson, October 22, [no year given] (C137/257).
121. Mundella Papers, Mundella to Leader, October 23, 1876 (AJM/RL/9/67/i–ii).
122. Glynne-Gladstone MSS, Leader to Gladstone, October 21, 1876 (Box 51); Gladstone, *Diaries*, IX, 165.
123. Devonshire Papers (8th Duke) 340/681, Chatsworth, Gladstone to Hartington, October 28, 1876; Shannon, *Bulgarian Agitation*, p. 248.
124. Shannon, *Bulgarian Agitation*, pp. 252–253.
125. Mundella Papers, Mundella to Leader, November 1, 1876 (AJM/RL/9/70/i).
126. Mundella Papers, Mundella to Wilson, November 3, 1876 (6P/81/28/i–ii).
127. Mundella Papers, Mundella to Leader, November 4, 1876 (AJM/RL/9/72/i).
128. Mundella Papers, Gladstone to Mundella, November 6, 1876 (6P/9/8/i).
129. Chesson Papers, Herbert to Chesson, November 6, [1876] (C 137/258); enclosure to Leader (C 137/259).
130. Liddon Papers 1876(2), Keble College Library, Oxford, Chesson to Liddon, November 11, 1876.
131. *Daily News*, November 18, 1876, p. 5, col. e.
132. Gladstone to Granville, November 8, 1876, #25, Ramm, *Political Correspondence*, I, 18.
133. Robert Blake, *Disraeli* (Garden City, N.Y.: Doubleday, 1968), p. 612.
134. Mundella Papers, Gladstone to Mundella, November 6, 1876 (6P/9/8/i–ii).
135. Chesson Papers, Herbert to Chesson, November 10, [1876] (C137/262).
136. Sir Thomas Powell Buxton, Jr., Papers, Rhodes House Library, Oxford, MSS British Empire 518, Freeman to Buxton, November 10, 1876 (C 109/40); Liddon Papers 1876(2), Herbert to Liddon, November 15, 1876; Herbert to Gladstone, November 16, 1876, Add. MS 44452, f. 136; Herbert to Gladstone, November 18, 1876, Add. MS. 44452, f. 137. See also Liddon Papers 1876(2), Herbert to Liddon, November 18, 1876.
137. Liddon Papers 1876(2), Chesson to Liddon, November 20, 1876; Herbert to Gladstone, November 23, 1876, Add. MS 44452, f. 272.

138. Mundella Papers, Mundella to Leader, December 7, 1876 (AJM/RL/9/76/i).

139. Liddon Papers 1876(2), Prospectus.

140. Mundella Papers, Gladstone to Herbert, November 22, 1876 (6P/9/12/i–ii).

141. Mundella Papers, Gladstone to Herbert, November 22, 1876, "Private" (6P/9/13). By the time Herbert received these letters, he was no longer functioning as honorary secretary, but he passed them both to Mundella (Herbert to Gladstone, November 23, 1876, Add. MS 44452, f. 272), and they had an influence, either in providing new ideas or in confirming plans already underway.

142. Liddon Papers 1876(2), Packet on the National Conference on the Eastern Question, November 30, 1876.

143. Mundella Papers, Mundella to Leader, December 7, 1876 (AJM/RL/9/76/i).

144. Mundella Papers, Gladstone to Mundella, November 6, 1876 (6P/9/8/ii); see also Gladstone, *Diaries*, IX, 166 for Gladstone's breakfast with a group of Nonconformists whom he recommended to Mundella in the letter cited above as "a most efficient body."

145. See Liddon Papers 1876(2) for the appeal of Albert Rutson to Liddon, November 21, 1876. Rutson said he would prefer a memorial to a conference, as less prescriptive, but the group involved was distinguished, and so he had decided to "venture to write" in order to ascertain Liddon's opinion.

146. A note in the *Daily News*, eloquent for what it did not say, urged tolerance of the Ritualists, since their position on the Eastern Question was so sound (December 4, 1876, p. 3, col. e).

147. Mundella to Gladstone, November 25, 1876, Add. MS 44258, f. 128.

148. Shannon, *Bulgarian Agitation*, pp. 194–198. See Gladstone's list of possible Catholic supporters in Mundella Papers, Gladstone to Mundella, November 26, 1876 (6P/9/15/i–ii and Annex).

149. Mundella Papers, W. Morris to Mundella, November 15, 1876 (6P/9/10/i). Gladstone suggested he might ask Tennyson; Gladstone to Mundella, November 26, 1876 (6P/9/15/i).

150. Mundella to Gladstone, November 25, 1876, Add. MS 44258, f. 128; November 26, 1876, Add. MS 44258, f. 131.

151. Armytage, *Mundella*, p. 171; Mundella Papers, F. Cavendish to Mundella, November 28, 1876 (6P/9/17); Gladstone to Mundella, November 30, 1876 (6P/9/20/i). Mundella decided against further approaches after a talk with Frederick Cavendish (Mundella to Gladstone, December 1, 1876, Add. MS 44258, f. 136).

152. Howell Collection, Bishopsgate Institute, London, International Affairs envelope, invitation, December 1, 1876. On Howell see F. M. Leventhal, *Respectable Rebel: George Howell and Victorian Working Class Politics* (London: Weidenfeld and Nicolson, 1971).

153. Broadhurst Papers, London School of Economics Library, F. W. Chesson to Henry Broadhurst, November 18, 1876, vol. 1, f. 18; Broadhurst Papers, Minutes of the Council of the Labour Representation League, December 5, 1876, p. 226.

154. Mundella Papers, Mundella to Wilson, December 15, 1876 (6P/81/32/ii). Leveson-Gower and Russell were related by marriage, and both were

connected to Granville; Leveson-Gower was Granville's brother and Russell was his son-in-law.

155. *Daily News*, December 9, 1876, p. 2, col. b.
156. Armytage, *Mundella*, pp. 174–175.
157. Mundella Papers, Gladstone to Mundella, November 6, 1876 (6P/9/8/ii).
158. Mundella to Gladstone, November 25, 1876, Add. MS 44258, f. 130.
159. Mundella Papers, Gladstone to Mundella, November 26, 1876 (6P/9/15/ii).
160. Mundella Papers, Shaftesbury to Mundella, November 28, 1876 (6P/9/18); December 2, 1876 (6P/9/21/i); December 5, 1876 (6P/9/23/i).
161. Mundella to Gladstone, December 1, 1876, Add. MS 44258, ff. 136–137.
162. Mundella to Gladstone, December 2, 1876, Add. MS 44258, f. 139.
163. Granville to Gladstone, November 27, 1876, #33 and December 6, 1876, #35, Ramm, *Political Correspondence*, I, 24–25.
164. See annex for regulations (Howell Collection, International Affairs Envelope, C).
165. See annex (Howell Collection, International Affairs Envelope, A).
166. *Manchester Guardian*, December 5, 1876, p. 5, cols. e-g.
167. Mundella Papers, Mundella to Wilson, December 3, 1876 (6P/81/29/i).
168. Liddon Papers 1876(2), George Rolleston to Liddon, December 5, 1876.
169. Pamela Horn, *Joseph Arch* (Kineton, Eng.: Roundwood Press, 1971), pp. 133–134.
170. J. P. Parry, *Democracy and Religion: Gladstone and the Liberal Party, 1867–1875* (Cambridge, Eng.: Cambridge University Press, 1986), pp. 233–234.
171. The *Daily News* carried a full account of the meeting on December 9, 1876, p. 2, col. b to p. 3, col. g. Buxton's speech appears on p. 2, col. d.
172. Ibid., p. 2, col. e.
173. Geoffrey Alderman, *The Jewish Community in British Politics* (Oxford: Clarendon Press, 1983), p. 32; *Daily News*, December 9, 1876, p. 2, col. f. After considerable discussion with Jewish leaders, Gladstone had already pledged himself to Simon's requirement (Devonshire Papers 340/681, Gladstone to Hartington, October 28, 1876).
174. Smelser, *Collective Behavior*, p. 299.
175. His speech is reported in the *Daily News*, December 9, 1876, p. 3, cols. b-g.
176. Gladstone, *Diaries*, IX, 176.
177. See Chapter 5.
178. *Daily News*, December 9, 1876, p. 3, col. a; and *Pall Mall Gazette*, December 9, 1876, p. 1, col. a to p. 2, col. a.
179. *Daily News*, December 9, 1876, p. 3, col. b.
180. Smelser, *Collective Behavior*, p. 308.
181. *Daily News*, December 9, 1876, p. 3, col. c.
182. Gladstone, *Diaries*, IX, 180.

8. A Shift in Focus

1. See Neil J. Smelser, *Theory of Collective Behavior* (New York: Free Press, 1963), p. 297.

2. This was his phrase at the St. James's Hall meeting.

3. The phrase is Stead's (Stead to Gladstone, February 8, 1878, British Library, Additional Manuscript 44303, f. 291).

4. See Eric Hobsbawm, *Primitive Rebels* (Manchester, Eng.: Manchester University Press, 1959) and Richard Price, *An Imperial War and the British Working Class* (London: Routledge and Kegan Paul, 1972), especially pp. 133–158.

5. Disraeli to Derby, September 8, 1876, Derby Papers (15th Earl), 920 DER(15) 16/2/2, Liverpool Record Office.

6. Disraeli to Corry, September 13, 1876, Disraeli Papers, B/XVI/B/1 (Box 69), Western Manuscripts, Bodleian Library, Oxford.

7. Disraeli to Derby, October 12, 1876, Derby Papers, 920 DER(15) 16/2/2.

8. Corry to Disraeli, September 19, 1876, Disraeli Papers, B/XVI/B/9 (Box 69).

9. Lord John Manners to Disraeli, September 7, 1876, "Private," Disraeli Papers, B/XX/M/196 (Box 106).

10. Cross to Disraeli, September 13, 1876, Disraeli Papers, B/XX/Cr/59 (Box 94).

11. Cross to Derby, September 13, 1876, "Private," Derby Papers, 920 DER(15) 16/2/5.

12. Lord John Manners to Disraeli, September 7, 1876, Disraeli Papers, B/XX/M/196 (Box 106).

13. Cross to Derby, September 13, 1876, "Private," Derby Papers, 920 DER(15) 16/2/5.

14. Corry to Disraeli, September 19, 1876, Disraeli Papers, B/XVI/B/9 (Box 69).

15. Lionel de Rothschild to Disraeli, September 8, 1876, Disraeli Papers, B/XXI/R/219 (Box 141).

16. B. H. Sumner, *Russia and the Balkans 1870–1880* (Hamden, Conn.: Archon Books, 1962; originally published 1937), pp. 220–221, 227.

17. Sumner, *Russia*, p. 200; Derby to Elliot, September 21, 1876, #316, *Sessional Papers: House of Commons* (Great Britain, 1877), vol. 90, pp. 237–238.

18. Richard Millman, *Britain and the Eastern Question, 1875–1878* (Oxford: Clarendon Press, 1979), pp. 194–195.

19. Ibid., pp. 196–197; another possible representative was Lyons, the ambassador to France.

20. *Pall Mall Gazette*, November 8, 1876, p. 1, col. a; *Daily Telegraph*, November 8, 1876, p. 4, col. f.

21. James Bentley, *Ritualism and Politics in Victorian Britain* (Oxford: Oxford University Press, 1978), pp. 11, 77.

22. See Robert Blake and Hugh Cecil, eds., *Salisbury: The Man and his Policies* (New York: St. Martin's Press, 1987).

23. Peter Marsh, ed., *The Conscience of the Victorian State* (Syracuse, N.Y.: Syracuse University Press, 1979), p. 67.

24. Gladstone to Granville, November 8, 1876, #25, in Agatha Ramm, ed., *The Political Correspondence of Mr. Gladstone and Lord Granville, 1876–1886*, 2 vols. (Oxford: Clarendon Press, 1962), I, 18.

25. *Punch*, January 6, 1877, vol. 71, pp. 301, 295, col. b.

26. Millman, *Eastern Question*, pp. 219–221.

27. Mundella to Gladstone, November 25, 1876, Add. MS 44258, f. 130.
28. Mundella Papers, Sheffield University Library, Mundella to Wilson, December 10, 1876 (6P/81/30/i–ii).
29. Mundella Papers (6P/66), Mundella to Leader, December 8, 1876 (AJM/RL/9/75/i).
30. Mundella Papers, Gladstone to Herbert, November 22, 1876 (6P/9/12/i–ii) and November 22, 1876, "Private" (6P/9/13).
31. A. Herbert to Gladstone, November 23, 1876, Add. MS 44452, f. 270.
32. Mundella Papers, Gladstone to Mundella, November 26, 1876 (6P/9/15/ii).
33. Gladstone to Frank Hill, October 18, 1876, Add. MS 44452, ff. 49–50.
34. Frank Hill to Gladstone, October 19, 1876, Add. MS 44452, ff. 57–58.
35. Mundella Papers, Gladstone to Mundella, January 6, 1877 (6P/10/1/ii) and [January 15, 1877?] (6P/10/2/ii).
36. Mundella Papers, Gladstone to Mundella, January 8, 1877 (6P/10/3/i).
37. Mundella Papers, Gladstone to Mundella (6P/10/10/ii). The archivists assign this letter to June, 1877, but internal evidence suggests the likelihood of a January date.
38. *Daily News*, December 9, 1876, p. 3, col. b.
39. Howell Collection, Bishopsgate Institute, London, Eastern Question Association, "Report for 1878," p. 2.
40. Membership list in Howell Collection, International Affairs Envelope D 1–4. Some names (Ambrose Phillips de Lisle for example) appear twice. Howell Collection, Eastern Question Association circular, April 24, 1877 (International Affairs Envelope, E 1–2).
41. See Liddon Papers 1876(2), Keble College Library, Oxford, J. Baxter Langley and M. Cathiall to Canon Liddon, November 6, 1876. National Federation of Liberal Associations, "Annual Report 1879: Statement of Treasurer's Receipts," in National Liberation Federation, *Annual Reports and Council Proceedings, 1877–1936* (Hassocks, Eng.: Harvester Press, 1975), after p. 18, reports receipts of £1180 11s. 10d. for 1879.
42. J. P. Parry, *Democracy and Religion: Gladstone and the Liberal Party, 1867–1875* (Cambridge, Eng.: Cambridge University Press, 1986), pp. 28, 421.
43. For these remarks, see the collection of early leaflets in the Howell Collection, International Affairs Envelope; Leaflet #15, an eight-page effort by Archibald Forbes ("The Evidence of A.F.," reprinted from *The Scotsman*, November 2, 1877) is in St. Deiniol's Library, Hawarden, (10/E/4). Dating of the leaflets is predicated on the fact that the second and third were based on speeches given in July 1877.
44. R. T. Shannon, *Gladstone and the Bulgarian Agitation 1876*, 2nd ed. (Hassocks, Eng.: Harvester Press, 1975; originally published 1963), p. 156, n. 2; the pamphlet can be found in Eastern Question Association, *Papers on the Eastern Question* (London: Cassell, Petter and Galpin, 1877).
45. Appears in *Papers on the Eastern Question Association*; see also *The Times*, January 17, 1877, p. 10, cols. a–b.
46. Gladstone to Catherine Gladstone, March 11 and March 30, 1877, Glynne-Gladstone MSS 779, ff. 150–151, St. Deiniol's Library, Hawarden;

George Carslake Thompson, *Public Opinion and Lord Beaconsfield, 1875–1880*, 2 vols. (London: Macmillan, 1886), II, 176, n. 2. The pamphlet, published in London by John Murray, may be found in St. Deiniol's Library, Hawarden.

47. William Ewart Gladstone, *Mr. Gladstone's Resolutions and Speech on the Eastern Question in the House of Commons May 7, 1877* (London: Cassell, Petter, and Galpin, 1877, for the Eastern Question Association).

48. See the price listed on the copy in St. Deiniol's Library (9X/N/7). For newspaper prices in general, see Lucy Brown, *Victorian News and Newspapers* (Oxford: Clarendon Press, 1985), pp. 52–53.

49. Glynne-Gladstone MSS, William Bernard to Gladstone, September 12, 1876 (Box 5).

50. For the price, see the copy in St. Deiniol's Library; for sales figures, Agatha Ramm, *William Ewart Gladstone* (Cardiff: University of Wales Press, 1989), p. 73, and Gladstone to Catherine Gladstone, March 30, 1877, Glynne-Gladstone MSS 779, f. 151. The pamphlet appeared on March 12 (Thompson, *Public Opinion*, II, 176, n. 2).

51. William Ewart Gladstone, *Speeches and Writings*, vol. 7, "Eastern Question Association," "Speech delivered at Hawarden, November 24th, 1877," back cover, in St. Deiniol's Library.

52. Glynne-Gladstone MSS, W. Forsyth to Gladstone, November 2, 1876, "Private" (Box 28).

53. Gladstone to Catherine Gladstone, March 11, 1877, Glynne-Gladstone MSS 779, f. 150.

54. Gladstone to Catherine Gladstone, January 7, 1877, Glynne-Gladstone MSS 779, f. 148.

55. Glynne-Gladstone MSS, J. H. Bell to Gladstone, January 10 and January 13, 1877 (Box 5).

56. Brown, *Victorian News*, pp. 52–53. Figures for *Daily News* are from 1871; for *Daily Telegraph*, from 1879.

57. Joseph Chamberlain Papers, Birmingham University Library, Chamberlain to Stead, October 1, 1878 (JC6/4K/25).

58. Sumner, *Russia*, p. 255 and n. 1.

59. Ibid., p. 258.

60. Ibid., pp. 266–267.

61. Millman, *Eastern Question*, pp. 260–261.

62. Sumner, *Russia*, pp. 270–271.

63. William Ewart Gladstone, *The Gladstone Diaries*, ed. M. R. D. Foot and H. C. G. Matthew, 11 vols. to date (Oxford: Clarendon Press, 1968–), IX, 209–210.

64. Gladstone to Granville, April 23, 1877, #54 and April 25, 1877, #55, Ramm, *Political Correspondence*, I, 35.

65. Gladstone, *Diaries*, IX, 214.

66. *Hansard Parliamentary Debates*, 3rd series, vol. 234, 1877, cols. 101–102.

67. Granville to Gladstone, April 27, 1877, #56, Ramm, *Political Correspondence*, I, 36 passing on a message from Salisbury transmitted by the violently proagitation Marquess of Bath.

68. Thompson, *Public Opinion,* II, 191; *Daily News,* April 30, 1877, p. 3, col. f; Howell Collection, Eastern Question Association circular, April 24, 1877 (International Affairs Envelope, E 1–2). In contrast, the executive council of the Workmen's Peace Association, in a statement published the same day, requested "the co-operation of the 400 branches, committees, and agents which the association has in different parts of the country" (see Thompson citation).

69. Broadhurst Papers, London School of Economics Library, Minutes of the Council of the Labour Representation League, April 20, 1877, pp. 249–250.

70. Ibid., n.d., p. 252.

71. Ibid., April 30, 1877, p. 253.

72. William Morris to Janey Morris, May 2, 1877, Add. MS 45338, f. 61–62. Morris was a pivotal figure in the agitation, as well as in Victorian life and letters generally, because he combined a gentlemanly career as a poet with experience as "a manufacturer and shopkeeper, though a very special one." He worked unusually closely with his artisans, and, like many of them, was an atheist (Peter Stansky, *Redesigning the World: William Morris, the 1880s, and the Arts and Crafts* [Princeton: Princeton University Press, 1985], pp. 3–5). He thus combined in his own person several divergent strands of the movement.

73. Broadhurst Papers, Labour Representation League, Minutes, n.d., pp. 252–253; *The Times,* May 3, 1877, p. 11, col. a; May 5, 1877, p. 13, col. d.

74. Broadhurst Papers, Labour Representation League, Minutes, May 5, 1877, pp. 254–255.

75. Ibid., May 11, 1877, p. 258.

76. *Daily News,* May 7, 1877, p. 5, col. c.

77. Ibid., May 8, 1877, p. 3, cols. f-g; *Standard,* May 8, 1877, p. 6, col. c.

78. *Standard,* May 14, 1877, p. 6, col. e.

79. Gladstone, *Diaries,* IX, 216–217.

80. Ramm, *Political Correspondence,* I, 44 n. 4 and House of Lords Record Office, *Reports of the Select Committee on Public Petitions 1877.* In addition there were five petitions against the resolutions and eleven which fell outside the period May 4–14 for a total of ninety-seven. Unfortunately Gladstone did not keep the letters and petitions he received. An overview of the material made by J. A. Godley (Ramm, *Political Correspondence,* I, 44 n. 4) is useful, although it gives impressions, not figures (J. A. Godley to Granville, June 5, 1877, Public Record Office 30/29/2613 9380). The records of the select committee can be analyzed statistically, but they include only about 20% of the petitions. Newspapers *(Daily News, Morning Post,* and *Standard)* were used to amplify these results, but because of their inevitable selectivity, the findings must be treated with caution. For an analysis of the source of the petitions, see Table 1 in Chapter 7.

81. Thompson, *Public Opinion,* II, 191; *Daily News,* April 30, 1877, p. 3, col. g.

82. Ramm, *Political Correspondence,* I, 215 and n. 8; *The Times,* May 2, 1877, p. 9, col. d.

83. *The Times*, May 4, 1877, p. 10, col. f. Newman Hall also organized his own meeting at the Congregational Church, Borough Rd., Southwark (ibid., May 7, 1877, p. 6, col. d).

84. Shannon, *Bulgarian Agitation*, p. 148. The figure for 1877 counts petitions to Parliament. Because Parliament was adjourned for much of 1876, communications in that year went to the Foreign Office instead. The 1877 number is reduced only to 15 percent if progovernment petitions are included (see Table 1, Chapter 7). All the petitions to Parliament in 1877 from religious bodies came from Nonconformists.

85. Ibid., p. 165 and n. 1.

86. Godley to Granville, June 5, 1877, PRO 30/29/26/3 9380, Crown Copyright.

87. In addition to the early involvement by the Labour Representation League and the Workmen's Peace Association, after the Parliamentary debate was over the national meeting of the National Agricultural Labourers' Union in London on May 15 considered a petition for neutrality (*Standard*, May 16, 1877, p. 2, col. f); a petition appears in House of Lords Record Office, *Report of the Select Committee on Public Petitions 1877*, p. 623, no. 8868, dated June 18, 1877. The National Agricultural Labourers' Union had also submitted a memorial in 1876 (Shannon, *Bulgarian Agitation*, p. 148).

88. Godley to Granville, June 5, 1877, Public Record Office, 30/29/26/3 9380 (Crown Copyright). Since the *Daily News*, the most faithful reporter of meetings, had a clear partisan interest in emphasizing Liberal participation, the figures gleaned from the newspapers (not surprisingly) suggest overwhelming involvement by Liberal associations.

89. See Table 1, Chapter 7.

90. All the opposition noted by the newspapers (in Sheffield, *Daily News*, May 7, 1877, p. 3, col. f and in Manchester, *Daily News*, May 7, 1877, p. 3, col. g) and all but one of the parliamentary petitions opposing the resolutions came from Conservative associations. The parliamentary petition in question may be the exception that proves the rule; it was evidently carried around for signature in Frome, where the leading Conservative, the Marquess of Bath, favored the agitation (House of Lords Record Office, *Report of the Select Committee on Public Petitions 1877*, p. 455 no. 6071).

91. See Godley to Granville, June 5, 1877, PRO 30/29/2613 9380.

92. *Daily News*, May 5, 1877, p. 2, col. e; Shannon, *Bulgarian Agitation*, p. 156. Unlike many pacifists, Richard was not prepared to say that war was always wrong.

93. According to Godley, one-half to one-third of the four hundred.

94. Gladstone to Granville, May 4, 1877, #58, Ramm, *Political Correspondence*, I, 36.

95. Gladstone, *Diaries*, IX, 216.

96. Hansard, vol. 234, cols. 366–369 (May 7, 1877).

97. Gladstone, *Diaries*, IX, 217 and n. 1.

98. Hansard, vol. 234, cols. 379–380.

99. Ibid., col. 827.

100. Mundella Papers (6P/67), Mundella to Leader, May 4, 1877 (AJM/RL/10/25/ii).
101. See Sullivan's comments (Hansard, vol. 234, col. 387).
102. Ibid., col. 472. Information about party affiliations and backgrounds of members is taken from *Who's Who of British Members of Parliament*, vol. 1, 1832–1885, ed. M. Stenton; vol. 2, 1886–1918, ed. M. Stenton and S. Lees (Hassocks, Eng.: Harvester Press, 1976).
103. Hansard, vol. 234, col. 435–436.
104. Ibid., cols. 402–403.
105. Ibid., cols. 439–440.
106. Ibid., col. 457.
107. Ibid., col. 663.
108. Ibid., col. 825. During a contentious career, Kenealy had earned a reputation for "erratic" conduct. He had been a prominent defender of the Tichborne Claimant, whose supporters figured among Disraeli's crankier adherents in 1877–1878; see article on Kenealy, *Dictionary of National Biography* (London: Oxford University Press, 1917–), X, 1298–99, and Hugh Cunningham, "Jingoism in 1877–78," *Victorian Studies*, 14 (1971), 432.
109. Hansard, vol. 234, col. 535–536.
110. Ibid., col. 800.
111. Ibid., col. 450.
112. Ibid., col. 676.
113. Ibid., cols. 956–957.
114. Ibid., col. 806.
115. Ibid., col. 670.
116. Almost the same polarization between working-class pacifists and middle-class leaders developed during the Boer War; see Richard Price, *An Imperial War and the British Working Class* (London: Routledge and Kegan Paul, 1972), pp. 71–74.
117. Hansard, vol. 234, col. 515.
118. Ibid., col. 909. Whether this figure is accurate or not, the British did rule more Muslims than any other government in the world, including the Porte: see William Ochsenwald, *Religion, Society, and the State in Arabia* (Columbus, Ohio: Ohio State University Press, 1984), p. 88.
119. See *Pall Mall Gazette*, November 22, 1876, p. 1, col. a to p. 2, col. a.
120. Millman, *Eastern Question*, pp. 274–280.
121. Thompson, *Public Opinion*, II, 200.
122. Hansard, vol. 234, cols. 808–816.
123. Ibid., col. 701.
124. T. A. Jenkins, *Gladstone, Whiggery, and the Liberal Party, 1874–1886* (Oxford: Clarendon Press, 1988), p. 66.
125. Hansard, vol. 234, cols. 655–658.
126. Ibid., col. 649.
127. Ibid., cols. 819–823.
128. Gladstone, *Diaries*, IX, 219.
129. Hansard, vol. 234, cols. 973–978.
130. Gladstone, *Diaries*, IX, 219.

131. *The Times,* May 19, 1877, p. 8, col. d.
132. Broadhurst Papers, Gladstone to Broadhurst, May 17, 1877, vol. 1, ff. 35–36. At Gladstone's suggestion, Broadhurst sent this letter to *The Times,* so that it might serve as a general "thank-you" from Gladstone for expressions of support during the recent crisis (*The Times,* May 19, 1877, p. 8, col. d).
133. Chesson Papers, Rhodes House Library, Oxford, MSS British Empire 518, A. Herbert to Chesson, May 14, 1877 (C137/263).
134. Macdonald to Gladstone, December 26, 1877, Glynne-Gladstone MSS 714.
135. Chamberlain Papers, Chamberlain to Stead, May 3, 1877, "Private" (JC6/4K/2).
136. Chamberlain Papers, Chamberlain to Stead, May 24, 1877, "Private" (JC6/4K/5).
137. Chamberlain Papers, Chamberlain to Dilke, October 10, 1876 (JC5/24/286).
138. See Chamberlain Papers, Chamberlain to Stead, May 18, 1876 (JC6/4K/4).
139. Gladstone to Granville, May 17, 1877, #61, Ramm, *Political Correspondence,* I, 38–39; the invitation had been proffered April 16 (Millman, *Eastern Question,* p. 286).
140. Chamberlain to Gladstone, May 24, 1877, Add. MS 44125, ff. 18–19.
141. Liddon to Madame Novikov, May 29, 1877, in *The M.P. for Russia,* ed. W. T. Stead, 2 vols. (New York: Putnam, 1909), I, 365.
142. George Baker, Mayor of Birmingham, to Gladstone, May 16, 1877, Add. MS 44454, f. 132.
143. Chamberlain to Gladstone, May 23, 1877, Add. MS 44125, f. 16; May 26, 1877, Add. MS 44125, f. 21.
144. Cunningham, "Jingoism," p. 435.
145. Chamberlain Papers, Chamberlain to Stead, May 18, 1877 (JC6/4K/4).
146. "Proceedings attending the formation of the National Federation of Liberal Associations with Report of Conference held in Birmingham on Thursday, May 31st, 1877," in National Liberal Federation, *Annual Reports,* pp. 14, 19. Hereafter "Proceedings."
147. Glynne-Gladstone MSS, Joseph Banner to Gladstone, May 27, 1877 (Box 3).
148. J. L. Garvin, *The Life of Joseph Chamberlain,* 4 vols. (London: Macmillan, 1932), I, 260. Gladstone himself estimated the crowd at 25,000 (Gladstone to Granville, June 1, 1877, #68, Ramm, *Political Correspondence,* I, 43).
149. Granville to Gladstone, May 18, 1877, #62, May 21, 1877, #64, Ramm, *Political Correspondence,* I, 39, 41; Gladstone to Granville, May 23, 1877, #65, ibid., p. 41.
150. "Proceedings," pp. 45–47.
151. Millman, *Eastern Question,* p. 292.
152. Francis H. Herrick, "The Origins of the National Liberal Federation," *Journal of Modern History,* 17 (1945), 116–117.
153. Ibid., p. 123.
154. Smelser, *Collective Behavior,* pp. 296–298.

155. National Federation of Liberal Associations, "Annual Report 1879," in National Liberal Federation, *Annual Reports,* p. 10.
156. Jenkins, *Whiggery,* pp. 285–286.
157. See Stead to Gladstone, January 6, 1878 and Gladstone to Stead, January 8, 1878, Add. MS 44303, ff. 264–266.

9. War and Counterprotest

1. Richard Millman, *Britain and the Eastern Question 1875–1878* (Oxford: Clarendon Press, 1979), p. 191.
2. Dwight E. Lee, *Great Britain and the Cyprus Convention Policy of 1878* (Cambridge, Mass.: Harvard University Press, 1934), pp. 32–36.
3. Robert Blake, *Disraeli* (Garden City, N.Y.: Doubleday, 1968), pp. 613–614; [Harriet Sarah (Loyd) Loyd-Lindsay, baroness Wantage], *Lord Wantage, V.C., K.C.B.: A Memoir by His Wife* (London: Smith, Elder, 1907), pp. 244–245.
4. Neil J. Smelser, *Theory of Collective Behavior* (New York: Free Press, 1963), p. 306, discusses what typically happens to unsuccessful social movements.
5. B. H. Sumner, *Russia and the Balkans, 1870–1880* (Hamden, Conn.: Archon Books, 1962; originally published 1937), pp. 303–304, 317–318, 335–341.
6. Gareth Stedman Jones, *Outcast London* (New York: Pantheon, 1984; originally published 1971), p. 77.
7. Stead to Gladstone, January 6, 1878, British Library, Additional Manuscript 44303, f. 264.
8. The major activity of High Churchmen was a "clerical declaration" got up by W. Denton, Canon Liddon, and Canon W. Bright which, with "no canvass," indeed "no machinery for canvassing," quickly attracted a thousand signatures (W. Denton to Gladstone, January 29, 1878, Glynne-Gladstone MSS 714, St. Deiniol's Library, Hawarden). This approach contrasts with that of 1876, when Canon Liddon, for example, was heavily involved in meetings and correspondence.
9. Mundella Papers, Sheffield University Library, Gladstone to Mundella, October 15, 1877 (6P/10/12/i–ii).
10. Mundella Papers, Gladstone to Mundella, November 27, 1877, "Private" (6P/10/13/i–ii).
11. Millman, *Eastern Question,* pp. 336–343.
12. Mundella Papers, Gladstone to Mundella, December 20, 1877 (6P/10/14/i–ii). Gladstone's instructions imply that the Eastern Question Association still had not developed its own branches around the country, but was dependent on existing, better organized groups.
13. Mundella Papers, Gladstone to Mundella, December 23, 1877 (6P/10/17/i–ii). The idea of protests from chambers of commerce was notably unsuccessful; see Table 1, Chapter 7.
14. See Mundella Papers, Gladstone to Mundella, January 3, 1878 (6P/11/2).
15. Gladstone to Schnadhorst, December 21, 1877, Add. MS 44295, f. 125.

16. Derby to Disraeli, January 28, 1878, Disraeli Papers, B/XX/S/1312 (Box 113), Western Manuscripts, Bodleian Library, Oxford.

17. Joseph Chamberlain Papers, Birmingham University Library, Chamberlain to Stead, December 19, 1877 (JC6/4K/7); Mundella Papers, Chamberlain to Mundella, December 22, 1877, telegram (6P/10/15). Telegram misnumbered 6P/10/13; envelope is correctly numbered 6P/10/15 Annex.

18. Mundella Papers, Chamberlain to Mundella, December 22, 1877 (6P/10/16/i–iv).

19. Stead to Gladstone, January 6, 1878, Add. MS 44303, f. 264. For Gladstone's approving reply, see Gladstone to Stead, January 8, 1878, Add. MS 44303, ff. 265–266.

20. Smelser, *Collective Behavior*, pp. 297–298, 302–303.

21. Freeman to Bryce, December 21, 1877 (MS Bryce 6, f. 153), Western Manuscripts, Bodleian Library, Oxford.

22. W. Morris to Janey Morris, December 20, [1877], Add. MS 45338, f. 84.

23. Mundella Papers, Mundella to Leader, December 20, 1877 (AJM/RL/10/63/ii).

24. W. Morris to Jenny and May Morris, Christmas Day, 1877, Add. MS 45339, f. 16.

25. W. Morris to Jenny and May Morris, Christmas Day, 1877, Add. MS 45339, ff. 16–17. Maltman Barry was a working-class agitator, friend of Marx, and suspected Tory agent; see Stan Shipley, *Club Life and Socialism in Mid-Victorian London* (Oxford: History Workshop, 1972), pp. 64–67.

26. *Standard*, December 31, 1877, p. 3, col. d; *Pall Mall Gazette*, December 31, 1877, p. 8, col. b.

27. *Daily News*, December 31, 1877, p. 2, col. b; *Morning Post*, January 1, 1878, p. 2, col. b.

28. Mundella to Gladstone, December 30, 1877, Glynne-Gladstone MSS 713.

29. Gladstone to H. J. Wilson, January 1, 1878, Glynne-Gladstone MSS 714.

30. Mundella to Gladstone, January 2, 1878, Glynne-Gladstone MSS 713.

31. Mundella Papers, Gladstone to Mundella, January 3, 1878 (6P/11/2) for refusal; Chamberlain to Gladstone, January 7, 1878, Glynne-Gladstone MSS 713 for authorization; Gladstone to Chamberlain, January 3, 1878, Add. MS 44125, f. 24.

32. Smelser, *Collective Behavior*, p. 298.

33. *Daily News*, January 1, 1878, p. 2, col. b. Chamberlain apparently provoked both these initiatives; see Mundella Papers, Chamberlain to Mundella, December 27, 1877 (6P/10/16/iv).

34. *Daily News*, January 29, 1878, p. 6, col. b; *Daily News*, January 4, 1878, p. 6, col. d. The Workmen's Peace Association, after circularizing its 500 branches (*Daily News*, December 22, 1878, p. 6, col. d), was able within a few days to record twenty-two meetings in urban centers, plus a series of village meetings (*Standard*, January 4, 1878, p. 3, col. d). And the Peace Society was not to be outdone; it is said to have sent more than 1,300 petitions to Parliament from local branches within a month. See A. C. F. Beales, *The History of Peace* (New York: Dial Press, 1931), p. 160. This was probably an enormous exaggeration. Very few of the petitions, either to

Parliament or to the Foreign Office, can be identified as coming from peace organizations, and the newspapers provide a similar picture (see Table 1, Chapter 7).

35. *Daily News,* January 5, 1878, p. 2, col. e; *Daily News,* December 8, 1877, p. 2, col. d; Pamela Horn, *Joseph Arch* (Kineton, Eng.: Roundwood Press, 1971), pp. 134–135.

36. *Daily News,* January 5, 1878, p. 2, col. d.

37. Petitions to the Foreign Office are at the Public Record Office bound in four volumes under the numbers FO 78/2930–33 (Crown Copyright). Their treatment in the records is similar to that of the petitions in the six volumes Shannon used (PRO FO 78/2551–56; see R. T. Shannon, *Gladstone and the Bulgarian Agitation, 1876,* 2nd ed. [Hassocks, Eng.: Harvester Press, 1975; originally published 1963], pp. 147–148). For petitions to the House of Commons, see House of Lords Record Office, *Reports of the Select Committee on Public Petitions 1878.* As a supplement, I have studied and tallied accounts of meetings and related activities in the *Daily News,* the *Morning Post,* and the *Standard;* although each newspaper's bias affects the kinds of meetings reported, the accounts give insights into what supposedly happened at the meetings, details which cannot be recovered elsewhere.

38. See Table 1, Chapter 7. The percentage of progovernment petitions to Parliament was lower.

39. See Table 1, Chapter 7.

40. *Daily News,* January 26, 1878, p. 3, col. c. Based on internal evidence, Leeds is another example.

41. See as examples of petitions which list occupations, the petition from Leith in PRO FO 78/2931, and the eight petitions from Kent and Surrey and the three from Merthyr Tydvil in PRO FO 78/2933.

42. See Table 1, Chapter 7.

43. *Daily Telegraph,* January 12, 1878, p. 3, col. g; January 8, 1878, p. 3, col. e; January 7, 1878, p. 2, col. b.

44. *Daily News,* December 24, 1877, p. 2, col. g; February 4, 1878, p. 6, col. f; February 18, 1878, p. 6, col. f.

45. Ibid., January 28, 1878, p. 2, col. b.

46. House of Lords Record Office, *Report of the Select Committee on Public Petitions 1878,* p. 1010.

47. *The Times,* February 4, 1878, p. 10, col. a.

48. *Pall Mall Gazette,* February 25, 1878, p. 8, col. b.

49. See Table 1, Chapter 7.

50. Horn, *Arch,* pp. 130–133.

51. Sidney and Beatrice Webb, *The History of Trade Unionism,* rev. ed. (New York: Longmans, Green, 1920), p. 331.

52. Petition from Chiddingstone, Kent, n.d, PRO FO 78/2933.

53. The eight petitions, in PRO FO 78/2933, originated in Westerham, Crockham Hill, Chiddingstone, and Beckenham in Kent, and Limpsfield in Surrey. They were transmitted to Gladstone by Henry F. Cox, of Nethenfield, Shortlands, Kent, on January 13 and January 18, 1878, Glynne-

Gladstone MSS 715 and 716. According to Cox, the signatures were collected during the week between January 3 and January 10 (letter of January 13, Glynne-Gladstone MSS 715).

54. See for example the five petitions from Dorset in PRO FO 78/2930: Canford Bottom, January 7; Woodlands, January 8; Tollard Farnham, January 3; Torrent Hinton, January 1; and Cranborne, January 9.

55. PRO FO 78/2932.

56. The *Pall Mall Gazette* objected to press reports that the Chamber of Commerce at Bristol had voted unanimously in favor of neutrality. Actually, there were only twelve people present, the resolution was adopted hastily at the beginning of the meeting and it was then sent directly to the National Press Association, in a modified form which increased its severity (quoted in *Daily Telegraph*, December 25, 1877, p. 2, col. f).

57. *Daily News*, February 9, 1878, p. 6, col. d. For the origins of the National Agricultural Labourers' Union, see Horn, *Arch*, pp. 45–47.

58. *Daily News*, January 8, 1878, p. 6, col. c.

59. Ibid., January 31, 1878, p. 3, col. f; September 18, 1876, p. 2, col. d; Royden Harrison, *Before the Socialists* (London: Routledge and Kegan Paul, 1965), p. 209; Jones, *Outcast London*, p. 167.

60. *Dictionary of National Biography*, XXII (London: Oxford University Press, 1917–), 879–882; *Standard*, January 8, 1878, p. 3, col. d.

61. *Daily News*, January 7, 1878, p. 6, col. g.

62. H. M. Hyndman, *The Record of an Adventurous Life* (London: Macmillan, 1911), p. 337 found her a more charismatic speaker than Bradlaugh; see in general Walter L. Arnstein, *The Bradlaugh Case* Oxford: Clarendon Press, 1965), p. 15, and for a discussion of the trial and its importance, pp. 20–23.

63. *Daily News*, January 26, 1878, p. 3, col. c.

64. Stead to Gladstone, January 27, 1878, Add. MS 44303, f. 283.

65. *Daily News*, January 5, 1878, p. 2, col. e.

66. Cf. Smelser, *Collective Behavior*, pp. 228–229, for the role of social movements in creating "temporary cleavages" which may lead to assignment of blame; p. 226 for the importance of scapegoating in hostile outbursts.

67. John M. MacKenzie, *Propaganda and Empire: The Manipulation of British Public Opinion, 1880–1960* (Manchester: Manchester University Press, 1985), pp. 40–66. It is no accident that the most telling expression of Jingoism was a music hall song. See also Smelser, *Collective Behavior*, p. 230.

68. *Standard*, October 9, 1876, p. 3, col. f.

69. The issue had aroused Gladstone's concern as early as the preceding summer, Gladstone to Shuvalov, July 20, 1877 (copy), Add. MS 44454, ff. 270–271. See on all this Joseph W. Hickey, "The Effect of Rhetoric on English Public Opinion during the Eastern Crisis of 1876–1878," M.A. diss., University of North Carolina at Greensboro, 1987, especially pp. 106–108; Alexander L. George, "The 'Operational Code': A Neglected Approach to the Study of Political Leaders and Decision-Making," *International Studies Quarterly*, 13 (1969), 216–217.

70. The degree of unrest in India, portrayed as serious by Lytton, the viceroy, seems to have been exaggerated. Lytton nurtured ambitious plans for a British advance on the Northwest Frontier and around Khelat, plans which Salisbury felt he had to cut back. Robert Blake and Hugh Cecil, eds., *Salisbury: The Man and his Policies* (New York: St. Martin's Press, 1987), pp. 128–130; Ram Lakhan Shukla, *Britain, India, and the Turkish Empire, 1853–1882* (New Delhi: People's Publishing House, 1973), pp. 94–120.

71. See Hugh Cunningham, "Jingoism in 1877–78," *Victorian Studies*, 14 (1971), 432.

72. Smelser, *Collective Behavior*, p. 226.

73. *Morning Post*, January 15, 1878, p. 5, col. f.

74. *Pall Mall Gazette*, January 11, 1878, p. 6, col. a.

75. W. Morris to Jenny Morris, January 14, 1878, Add. MS 45339, f. 23; *Pall Mall Gazette*, January 11, 1878, p. 4, col. b, where Sutherland's remarks were called "language of . . . wholesome plainness."

76. W. D. Sweet to Gladstone, January 31, 1878, Glynne-Gladstone MSS 714. There is a large file of hate letters from this period at Hawarden in Glynne-Gladstone MSS 702.

77. "A Conservative" to Gladstone, May 9, 1878, Glynne-Gladstone MSS 702.

78. See Cunningham, "Jingoism," p. 448.

79. For a most helpful summary of the opposition to the agitation see ibid., p. 453.

80. Ibid., pp. 434, 439.

81. Ibid., pp. 449–450, 453; *Morning Post*, February 1, 1878, p. 7, col. b. A similar observation was made by Price about the Jingo crowds during the Boer War; see Richard Price, *An Imperial War and the British Working Class* (London: Routledge and Kegan Paul, 1972), p. 147. It was said that before the meeting in Woolwich, the workers at the Arsenal were reminded that their jobs depended on brisk business in the weapons industry. Letters were supposedly sent out, over the signature of Edwin Hughes, a solicitor who acted as agent for the Conservatives in Plumstead and in the City; they read: "I understand that there is to be a public meeting . . . to protest against the expenditure of any more money on warlike stores. I think Woolwich ought to be the last place to pass such a resolution, and you should get up a party to go down and vote against it." (*Daily News*, February 4, 1878, p. 6, col. g.)

82. Cunningham, "Jingoism," pp. 431–432, 451. Apart from a few individuals like Lord Strathenden and Campbell, Urquhart's influence on the protest seems to have been minimal; at least participation by the few remaining foreign affairs committees was statistically negligible. A similarly tantalizing but minor role was played by some of the Orange Lodges, whose anti-Irish Catholic sentiments encouraged nationalism (see Table 1, Chapter 7).

83. Donald C. Richter, *Riotous Victorians* (Athens, Ohio: Ohio University Press, 1981), pp. 103–132.

84. The medical students reportedly were mobilized for several London demonstrations. Before the aborted meeting at the Agricultural Hall in February, a "big, bluff-looking gentleman" (possibly Ashmead Bartlett, a protester of Conservative background who had become disillusioned by the sight of battlefields in the Balkans; Cunningham, "Jingoism," pp. 439–440), was said to have put up a notice in the library at University College Hospital (William S. Tuke, University College Hospital, in Broadhurst Papers, London School of Economics Library, vol. 1, no. 34). It read: "On Thursday, at eight o'clock, *the traitor Gladstone will (or thinks he will) hold a meeting in favour of Russia at the Agricultural-hall. Shall this be? No! Come early and get front seats, and treat him as his treachery deserves."* (Gladstone to Treasurer of Guy's Hospital, February 23, 1878, Add. MS 44456, f. 112.) Gladstone took the treasurer to task for his role (on the basis of a *Daily News* article); the treasurer responded evasively and refused to issue a formal denial of involvement (H. L. Eason, "Students and Politics," *Guy's Hospital Gazette*, December 19, 1936, pp. 547–548, Add. MS 44456, f. 113). On the part played by the medical students in general, see Cunningham, "Jingoism," pp. 450–451.

85. Cunningham, "Jingoism," p. 446. For a discussion of hostile outbursts, see Smelser, *Collective Behavior*, pp. 222–269. As before, I analyzed the *Daily News*, the *Standard*, and the *Morning Post*.

86. When the Liberals of the City of London Neutrality Committee arranged for a meeting at 3:00 on January 31 in the Cannon Street Hotel, many individuals turned up with "anonymous postcards inviting them to a meeting called for 2 o'clock" (*Daily News*, February 1, 1878, p. 3, col. f).

87. *Daily News*, January 31, 1878, p. 3, col. g; *Standard*, January 28, 1878, p. 3, col. e.

88. See the *Standard's* comments on the meeting in Bayswater (February 6, 1878, p. 3, col. e).

89. E. P. Thompson, *William Morris*, rev. ed. (New York: Pantheon, 1977; originally published 1955), pp. 218–219.

90. *Morning Post*, February 13, 1878, p. 5, col. a; *Standard*, February 13, 1878, p. 6, col. d, describing the February 12 meeting at Birmingham.

91. *Daily News*, February 11, 1878, p. 3, col. a.

92. *Standard*, February 11, 1878, p. 3, col. c.

93. Government supporters favored "Rule, Britannia," with special emphasis on the line, "Britons never shall be slaves;" almost as frequently heard was the music hall ditty sung by Macdermott:

> We don't want to fight;
> But by jingo if we do,
> We've got the men, we've got the ships,
> We've got the money too.

(John Bartlett, *Familiar Quotations*, 11th ed., Boston: Little Brown, 1937, originally published 1882, p. 562.) The protesters were not slow to respond. A parody on Macdermott ran in the *Morning Post*, January 30, 1878, p. 3, col. c:

> We don't want to fight;
> But by jingo if we do,
> We'll have two shillings income tax,
> And a d——d good licking, too!

94. Cunningham ("Jingoism," p. 446) asserts that "the successful assault on meetings" generally occurred in the West Midlands. The newspapers suggest that the majority of such episodes took place in London. Such evidence from London-based newspapers is not necessarily convincing. More helpful is the observation that opposition typically occurred in large cities which had been divided about the protest (London, Manchester, Gateshead), or where a locally prominent figure had taken a strong stand in favor (Sheffield, Mundella; Bristol, Samuel Morley).

95. For confirmation of this opinion, see Cunningham, "Jingoism," p. 452. Richter *(Riotous Victorians,* p. 163) points out that in addition to election campaigns, disorder attended many nonpolitical occasions, such as processions of the Salvation Army or the Orange Lodges. He did not, however, find violence attached to "agitations championing any serious political or social cause."

96. Cunningham, "Jingoism," p. 446.

97. *The Times,* January 31, 1878, p. 5, col. d.

98. *Morning Post,* February 6, 1878, p. 5, col. f.

99. *The Times,* February 4, 1878, p. 10, col. a; *Manchester Guardian,* February 2, 1878, p. 5, col. d. This restless behavior, moving "from object to object," is typical of hostile outbursts (Smelser, *Collective Behavior,* pp. 260–261).

100. *Morning Post,* February 11, 1878, p. 3, col. c.

101. Cunningham, "Jingoism," pp. 448–449.

102. Cf. ibid., p. 446.

103. *Daily News,* January 1, 1878, p. 2, col. b; January 2, 1878, p. 3, col. d.

104. Ibid., January 3, 1878, p. 2, cols. e-f.

105. *Daily Telegraph,* January 9, 1878, p. 3, col. a.

106. *Daily News,* January 10, 1878, p. 6, col. e.

107. Ibid., January 12, 1878, p. 6, col. e.

108. *The Times,* January 17, 1878, p. 6, cols. b-c; *Daily News,* January 17, 1878, p. 2, cols. c-f.

109. William Morris to Janey Morris, January 19, 1878, Add. MS 45338, f. 91.

110. *Standard,* January 17, 1878, p. 3, cols. f-g.

111. See Smelser, *Collective Behavior,* p. 265: "when authorities are . . . actively supportive of one side in a conflict, they give a green light to those bent on hostile expression."

112. *Daily News,* January 2, 1878, p. 3, cols. c-d; *Daily Telegraph,* January 2, 1878, p. 3, col. c.

113. Millman, *Eastern Question,* pp. 353–354.

114. *Daily Telegraph,* January 4, 1878, p. 3, col. f.

115. Cunningham, "Jingoism," pp. 433–434.

116. January 19, 1878, Add. MS 45338, f. 90.

117. *Daily News,* January 19, 1878, p. 2, col. g; January 26, 1878, p. 3, col. c.

118. Sumner, *Russia*, pp. 353–355; Millman, *Eastern Question*, pp. 366–370. Derby returned on January 27 (Millman, *Eastern Question*, p. 370), but Carnarvon was gone for good.

119. *Daily News*, January 28, 1878, p. 2, cols. a-b.

120. *Hansard's Parliamentary Debates*, 3rd series, vol. 237, 1878, cols. 435–436.

121. Ibid., cols. 470–472. It would not be easy to spend such a sum in such a short time: see *Daily News*, March 18, 1878, p. 6, col. d for an instance of payment in advance in order to commit money. Such practical considerations support the interpretation that the vote of credit was arranged more for diplomatic effect than for serious military purposes.

122. Ibid., cols. 536–561.

123. Ibid., col. 564.

124. Ibid., col. 565.

125. Ibid., cols. 574–575.

126. See Figure 3 above.

127. *Daily News*, January 31, 1878, p. 3, col. f.

128. Ibid., January 30, 1878, p. 6, col. f. For Morley's refusal and subsequent activities, see *Daily News*, February 1, 1878, p. 3, cols. e-g and *The Times*, February 1, 1878, p. 12, col. a. Meanwhile, a meeting of the Workmen's Neutrality Committee had called for protest meetings "in all parts of the metropolis" (*Daily News*, January 29, 1878, p. 6, col. b).

129. *The Times*, February 1, 1878, p. 12, col. a.

130. William Morris to Janey Morris, February 1, 1878, Add. MS 45338, f. 95.

131. *The Times*, February 1, 1878, p. 12, cols. a-b; *Pall Mall Gazette*, February 2, 1878, p. 5, col. a.

132. *Daily News*, February 1, 1878, p. 3, cols. e-f.

133. *The Times*, February 4, 1878, p. 10, col. b. The culprit, Robert Thomas Wilmot, a builder, was brought before the magistrates, pleaded guilty to an "impulse of the moment," was accused of drunkeness by the police and was finally discharged upon the intercession of the Lord Mayor (*Pall Mall Gazette*, February 15, 1878, p. 7, cols. a-b).

134. Millman, *Eastern Question*, pp. 374, 377. Apparently the Ottoman plenipotentiary, Server Pasha, transmitted the news of an armistice, but did not want to admit that in order to obtain it, he had had to agree to allow the Russians to occupy the Catalca (Tchataldja) lines, the forward defense of Constantinople itself. Consequently, the completely legitimate Russian advance was as much a mystery in Constantinople as elsewhere until Server arrived in the capital; Millman, *Eastern Question*, pp. 379 n. 17, 582.

135. See Hansard, vol. 237, cols. 749, 775.

136. Millman, *Eastern Question*, pp. 377–378; Hansard, vol. 237, cols. 956–59.

137. Smelser, *Collective Behavior*, pp. 140, 142, 146–147.

138. William Morris to Jenny Morris, February 11, 1878, Add. MS 45339, f. 25; Hansard, vol. 237, col. 1310; *Pall Mall Gazette*, February 8, 1878, p. 6, col. a; *Morning Post*, February 8, 1878, p. 5, col. c; Millman, *Eastern Question*, pp. 379–381. According to Millman, news of the Russian advance on Constantinople was published as early as the evening of February 6.

139. Millman, *Eastern Question*, p. 382.
140. *Daily News*, February 11, 1878, p. 3, cols. a–b; February 12, 1878, p. 3, col. f; *Morning Post*, February 11, 1878, p. 3, col. b.
141. Hansard, vol. 237, col. 1417; Millman, *Eastern Question*, pp. 382–383.
142. *Daily News*, February 4, 1878, p. 6, col. g.
143. William Morris to Janey Morris, February 20, 1878, Add. MS 45338, f. 101.
144. Broadhurst Papers, Gladstone to Henry Broadhurst, February 18 and 19, 1878, Item #33, vol. 1, ff. 45–48. See also William Ewart Gladstone, *The Gladstone Diaries*, ed. M. R. D. Foot and H. C. G. Matthew, 11 vols. to date (Oxford: Clarendon Press, 1968–), IX, 291–292.
145. Mundella Papers, Gladstone to Mundella, February 19, 1878 (6P/11/9/i). For arrangements for admission by ticket, see E. H. Bayley to Gladstone, February 19, 1878 (Southwark Liberal Association), Glynne-Gladstone MS 715.
146. *Daily News*, February 23, 1878, p. 5, col. e; *The Times*, February 26, 1878, p. 11, col. d. Quotes are from the *Daily News*. Broadhurst divulged these details after the meeting had been called off, to justify his objections to the cancellation. As Agatha Ramm has pointed out to the author, with five thousand stewards in the audience, one would have to wonder about the proportion of stewards to listeners.
147. Gladstone, *Diaries*, IX, 292.
148. Gladstone to Granville, February 19, 1878, #105, Agatha Ramm, ed., *The Political Correspondence of Mr. Gladstone and Lord Granville 1876–1886*, 2 vols. (Oxford: Clarendon Press, 1962), I, 69.
149. William Morris to Janey Morris, February 20, 1878, Add. MS 45338, f. 101.
150. Mundella Papers, Westminster and Shaftesbury to Mundella, February 17, 1878 (6P/11/8/i–ii).
151. Sumner, *Russia*, p. 381; Millman, *Eastern Question*, p. 396.
152. William Morris to Janey Morris, February 20, 1878, Add. MS 45338, f. 102.
153. *Daily News*, February 21, 1878, p. 3, col. c.
154. Gladstone, *Diaries*, IX, 292.
155. William Morris to Janey Morris, February 20, 1878, Add. MS 45338, f. 101.
156. Smelser, *Collective Behavior*, p. 304. (His example here is the women's suffrage movement in England.)
157. *Daily News*, February 19, 1878, p. 2, col. f.
158. S. Hutchinson Harris, *Auberon Herbert; Crusader for Liberty* (London: Williams and Norgate, 1943), p. 197.
159. *Daily News*, February 22, 1878, p. 6, col. e; February 23, 1878, p. 3, col. a.
160. *Pall Mall Gazette*, February 25, 1878, p. 8, col. b.
161. *Daily News*, February 25, 1878, p. 2, cols. a–e.
162. *The Times*, February 25, 1878, p. 10, col. a.
163. *Pall Mall Gazette*, February 26, 1878, p. 6, cols. a–b; *Standard*, February 25, 1878, p. 3, col. d.

164. Harris, *Herbert,* pp. 19–38; *The Times,* February 26, 1878, p. 11, col. d.
165. Henry Broadhurst, *Henry Broadhurst, M.P.: The Story of His Life from a Stonemason's Bench to the Treasury Bench* (London: Hutchinson, 1901) p. 86. Broadhurst said that he dropped out as soon as Bradlaugh insisted that the meeting be held on Sunday; this meant that Nonconformist working men would not come.
166. *Pall Mall Gazette,* February 26, 1878, p. 9, col. a.
167. Harris, *Herbert,* p. 200.
168. *Daily News,* March 11, 1878, p. 3, cols. a-c.
169. Gladstone, *Diaries,* IX, 297. Gladstone considered the crowd "in the main friendly," but the *Pall Mall Gazette* called it "threatening" and said that the Gladstones' final departure was monitored by "an escort of four mounted constables" (ibid., n. 5).
170. *Daily News,* April 5, 1878, p. 3, col. b (letter to the editor from Auberon Herbert).
171. Ibid., April 8, 1878, p. 2, col. d.
172. Ibid., March 13, 1878, p. 3, col. d, quoting the labor leader G. J. Holyoake.
173. *Morning Post,* January 30, 1878, p. 6, col. d.
174. Article from the *Standard,* January 30, 1878, Glynne-Gladstone MSS 716.
175. Chamberlain Papers, Chamberlain to Stead, January 30, 1878, Copy, "Private" (JC6/4K/15).
176. Mundella Papers (6P/68), Mundella to Leader, January 25, 1878 (AJM/RL/ 11/10/i–iii); Cunningham, "Jingoism," pp. 434–435.
177. Mundella Papers, Goldwin Smith to Mundella, February 17, [1878] (6P/ 11/7/ii).
178. Mundella Papers (6P/68), Mundella to Leader, January 30, 1878 (AJM/RL/ 11/13/i–ii).
179. Mundella Papers (6P/68), Herbert to Leader, January 30, [1878] (AJM/RL/ 11/13/Annex i–iv).
180. Mundella Papers (6P/68), Mundella to Leader, January 30, 1878 (AJM/RL/ 11/13/i–ii).
181. Chamberlain Papers, Chamberlain to Stead, March 27, 1878, Copy, "Private" (JC6/4K/18).
182. Sumner, *Russia,* p. 389.
183. Millman, *Eastern Question,* pp. 404–406.
184. Lee, *Cyprus Convention,* p. 68.
185. Sumner, *Russia,* pp. 389–394; Millman, *Eastern Question,* pp. 407–413. Details of the military plans were not made public until April (see George Carslake Thompson, *Public Opinion and Lord Beaconsfield, 1875–1880,* 2 vols. [London: Macmillan, 1886], II, 409, 415), but Derby's departure was an unmistakable sign of trouble.
186. William Morris to Jenny Morris, March 18, 1878, Add. MS 45339, f. 29.
187. *Daily News,* April 2, 1878, p. 6, col. c.
188. G. C. Thompson, *Public Opinion,* II, 420–421; R. A. J. Walling, ed., *The Diaries of John Bright* (New York: Morrow, 1931), p. 406; *Daily News,* April 2, 1878, p. 5, col. c; April 4, 1878, p. 2, cols. c-g.
189. National Federation of Liberal Associations, "Annual Report 1879," in

National Liberal Federation, *Annual Reports and Council Proceedings, 1877–1936* (Hassocks, Eng.: Harvester Press, 1975), pp. 13–15; *Daily News*, April 4, 1878, p. 2, cols. d-g.

190. *Daily News*, April 11, 1878, p. 3, cols. a-b.
191. Ramm, *Political Correspondence*, I, 70 n. 3.
192. Gladstone, *Diaries*, IX, 305.
193. *Daily News*, April 11, 1878, p. 3, col. c.
194. Ibid., April 2, 1878, p. 6, col. c; April 19, 1878, p. 2, cols. a-e.
195. Gladstone, *Diaries*, IX, 307.
196. House of Lords Record Office, *Report of the Select Committee on Public Petitions 1878*.
197. Broadhurst Papers, "Minutes of the Council of the Labour Representation League," March 15 and April 12, 1878, pp. 284–287; petition appears in House of Lords Record Office, *Report of the Select Committee on Public Petitions 1878*, p. 493, #8689.
198. See *Report 1878*, "Petitions for using every effort to avoid war," pp. 548–549 (April 4–May 7, 1878, #9758–98); out of 41 petitions, 32 were similar. Ibid., pp. 496–499 (April 4–9, 1878, #8744–8866); out of 123 petitions, 110 were similar.
199. *Daily News*, April 4, 1878, p. 6, col. d; *The Times*, April 8, 1878, p. 8, col. c.
200. Ibid., April 8, 1878, p. 4, col. d and p. 5, col. c.
201. Ibid., May 4, 1878, p. 5, col. d.
202. G. C. Thompson, *Public Opinion*, II, 422.
203. Millman, *Eastern Question*, pp. 423, 429–431.
204. *The Times*, April 16, 1878, p. 8, col. c; *Daily News*, April 9, 1878, p. 4, col. e.
205. *Daily News*, April 13, 1878, p. 4, col. b.
206. Ibid., April 16, 1878, p. 4, col. c.
207. Ibid., April 26, 1878, p. 4, col. c; May 14, 1878, p. 3, col. e; p. 4, col. c.
208. Ibid., May 23, 1878, p. 2, col. b.
209. Ibid., May 24, 1878, p. 2, col. c.
210. Ruth Bogin, "Petitioning and the New Moral Economy of Post-Revolutionary America," *William and Mary Quarterly*, 45 (1988), 420–422, points out that "petitions, by their very nature, acknowledged the power of the rulers and the dependence of the aggrieved," and hence, if unsuccessful, were usually followed by an outbreak like Shays's Rebellion or the Whiskey Rebellion. I am indebted to my colleague, Professor Robert Calhoon, for this reference.

10. Conclusion

1. Yuluğ Tekin Kurat, *Henry Layard'in Istanbul Elçiliği, 1877–1880* (Ankara: Ankara Üniversitesi Basimevi, 1968), p. 214.
2. See B. H. Sumner, *Russia and the Balkans, 1870–1880* (Hamden, Conn.: Archon Books, 1962; originally published 1937), pp. 355–359, 372–381.
3. He owned 57,000 acres in Lancashire with an annual rent of £156,735

(*The Great Landowners of Great Britain and Ireland,* 4th ed., London: 1883). I am indebted to Dr. Robert C. Shipkey for this reference.

4. W. Hart Dyke to Disraeli, January 25, 1878, "Confidential," Disraeli Papers, B/XX/S/1308 (Box 113), Western Manuscripts, Bodleian Library, Oxford.

5. Disraeli to Queen Victoria, January 26, 1878, quoted in W. F. Monypenny and G. E. Buckle, *The Life of Benjamin Disraeli, Earl of Beaconsfield,* 6 vols. (London: J. Murray, 1910–1920), VI, 234.

6. Derby to Lord Wilton, July 1, 1877, Derby Papers (15th Earl), 920 DER(15) 16/2/13, Liverpool Record Office.

7. Sumner, *Russia,* pp. 396–398.

8. M. S. Anderson, *The Eastern Question, 1774–1923* (London: Macmillan, 1966), pp. 211–216; Dwight E. Lee, *Great Britain and the Cyprus Convention Policy of 1878* (Cambridge, Mass.: Harvard University Press, 1934), pp. 68–85.

9. Salisbury to Layard, April 18, 1878, quoted in Lee, *Cyprus Convention,* p. 75.

10. Kurat, *Layard,* pp. 220, 222.

11. Lee, *Cyprus Convention,* pp. 142–157; Şevket Pamuk, *The Ottoman Empire and European Capitalism, 1820–1913* (Cambridge, Eng.: Cambridge University Press, 1987), pp. 73–76.

12. William Ewart Gladstone, "Electoral Facts," *Nineteenth Century,* IV (July–December 1878), 961, 964–968; W. C. Lubenow, *Parliamentary Politics and the Home Rule Crisis* (Oxford: Clarendon Press, 1988), pp. 160–161. Lubenow's remarks seem particularly applicable to the Conservatives in their many years out of office after the repeal of the Corn Laws; but the tradition remained in the 1870s and 1880s.

13. Some of the younger High Churchmen did stay with Gladstone through the Home Rule crisis: see J. P. Parry, *Democracy and Religion: Gladstone and the Liberal Party, 1867–1875* (Cambridge, Eng.: Cambridge University Press, 1986), p. 439.

14. Pamela Horn, *Joseph Arch* (Kineton, Eng.: Roundwood Press, 1971), p. 128; Joseph Arch, *Joseph Arch. The Story of His Life Told by Himself* (New York: Garland, 1984; reprint of 2nd ed., originally published 1898), pp. 315–317, 324–325.

15. Cf. Horn, *Arch,* p. 123.

16. Ibid., pp. 167, 171.

17. Henry Broadhurst, *Henry Broadhurst, M.P.: The Story of His Life from a Stonemason's Bench to the Treasury Bench* (London: Hutchinson, 1901), p. 88.

18. Ibid., p. 95.

19. Ibid., p. 188.

20. Ibid., p. 189.

21. Ibid., p. 8.

22. Stan Shipley, *Club Life and Socialism in Mid-Victorian London* (Oxford: History Workshop, 1972), p. 74.

23. William Ewart Gladstone, *The Gladstone Diaries,* ed. M. R. D. Foot and

H. C. G. Matthew, 11 vols. to date (Oxford: Clarendon Press, 1968–), IX, 374.

24. Ibid., p. 471.
25. See T. A. Jenkins, "Gladstone, the Whigs, and the Leadership of the Liberal Party, 1879–1880," *Historical Journal*, 27 (1984), 337–360.
26. T. A. Jenkins, *Gladstone, Whiggery, and the Liberal Party, 1874–1886* (Oxford: Clarendon Press, 1988), pp. 230–236.
27. Ibid., pp. 230–236, 248.
28. Ibid., pp. 230–232.
29. R. T. Shannon, *Gladstone and the Bulgarian Agitation, 1876*, 2nd ed. (Hassocks, Eng.: Harvester Press, 1975; originally published 1963), pp. 274–281.
30. Gladstone, *Diaries*, IX, 656.

Index